The Strange History of

BONNIE *and* CLYDE

The Strange History of

BONNIE *and* CLYDE

John Treherne

Cooper Square Press

First Cooper Square Press edition 2000

This Cooper Square Press paperback edition of *The Strange History of Bonnie and Clyde* is an unabridged republication of the edition published in Briarcliff Manor, New York, in 1985.

Designed by Louis A. Ditizio

Published by Cooper Square Press
An Imprint of the Rowman & Littlefield Publishing Group
150 Fifth Avenue, Suite 911
New York, New York 10011

Distributed by National Book Network

Library of Congress Cataloging-in-Publication Data

Treherne, J. E.
    The strange history of Bonnie and Clyde / John Treherne.—1st Cooper Square Press ed.
        p. cm.
    Originally published: New York : Stein and Day, 1985, c1984.
    Includes bibliographical references.
    ISBN 0-8154-1106-5 (alk. paper)
    1. Parker, Bonnie, 1910–1934. 2. Barrow, Clyde, 1909–1934.
    3. Criminals—United States—Biography. I. Title: Bonnie and Clyde.

HV6425 ,T73 2000
364.15'52'0922—dc21
[B]   00-043094

♾™ The paper used in this publication meets the minimum requirements of American National Standard for Information Sciences—Permanence of Paper for Printed Library Materials, ANSI/NISO Z39.48-1992. Manufactured in the United States of America.

This book is dedicated to the memory of:

John N. Bucher of Hillsboro, Texas. Died April 27, 1932.

Eugene Moore of Atoka, Oklahoma. Died August 5, 1932.

Howard Hall of Sherman, Texas. Died October 11, 1932.

Doyle Johnson of Temple, Texas. Died December 25, 1932.

Malcolm Davis of Dallas, Texas. Died January 6, 1933.

Harry McGinnis of Joplin, Missouri. Died April 13, 1933.

Wes Harryman of Joplin, Missouri. Died April 13, 1933

Henry D. Humphrey of Alma, Arkansas. Died June 23, 1933.

Joseph Crowson of Huntsville, Texas. Died January 16, 1934.

E. B. Wheeler of Grapevine, Texas. Died April 1, 1934.

H. D. Murphy of Grapevine, Texas. Died April 1, 1934.

Cal Campbell of Commerce, Oklahoma. Died April 6, 1934.

Contents

Illustrations

FIGURES

MAPS

Acknowledgments

The writing of this book was made pleasurable by the help and friendship of many people on both sides of the Atlantic. I am particularly grateful for the kindness that I received in Dallas, especially to Raj and Barbara Sohal, under whose hospitable roof I stayed and who helped me in my research; to John Neal Phillips, who although himself engaged in writing a book on Ralph Fults shared so much of his local knowledge with me, and to André Phillips for cooking me Bonnie's favorite meal of red beans and cabbage. It is a pleasure to thank Randy Stanley and Fran Lundy for inviting me to and helping with my research at Joplin, Missouri, and to United States Marshal Clint Peoples for telling me about his involvement, half a century ago, with the people and events described in this book. My visits to the southwestern United States were also facilitated by many other kind folk, who helped me and taught me the meaning of Southern hospitality, notably: Patty Benoit (Temple, Texas), Charlie Bonner (Atoka, Oklahoma), Lucille Boykin (Dallas, Texas), Ed Cave (Kaufman, Texas), "Duke" Ellis (Stringtown, Oklahoma), Teresa Fox (Fort Smith, Arkansas), Gaines de Graffenried (Waco, Texas), Kathy Gravell (Hillsboro, Texas), Casey Greene (Dallas, Texas), Betty Homan (Des Moines, Iowa), Peter Kurilecz (Dallas, Texas), Bill Lundy and Donald Pierce (Joplin, Missouri), Carol Waller (Platte City,

Missouri), Henry Wells (Wellington, Texas), John Winters (Stringtown, Oklahoma). I received much invaluable help from various Cambridge colleagues and friends. I am particularly grateful to Paul Chipchase for patiently reading and commenting on the draft chapters as they were produced and to Tony Colwell of Jonathan Cape for his generous professional help. I benefited from the expert advice of the professor of criminology Donald West and of Sir John Butterfield and Sir Edmund Leach. Professor J. C. Holt instructed me on the growth of the legend of Robin Hood and Geoffrey Ashe provided valuable insight on Arthurian matters. I also thank Pete Tucker for educating me about American cars of the late 1920s and early 1930s and especially for letting me tinker with his precious 1934 Ford V-8; and Margaret Scott, of Leicester Polytechnic, for talking to me about clothes and fashion in the 1930s and 1960s; and Peter Seward for invaluable guidance on cinematographic matters. I am grateful to Patterson Smith (of Montclair, New Jersey) and John Hammond (of Ely, Cambridgeshire) for obtaining some very scarce books for me and to the staffs of the libraries and institutions which I used for my research, notably: the Library of the British Film Institute, the British Library, Cambridge City Library, Cambridge University Library, Dallas Historical Society, Dallas Public Library, Des Moines Public Library, Fondren Library of Southern Methodist University (Dallas, Texas), Fort Smith Public Library, the Homer Garrison Museum and Hall of Fame (Fort Fisher, Waco, Texas), the Italian Institute in the United Kingdom, Joplin City Library, Hillsboro City Library, and the Southwest Historical Wax Museum (Grand Prairie, Texas). Finally I thank Margaret Clements for her patient typing of the manuscript of this book.

The following photographs are from the collection of the Texas/Dallas History and Archives Division, Dallas Public Library: 1, 3, 4, 5, 7, 8, 9, 10, 12, 13, 15, 17, 18, 19, 20, 21, 23, 24, 25, and 26. Plates 28 to 32 were supplied courtesy of the National Film Archive Stills Library. Plate 1 is reproduced by permission of Warner Brothers and Tetira-Hiller Productions © 1967 (All rights reserved); plate 29 by permission of J. E. D.

Productions Corp., New York; plate 30 by permission of MCA, Universal City, California; plate 31 by permission of Lorimar, Culver City, California; plate 32 by permission of Samuel Z. Arkoff © 1958; plate 33 by permission of Achille Manzotti and Fasco Film ©; plates 6 and 11 were supplied by the BBC Hulton Picture Library; plate 16 was provided by Associated Press; plate 22 appears by permission of Clint Peoples. Plates 2, 14, and 27 were taken by the author. Fig. 1 is reproduced by courtesy of the Edison Institute, Dearborn, Michigan; Fig. 2 © 1933 by The New York Times Company, reprinted by permission; Figs. 3 and 4 are reprinted with the permission of the *Dallas Morning News*; Figs. 5, 6, 7, 8, and 9 are from the Texas/Dallas History and Archives Division, Dallas Public Library.

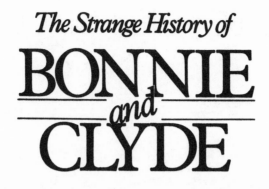

The Strange History of
BONNIE *and* CLYDE

THE BONNIE AND CLYDE COUNTRY

1

Guns,
Carrots,
And
Legends

NOT FAR FROM the sleepy township of Grapevine, Texas, on a sunny Easter Sunday afternoon, two uniformed police officers lay in the mud of a quiet country road. They had been hit at close range by shotgun blasts; one of them was still conscious. A short blonde woman stood looking down at the dying man, cradling a gun. When the police officer stirred slightly in pain, she brought the weapon to her shoulder and fired twice into his face. Then she burst out laughing and turned to the young man at her side, exclaiming, "Look-a-there, his head bounced just like a rubber ball."

THAT DAY SHE had been anxious about a pet rabbit called Sonny Boy. It was an Easter present for her mother. It lived in the backseat of the car along with a great many guns and ate carrots. The car smelled of it, and the young man who was her lover complained bitterly.

Bathing a rabbit is not an easy matter for traveling people. On the afternoon of March 31, 1934, they had parked the car and doused the evil-smelling creature in the muddy freshwater of North Texas. The rabbit leaped and struggled while they soaped and rinsed it in icy water and dried it delicately in a towel. Back in the car the frightened animal, chilled to the bone, had lost consciousness. The blonde woman grew agitated, and they had to stop the car again to light a fire and revive the creature.

There was no one about. The man collected a small heap of sticks and sat by the flames turning the limp rabbit gently from side to side to stop it singeing, burning his own eyebrows in the process. The woman fondled the rabbit, and at last it began to stir. The fear that they would kill Sonny Boy with cleanliness worried her for the rest of the day.

That Sunday afternoon they had an appointment to keep. By a complicated and secret arrangement, they were to meet the blonde woman's mother on a quiet side road one hundred yards from the main highway between Grapevine and Roanoke. When they reached the rendezvous, the Easter rabbit was put out to eat grass at the roadside. As the day wore on and the sun warmed them, the man grew bored and went to sleep in the car. The blonde woman took the rabbit on the front seat with her and was grooming and soothing it until she heard faintly the noise of approaching vehicles. It was not her mother's car. She woke the man and whispered, "It's the law."

As the two burly, blue-clad officers parked their motorcycles and strolled over to them, there was a burst of gunfire from the car, and both policemen were hit and knocked to the ground.

The scene was watched from a safe distance by an elderly farmer who had been taking the air under a tree after his Easter Sunday dinner. He said he watched Bonnie Parker finish off the wounded policeman and make his head bounce. He recorded her exclamation for posterity, adding one more violent and dubious episode to a twentieth-century legend.

SEVEN WEEKS AFTER bathing Sonny Boy, Bonnie Parker and Clyde Barrow were lying dead in a lonely Louisiana road. A large, excited crowd, men in shirt-sleeves and women in summer dresses, quickly gathered around their bullet-shattered car. Children dipped their hands in the blood and men tried to prize fragments from their still-warm bodies. Within hours, nine thousand people—sightseers, newspapermen, officials—had crowded into the nearby normally peaceful town, and the roads were choked with vehicles.

Later that day, the two bullet-riddled bodies were taken from that quiet corner of Louisiana and were driven across the familiar Texas roads, their refuge for so many dangerous months: westward along straight, pine-fringed roads, through hardwood forests, past the place where they had played with fireworks on the previous Christmas Day, through the east Texas oil fields and across rolling blackland prairies toward their homes in West Dallas.

The corpses were put on public view. Thirty thousand people filed past Clyde's body as it lay dressed in a light gray suit with a pearl tiepin and a stiff collar, and forty thousand queued to gaze at the woman who had chosen to share his crimes and to die at his side.

Excited people pushed and shoved on the tree-shaded lawns to watch Bonnie's coffin carried in brilliant sunshine up the steps and through the classical portico of the McKamy-Campbell Funeral Home in Dallas on the afternoon of May 26, 1934. On the previous day the press of the crowd had been so great at Clyde's burial that his family were forced to the lip of the open grave and narrowly escaped being pushed in as a low-flying airplane dropped a gigantic wreath.

Half a century later, someone had taken the trouble to place some cheap plastic roses on Bonnie's grave at the Crown Hill Cemetery, near Love Airfield, and people still walk over the rough, soggy grass to stand by a low, clipped hedge and read her epitaph:

> As the flowers are made sweeter
> By the sunshine and the dew,
> So this world is made brighter
> By the likes of folk like you.

DESPITE THE ENORMITY of their crimes, there was much public sympathy for Bonnie and Clyde, and in scattered townships on the wide Texas plains the eyes of old men still shine as they recall any number of firmly believed but clearly fictional events in the life of the multiple murderer and his girl. The teller's window from a minor Texas bank that they robbed is a cherished object stored in the basement of the Dallas Historical Society, their wax effigies a prominent exhibit at the Southwest Historical Wax Museum at Grand Prairie; Clyde's pocket watch and sawn-off shotgun are enshrined in the Hall of Fame at the Texas Rangers Museum at Waco. The desire for relics associated with Bonnie and Clyde has extended in space and time to include the bricks from a building in which they had spent just two nights, thirty years before. In 1964 these prized objects were sold for a dollar apiece. One little girl persuaded her parents to buy a venetian blind from the demolished building in Platte City, Missouri, because she "wanted to remember how sorry she felt for Bonnie and Clyde"!

The legend of Bonnie and Clyde was born of the anxiety and fear that accompanied the crime wave of the early 1930s in the American southwest. After their deaths it grew with the gossip of ordinary people, in the pages of pulp magazines, through several movie films, pop songs, even a fashion craze. The legend has many versions: they were fugitives fleeing from injustice; they were attractive and handsome or rat-faced killers; they were tough and resourceful or incompetent clowns; vulgar or stylish; champions of the oppressed or greedy robbers.

Like most legends, Bonnie and Clyde's thrived on uncertainty. And there was a great deal of that. After all, it was peculiarly difficult in the midst of a disastrous national crime wave to obtain reliable information about two particularly elusive and violent fugitives. Further confusion was added by the contradictory testimonies of some participants, notably the members of their families, who were at pains to present them as wronged, attractive, and charming, and the lawmen, who wished to convey exactly the opposite.

It was this uncertainty that enabled the legend-makers—the small-town gossips, participants, journalists, and film-makers —to select the versions that were most suitable for their storytelling. Changing public attitudes also affected the growth of their legend. The Hollywood movie-makers, like the professional balladeers and minstrels of the fourteenth and fifteenth centuries describing the exploits of Robin Hood, adapted their stories of Bonnie and Clyde to the audiences of the time: from the first film made for cinema audiences of the Great Depression to the latest Italian version of the legend, *Bonnie e Clyde all'italiana* (1983), in which the two fugitives are reduced to incompetent clowns. But it was Arthur Penn's screen masterpiece made in the nonconformist 1960s that more than anything else in recent times successfully adapted and so sustained the legend. It led to a novel based on the film and a book about the film, several pop tunes and even influenced the way people dressed in the late 1960s. Bonnie and Clyde sweatshirts were worn in Greenwich Village. Faye Dunaway, in her role as Bonnie, was rated one of the Ten Best Dressed Women of the Year. The Bonnie and Clyde look became the rage on both sides of the Atlantic, and the pages of glossy fashion magazines were filled with photographs of slim young ladies wearing Bonnie berets. Underwear advertisements in *Vogue* showed scantily dressed women brandishing revolvers; teenagers rioted in Westport, Connecticut, dressed in Bonnie and Clyde clothes; Brigitte Bardot sang of them in Paris; American intellectuals used them as symbols of protest against the Vietnam War.

Such spectacular growth of a legend is perhaps a surprising phenomenon in the middle years of twentieth-century civilization. Yet, as we shall see, the transformation of the humble Dallas waitress and her jug-eared boyfriend occurred by essentially the same processes that produced the legend of the outlaw of Sherwood. It was Bonnie Parker who supplied the unique ingredient: the image of the tiny feminine figure with a machine-gun, who chose to die with the man she loved. It was as though Annie Oakley had teamed up with Billy the Kid, or as if Maid Marian had fought with bow and arrow beside her Hood.

Bonnie must have had some inkling of the furor that would follow her violent death, for she took a hand in the myth making and, toward the end of her brief life, even spoke of her duty to "her public." Even so, she could have had no conception of the extent or the ramifications of the legend that would become familiar to millions of people throughout the world. Still, she could not fail to be aware of the varied and curious public attitudes to the two fugitives as they drove for so many thousands of miles along the roads of the American southwest. She must, in particular, have derived some sardonic amusement (for she had an excellent sense of humor) from one choice example—the unsolicited opinion of a Dallas lawyer concerning the events that took place after the bathing and reviving of Sonny Boy during the Easter of 1934:

> Officers can expect anything to happen if they stick their noses into something that isn't their business. Whoever was in that car was off the highway, a hundred yards or more when those two uniformed officers came towards them. They didn't know what the officers might do to them so they fired.

2

GOLDEN-HEARTED GIRL

THE TOWNSHIP OF Rowena is a tiny speck on the vast Texas plains that had once been cattle country, in a fork of the old Dodge City Trail. The two routes converged eighty-five miles to the northwest, and over them countless great herds of cattle had been driven on their northward journey to the Kansas railheads. By 1910, however, when Bonnie Parker was born, cattlemen had given place to farmers and Rowena, with a population of six hundred, was the center of a flourishing agricultural community, growing cotton and grain and rearing cows and poultry.

The Parkers were comfortably off. Henry Parker was a bricklayer and earned enough money to keep his family in the condition of narrow respectability thought proper in a little Texas town in 1910. Mr. and Mrs. Parker were devout churchgoers, but apart from attending the Rowena Baptist Church, their only social diversions were occasional picnics and village socials and suppers.

Bonnie was a healthy baby, with cotton-colored hair and big blue eyes, and grew into a mischievous, high-spirited girl who severely taxed the patience of her elder brother, Hubert—a quiet, rather serious boy known in the family as Buster. Buster became Bonnie's self-appointed guardian and, at the age of

five, used proudly to escort his three-year-old sister, resplend-
ent in ruffles and starched bows, to Sunday school. Bonnie once
disgraced him at a school concert by singing a disreputable
song in her tiny piping voice, and Buster found this hard to
forgive.

In 1913 Buster and Bonnie acquired a sister, Billie, who was
thoroughly spoiled and petted by their grandmother; Bonnie,
however, remained her father's favorite. A visiting uncle
taught her to swear, and Mr. Parker tolerated this and thought
it amusing, though poor Buster was chastized by his father for
very minor transgressions. It was left to Emma Parker to
discipline Bonnie with a hairbrush.

The contented and uneventful family life of the Parkers in
Rowena was shattered when Bonnie's father died in 1914,
leaving his widow with three small children and no adequate
income. Emma Parker was forced to move the family to her
mother's home in Cement City, a semirural collection of scattered wooden houses near a cement works on the outskirts of
Dallas—then one of the toughest parts of the city and a haunt of
criminals. There she got a job, while her mother looked after
the children.

It was in her grandmother's home at this time that Bonnie
first met her cousin Bess (the daughter of Emma Parker's
sister), who was three years older than Bonnie but small for her
age. They were a wild pair and became firm friends. Emma
Parker recalled that her mother's and her sister's houses "were
generally in a stew from morning to night" as a result of their
pranks, despite frequent application of the hairbrush.

Bess and Bonnie usually played alone together, for Billie was
far too young for them (and reported their naughtinesses to her
doting grandmother), while Buster was much too serious to
join in. The two girls removed their hated long winter underwear two months before they were supposed to and hid it
between the featherbed and the mattress. They intensely dis-
liked the bags containing asafetida (a particularly smelly plant
gum believed to have medicinal properties) that their grandmother insisted they should hang around their necks. Bonnie
and Bess cut the suspending strings with a butcher's knife, but

they refused to help Billie get rid of her asafetida bag, for they knew that she would tell their grandmother and get them another spanking.

They played at being circus acrobats in their grandmother's barn; they lit fires in a wigwam made of sacks and roasted stolen potatoes in it; they set fire to the garden fence, and the whole family had to put out the blaze with saucepans of water before Bonnie and Bess got such a spanking they could not sit down for a week. They played at being opera singers on top of the pigpen; they stole some of their grandfather's snuff and drank his homemade green wine that they discovered in the hayloft, and Bonnie became drunk and insensible.

Strangely, in the light of subsequent events, Bonnie as a child was terrified of guns. For this reason she was very apprehensive when she and Bess had to help out by making the beds, for their grandfather kept a large old-fashioned pistol beneath his pillow. Bonnie would never touch the weapon, and it was always Bess who carried it to the dresser, where it was placed while they made the bed. Bess remembered that Bonnie would scream with terror if she inadvertently touched the pistol while she was making her grandfather's bed.

Bess described Bonnie as "the tenderest-hearted little thing that I ever saw. All you had to do to make Bonnie cry was to start a sob-story and begin bawling yourself. In five minutes Bonnie would be weeping copiously and ready to give you anything on earth she had if she thought it would help out." Bonnie was fanatically devoted to her hard-pressed mother and, unlike young Billie, tried to help Mrs. Parker by such small acts as tidying up her clothes after she had hurriedly changed and dashed to work in the morning. Bess noticed that Bonnie would pat and lovingly caress Emma Parker's hastily thrown-down clothes before neatly folding them and putting them away.

BONNIE WAS SENT to school at the age of six. She was intelligent and had no difficulties with her lessons and was able to look after herself in the playground. She could beat the bigger boys, and if she got into difficulties, there was always cousin Bess to rush to her aid.

Bonnie was always near the top of the class and won a variety of school prizes for essay writing and spelling; she was once the star of a spelling competition with a neighboring school and was awarded a medal for the city championship. She also excelled in elocution and loved the weekly acting lessons.

Bonnie's childish good looks and precocious ways led to her being hired at the age of seven by some of the candidates in the Cement City elections, for according to Bess, Bonnie's presence always attracted a crowd for the politicians to harangue. She enjoyed these public appearances as much as she did her theatrical performances at school. She was an exhibitionist and soon after entering elementary school caused a commotion at one of the Friday afternoon programs for the parents. Her mother was in the audience, and Bonnie had the part of a pickaninny in a crowd of other child actors. Her bright hair was covered with a stocking cap, and her face was carefully blackened with soot, but one of the small boys in the cast could not resist pulling the cap from her head during the performance. Bonnie was mortified. She burst into tears, dirtying her dress with the soot and leaving white streaks on her face. When the culprit sniggered, Bonnie turned on him and, her mother said, "tore into him right before everyone." This caused considerable merriment in the audience, which encouraged Bonnie to give an impromptu series of cartwheels and somersaults while the program broke up in near riot.

While still at elementary school Bonnie acquired a number of young admirers, and their gifts of candy bars, apples, and chewing gum filled her school satchel. Her favorite was a boy called Noel. Unfortunately, Noel annoyed the ten-year-old Bonnie by some unexplained incident at school. She followed him on his way home and confronted him outside the drugstore, where she jumped on the boy, clawing and kicking at him, holding a piece of razor blade in her hand and threatening to cut his throat if he ever troubled her again. The weeping boy was eventually saved by a passing woman who separated the two struggling children.

On another occasion Bonnie and Bess gave a beating to two sisters in their class who, they believed, were stealing their pencils. They lured the sisters to a lonely gravel pit for the purpose. The next day the sisters reappeared with their big brother. Bonnie and Bess attacked all three and vanquished them—a victory that, according to Bess, terminated pencil stealing at their school.

As a child Bonnie Parker was clearly capable of violent behavior but not to an abnormal degree for a child brought up in a rough "poor white" community. She was warm and spontaneous and was capable of deep affection, especially for her mother and her family. She was also intelligent and showed signs of an artistic temperament, but she was an exhibitionist whose behavior could be easily influenced, sometimes in a violent way, by her audience.

ALTHOUGH SHE WAS popular with the neighborhood boys, Bonnie did not appear to be particularly interested in the opposite sex until she was fifteen years old, and then, with typical impetuosity, she developed a grand passion for another pupil at her school, Roy Thornton. With characteristic showmanship, she had his name tattooed on her thigh, and after overcoming her mother's opposition, Bonnie married her young lover, a year later, when she was only sixteen.

Bonnie and Roy lived in a house that was only two blocks away from her former home, but even though she was so close at hand, Bonnie was immediately overwhelmed at being separated from her mother, whom she found she needed constantly. Each night Bonnie and Roy would call on Emma Parker, and frequently Bonnie would beg her mother to come to the new house and spend the night there.

Mrs. Parker recalled that Bonnie was often ill at this time. It was winter, and her husband refused to take her through the snow to visit her mother. Once Bonnie woke up in the night from a dream in which her mother was dying and became so distraught that she forced Roy to walk through a blizzard to reassure her that her mother was safe and well. Such was the intensity of Bonnie's need for her mother that Mrs. Parker eventually suggested that Bonnie and Roy should move in with her. This invitation was gratefully accepted—even by Roy, who must have found the constant journeyings between the two homes very trying.

In 1926 they all moved to a rented house in Olive Street, Dallas. After they had been there for a few months, Roy Thornton, perhaps not surprisingly in view of Bonnie's intense attachment to her mother, became discontented with life in the shared house. He began to stay away, sometimes for days at a time: In 1927 he left home for ten days in August, for eighteen days in October, and in December of that year he left again. Emma Parker describes how he would "just walk off and leave her for a month or so, and then come strolling back some afternoon, expecting a big welcome, which he invariably got."

Bonnie was wounded by Roy's attitude to the marriage and devastated by his periods of absence from their home. His conduct is not hard to explain, for marriage to a strong-minded girl who could not cut herself free from her mother must have been extremely wearing. Furthermore, as would later transpire, Roy had other compelling reasons for periodically deserting Bonnie.

Bonnie attempted to console herself in her loneliness with a diary.

BONNIE'S JOURNAL

Dear Diary,
    Before opening this year's diary, I wish to tell you that I have a roaming husband with a roaming mind. We are separated again for the third and last time. The first time, August 9–19, 1927; the second time, October 1–19, 1927; and the third time, December 5, 1927. I love him very much and miss him terribly. But I intend doing my duty. I am not going to take him back. I am running around with Rosa Mary Judy and she is somewhat a consolation to me. We have resolved this New Year's to take no men or nothing seriously. Let all men go to hell! But we are not going to sit back and let the world sweep by us.

January 1, 1928. New years nite. 12:00
   The bells are ringing, the old year has gone, and my heart
has gone with it. I have been the happiest and most miserable
woman this last year. I wish the old year would have taken my
past with it. I mean all my memories, but I can't forget Roy. I
am very blue tonight. No word from him. I feel he has gone for
good. . . .

For seventeen days Bonnie continued her diary, recording the
emptiness of her life—occasional visits to the movies (she saw
Ronald Colman and Vilma Banky in *A Night of Love* and
Florence Vidor and Clive Brook in *Afraid to Love*), an unsuccessful date, her desperate boredom, and, constantly, her longing for her young husband. And then, after writing the date—
January 17, 1928—nothing more. Emma Parker could do little
to comfort her daughter in her desperation, for however badly
Roy Thornton treated her, Bonnie wanted him back: there was
no question of "sending him packing" as her indignant mother
advised.

   Not long after this, Bonnie took a job in a busy café in the
center of Dallas. Marco's Café was on Main Street, two blocks
from the Dallas courthouse, and many of the customers were
lawyers and city officials, some of whom Bonnie would later
encounter in very different circumstances. Little Bonnie—still
less than five feet tall—bustled about energetically, waiting at
the tables and acting as cashier. She enjoyed the busy life of the
café (which advertised "Pure Foods, Quick Service, Popular
Prices") and made a number of friends there. The manager,
too, was pleased that his lively young waitress should attract
more customers but was very annoyed when he discovered that
she allowed many of them to get away without paying—if she
thought they were short of cash or down on their luck. The
manager told her mother that he was worried that Bonnie was
also paying for meals for "courthouse bums" out of her own
wages, but Mrs. Parker realized that she would continue to
hand out free food despite her promises to the contrary. Bonnie
usually had so little money left from her wages that she could

not even replace her worn-out clothes and Mrs. Parker would have to go out and buy new clothes from her meager earnings for her overgenerous daughter.

Bonnie's impulsive charity, as described by her mother, was certainly unusual, but to Mrs. Parker it was just another case of "Bonnie's heart," which was "as big as the courthouse" from which the recipients of her largesse chiefly came. It was, however, an unfortunate generosity, an aspect of Bonnie's showmanship rather than genuine philanthropy. A poor and inexperienced girl, with a troubled marriage, working at a humdrum job in a crowded Dallas café could at least attract admiring attention and gratitude, as she evidently did. Perhaps it gave her a certain sense of power to be the golden-hearted young girl who gave away her wages to the customers of Marco's Café; perhaps it also appealed to her sense of theater.

Bonnie was also popular with the neighborhood children in Olive Street, Dallas. She had a passion for babies and often had a strong desire to "borrow them" for a few days. Once with her sister, Billie, she organized an impromptu children's party at home, and their mother returned that evening to find the house full of small ice-cream-eating children.

Bonnie Parker was eighteen years old when Roy Thornton returned, in early 1929, from his longest period of desertion, lasting for more than a year. Despite her occasional dates, Bonnie had not fallen in love with any other man during these lonely months, but she found that her affection for her husband had dwindled and quickly realized that she no longer loved him at all. Their relationship ended when Bonnie, no doubt with her mother's enthusiastic support, turned Roy Thornton out of their house. She continued with her job at Marco's Café. The family was still together: her brother, Buster, lived in the house in Olive Street (although he did not figure greatly in her life at that time), and Billie now had a husband, Fred, who had moved into the Parker home.

Some months after she had thrown out Roy Thornton, Bonnie learned that he had been involved in a robbery in Red Oak, a small town some twenty miles south of Dallas.* He was tried, convicted, and jailed for five years. Bonnie was not particularly shocked by the news of his crime: she was, after all, living in a very rough part of the city and, despite her family's wish for respectability, was undoubtedly familiar with criminals, understood their way of life, and must have known of her husband's criminality. Her mother said that Bonnie felt exceedingly sorry for Roy but did not divorce him for she felt, with a strange loyalty, that it would look "sort of dirty" to file a petition for divorce while Thornton was in jail.

In November, 1929 Marco's Café closed down, and Bonnie got a job as a waitress at another café on Houston Street and, again, quickly became very popular with the customers. One of these was a young post-office worker, Ted Hinton, whose life would later be tragically linked to that of the vivacious young waitress. He remembered, years later, how Bonnie had told him that she would like to be a singer, an actress, or even a poet.

Bonnie left her job at the café on Houston Street just as the Great Depression was starting and even in prosperous Dallas unemployment was rising. She could not find another job. She returned to a life spent mostly at home, enlivened only by occasional movie shows, dates, and visits to friends.

In January, 1930 Bonnie, still without a job, went to stay with a girlfriend in West Dallas. Her friend had a broken arm and Bonnie was helping with the housework. One evening a young man called, and Bonnie met him in the kitchen; he was slim, about five feet six inches tall, with a puckish face and prominent ears.

In the second week in January, Emma Parker called on Bonnie's friend and saw the young man for the first time: "He was in the kitchen with a big cook apron on, mixing up some hot chocolate, a drink of which he was very fond. I knew there

---

*Thornton was, in fact, an experienced "torch man"; a criminal acquaintance said that he "knew a lot about burning holes in bank vaults." He would appear in a very unexpected role thirty years later, as a rival of Clyde Barrow, in Shpetner's movie *The Bonnie Parker Story.*

was something between them the minute Bonnie introduced him to me. I could tell it in Bonnie's eyes and her voice and the way she kept touching his sleeve as she talked. I knew too that it was different from the young girl love she had given Roy."

The slim young man was Clyde Barrow.

3

THE
ROOT
SQUARE
GANG

CLYDE BARROW'S FAMILY was poorer than Bonnie Parker's. He was born on March 24, 1909, in a ramshackle clapboard farmhouse, half a mile from the nearest neighbor, three miles from the tiny Texas township of Telico, and thirty miles southeast of Dallas (then a city of less than one hundred thousand inhabitants). Before the Civil War Telico was intended to be the metropolis of northern Texas, but the plans never materialized and it remained an isolated community of barely a hundred souls, windswept or baking in the summer heat, set in a wide landscape of rolling black prairie.

Clyde Barrow's father, Henry, was an illiterate tenant farmer, a taciturn man with huge work-roughened hands. The family was desperately poor, and Clyde's father was forced to work in the fields during all the hours of daylight. They were poorly clothed, rarely had enough to eat, and enjoyed virtually no social diversions to break the monotonous routine of their life.

Mrs. Barrow, a tiny, careworn woman, bore eight children— Clyde was the sixth. His sister Nell, five years old when he was born, thought him adorable and delighted to sit and hug him. When he was six months old, her love had grown so fierce that she squeezed him almost to death. The baby went blue around the mouth and fell back limp and unconscious: it took three hours for Mrs. Barrow and the neighbors to revive him, and it was three days before he fully recovered from Nell's excess of love.

Although their mother and father were both quick-tempered and worked to the limits of their endurance, Nell could not remember any of the Barrow children ever being punished by their parents. She was certainly not spanked for squeezing the breath out of her baby brother, nor was she punished on an occasion some years later when, while they were out swimming, she failed to notice that the little boy was close to drowning. Once again Clyde was limp and unconscious as he was dragged on to the bank of the creek. Nell and her cousins revived him by rolling him on a bank of leaves and moving his arms about.

As a small boy Clyde was unusually adventurous and, according to Nell, "was never afraid of anything." At the age of five he disappeared one morning from the farm and could not be found. Even his taciturn father grew anxious and left the fields to join in the hunt. Mrs. Barrow was frantic, and Nell sobbed continually as they searched the neighborhood for the lost child. At dusk Clyde reappeared riding on a wagon, quite unmoved by the tears and scoldings that greeted him, and said disdainfully, "Shucks! A man gave me some pennies and I couldn't spend 'em till I got to town, could I? So I des walked in." He got off scot-free for this, too.

IN HER ACCOUNT of his early childhood, Nell paints a charming but quite unconvincing picture of Clyde's accidents and adventures on the squalid farm in Telico. A more convincing interpretation is that of early neglect by tired, overworked parents and of a toddler left to the occasional attentions of a small sister. This care was so inexpert that he nearly perished on at least two occasions, was never guided or corrected, and was left to wander inadequately clothed and unsupervised across the bleak surrounding countryside. Nell was probably nearer to the truth when years later she said of Clyde, "how few good times he'd had when growing up."

The highlights of Clyde's impoverished childhood were the very occasional visits to the little movie house in a nearby town. He was thrilled by the adventures of the cowboy outlaws he saw on the flickering screen, and in his play he imagined himself to be Jesse James or Cole Younger, both of whom had brought off a number of famous robberies in Texas. Their exploits were, in fact, still being recreated by the Cole Younger-Frank James Wild West Show during Clyde's childhood years. The last of the old Western outlaws, Henry Starr, was in fact shot down, during a bank robbery in Harrison, Arkansas, on February 18, 1921, when Clyde was nearly twelve years old. These cowboy criminals were almost his contemporaries—not figures from the remote past such as the American gangsters of the 1930s would appear to a modern child. The silent movies that enthralled the young Clyde followed the peculiar moral code of the Wild West—a code that wrapped a murderous criminal such as Jesse James in the heroic aura of Robin Hood and despised as a traitor and a coward the law officer such as Charley Ford who brought James's criminal career to an end. These sentiments would not have been at any marked variance with the simple values of Clyde's family. According to Nell, family disputes were frequent and usually led to fierce rows or fights between the children, but if they were threatened from the outside, then the overriding family loyalty made them draw together to present a solid front no matter what the rights or wrongs of the matter or the size and number of the adversaries.

In their games as Western outlaws, it was always Clyde Barrow who took the part of the leading gunfighter, usually Jesse James, and the long-suffering Nell had to be content with the part of the coward or, when the game was cowboys and Indians, a redskin. Nell, five years older than Clyde, was not altogether happy with this arrangement, "but Clyde was going to be the big shot if we played, and if I kicked about it, we didn't play. It was very dull when Clyde refused to play, therefore I went on being cowards and redskins."

Both Nell and Clyde hated school, but it was not until Clyde reached school age that Nell was persuaded to play truant; it had never even occurred to her before. On the days they stayed away, they took their school lunch with them into the nearby woods in the flatlands of the creek bottoms to play at gunfighting and Indian slaughter.

The Barrow children also amused themselves with the farm animals, and Clyde would ride the calves until, in Nell's words, "they could hardly totter." His parents were not bothered by this but objected strongly to his riding milking cows or fattening pigs. With his older brother, Marvin Ivan (invariably known as Buck), Clyde would use the chickens for cockfighting and, occasionally, birds that Buck stole from neighboring farms; Nell was very indignant at the suggestion that Clyde also stole chickens for this purpose.

Clyde Barrow did, however, reveal an innate cruelty when as a child he was seen by some neighbors "torturing pet animals." He was apparently in trouble on this score on several occasions, for one of his pastimes was to break a captured bird's wing and watch the wounded creature attempt to fly. Another was to half wring the necks of chickens and enjoy their prolonged agony.

Much of Clyde's play, in fact, seems to have possessed an underlying violence: imaginary gun fights, cockfighting, tormenting calves, and torturing birds. Farm life was hard, and maybe this kind of play prepared him for it. Certainly the children had to work as soon as they were able (hoeing corn, chopping cotton, and doing household chores), and even this allowed them just to survive on the edge of destitution: there were no luxuries in the Barrow home, and food and clothing were at subsistence level.

To save money, Mr. and Mrs. Barrow would frequently banish the children to various relations in the general vicinity of Dallas. When Clyde was six and Nell eleven years old, they were sent to stay with their father's uncle at his farm near Corsicana, a prosperous oil town in rich farmlands some twenty miles from Telico. According to Nell, this uncle was "crazy" about them both and they liked him, his house, and their cousins, who were about their own age. As at home, they worked on the farm and, in Nell's words, "hunted some, and played a lot," but their education was severely neglected, and they seem not to have gone to school at all during their visits to the farm near Corsicana. Their stays with this favorite uncle would last for about three months, and then they would return to the shabby wooden home near Telico.

After three years of shuttling between home and the farm at Corsicana, they were sent to stay with another uncle on a ranch at Mabank, twenty-five miles east of Telico. Here, to their dismay, they were sent to school, though there were compensations, such as horses to ride. However, their aunt was "very stingy" and had evolved a most economical regime for consuming the pigs that they reared on the ranch. The pigs were slaughtered in the autumn, and the aunt would smoke all the best joints and make sausages from the remaining meat. The trouble was that, though they ate the smoked ham only infrequently, they had the sausages very frequently indeed—three times a day. The Barrow children soon became thoroughly bored with this exclusive diet, and Clyde devised a plan to steal sausages and feed them to the many dogs belonging to the ranch until the poor animals, in Nell's words, "puffed up like balloons and walked funny." But the plan misfired, for no matter how many dogs they distended, the supply of sausages was inexhaustible and the menu at the ranch remained unchanged.

Clyde and Nell left the ranch, partly as a consequence of the diet, and moved on to yet another uncle, who lived in Kerens, a town east of Corsicana. This man was the strictest of all the uncles, for he was a disciplinarian and made the two children work hard; they had to get up before dawn to look after the farm animals or labor for long hours in the fields. Clyde particularly hated their life on the farm in Kerens, but fortunately for him and Nell, their father gave up his unequal struggle with the farm near Telico and moved with his wife into West Dallas, then one of the roughest areas in that part of Texas.

Clyde Barrow was twelve years old, skinny and small for his age, when he moved to West Dallas with his seventeen-year-old sister. The district into which they moved was in the part of the city where "poor whites and thugs hung out," according to one contemporary description. It was an area of low timber-framed buildings set along a grid of wide dirt roads on flat-lands near the muddy Trinity River, which occasionally spilled into the untidy yards and scruffy streets to give the district its nickname the Bog. However, to a boy reared in poverty on an isolated Texas farm, even the Bog must have seemed an exciting and fascinating place.

The first home of the Barrow family in the Bog was a make-shift camp on the grass beneath one of the drafty arches of the long Houston Street Viaduct. Nell soon found a job and went to live nearer to her work in the city, and the rest of the Barrow family eventually acquired a home when Henry Barrow started his own business, a clapboard filling station on Eagle Ford Road, which he combined with a small store selling groceries, cooked meats, and Coca-Cola. Clyde was sent to the Cedar Valley School in West Dallas. He had always hated school and left at the first opportunity, at the age of sixteen. Before the Great Depression, Dallas was one of the most rapidly growing and prosperous cities in the United States, and he had little difficulty in finding a job. In fact, he had many of them, including one as a Western Union messenger. Western Union messengers were a rough lot at the time, and some combined petty larceny with their normal duties. Ted Hinton, who was a Dallas messenger boy, recalled that of his counter-parts, twelve ended up in prison and four in the electric chair.

Clyde Barrow later took a job with Proctor and Gamble. Nell, who had married by this time (she was now Mrs. Cowan and lived on Pear Street, South Dallas), recalls that her broth-er used his earnings to buy an old car, "a stripped-down speed-ster," which cost him fifty dollars. Clyde decided to use his newly acquired mobility to drive down to his sister's home and move in with her and her husband. Nell was delighted at this turn of events, for her husband, who worked as a musician in a dance band, was frequently away from home and she was very lonely. The arrival of her lively teenage brother changed all that, and they quickly resumed their old easygoing relation-ship. In Nell's eyes her brother was not a budding criminal but a "very handsome boy" and "a joy to have in the house." She said

that they "pranked together like two kids." Clyde even took
over the absent Mr. Cowan's saxophone and started learning to
play it, distressing Nell and the neighbors with his efforts.

Nell and her brother also bought themselves a ukulele, a
fashionable instrument of the day. They had to scrape around
for the last few cents to raise the necessary $1.98, and to buy it
they had to walk four miles into the city and back. When they
got the instrument home, they realized that they did not know
how to tune it, but Clyde solved this problem by a stratagem
that clearly enhanced his standing still further in his adoring
sister's eyes. To obtain the necessary expertise, Clyde borrowed
a few more cents and telephoned a nearby drugstore, asking
them to send round two ice creams. When the black delivery
boy appeared, Clyde got him to show them how to tune the
instrument and then to play the "St. Louis Blues" for them as
they sat on the front steps of Nell's house on Pear Street.

Clyde still kept one of his childhood practices during his
early manhood in South Dallas, for he would occasionally play
hooky from work. One spring day Nell discovered her brother
at home with a bandaged wrist; he told her that he had
sprained it, that it was painful, and that he had had to leave
work. Nell said that she "half scolded" Clyde for this dishonesty
when shortly afterward she found him putting on a necktie and
using his supposedly injured wrist with perfect ease, but she
soon relented, for she knew "how Clyde loved a good time." The
truant drove out into the spring sunshine in his old car to enjoy
the stolen day and did not return until late that night. Nell
could see that something was wrong as soon as he entered the
room. Clyde told her that he had been speeding in his car, had
been spotted by a policeman, and had escaped but feared that
the policeman had taken his car number and would call for
him. He begged his sister not to "tell on him." She recalled, "I
promised that I wouldn't. I never broke that promise. I never
told on him about anything till the day he died." Fortunately
for Clyde, the police never called about his driving offense.

Besides experimenting with cars, Clyde was also learning
about girls; his first conquest was a schoolgirl called Anne,
from the Forest Avenue High School. They met in late 1925.

The girl's mother was opposed to the affair, but it lasted until Anne graduated from high school. Nell was proud that her brother should have attracted a girl who could graduate from high school: "Clyde's delightful personality and his ability to make people like him was attested over and over by the fact that although he had almost no education and no background, the most respectable and educated people were his friends, and the nicest girls fell in love with him."

Clyde met Anne when he was working at Proctor and Gamble. Her brother worked with Clyde and took Clyde home with him, where he met Anne and instantly fell in love with her. He had planned to marry Anne as soon as she finished school. Surprisingly her parents did not object to the proposed marriage; they did not appear to know about the minor juvenile offenses that Nell's adored brother had got mixed up in.

In the spring of 1926, Clyde and Anne quarreled, for he was quick-tempered, headstrong, and often upset her. Anne was not prepared to be treated in this way and took herself off to stay with an aunt at a farm in undulating wooded plains near the small town of San Augustine, 170 miles southeast of Dallas, close to the Louisiana border.

Clyde was full of remorse at his treatment of Anne and missed her terribly. According to his sister, he decided to rent a car for the afternoon (his own car no longer worked) and drive to San Augustine. He persuaded the girl's mother to come along as well, to visit her San Augustine relations and, he hoped, improve his chances of reconciling Anne. The two estranged lovers made up their differences very quickly, and Anne's mother also enjoyed her unexpected visit to San Augustine; things went so well that they all stayed on for two more days.

Meanwhile, the manager of the rental company was getting anxious about the car Clyde Barrow had rented. The police were informed of its disappearance and eventually tracked Clyde down to the farmhouse in San Augustine. Clyde did not wait for an interview but ran out of the farmhouse and across the surrounding fields as the policemen drew their pistols and fired two shots after him. Clyde hid in some nearby woods until they left and returned to the farmhouse after dusk, to a tearful

Anne and a very frosty reception from Anne's mother and her relations.

Nell Cowan later maintained that this rather absurd incident was the primary cause of her brother's embarking on a criminal career. According to her, he was at this time just a high-spirited boy and his behavior in running from a police inquiry about the nonreturn of a rented car was merely because "he didn't like rows and it was easier to run away." This is an unconvincing explanation from a woman who said that her brother "was never afraid of anything." Furthermore, it is unlikely that he really believed that he could drive for 340 miles and have time to win back Anne in an afternoon. It seems likelier that his conduct when the police arrived at the farmhouse was a consequence of the minor juvenile offenses that Anne certainly knew about. This would accord more convincingly with the behavior of a youthful hellraiser who, according to the neighbors, "had gotten into trouble several times" for, among other things, torturing animals.

Barrow's subsequent conduct, immediately after the incident at the San Augustine farmhouse, is also difficult to reconcile with Nell's picture of the innocent youth trapped into a criminal career by a single unconsidered brush with the police. If this were the case, why within a few hours would he steal a car to try to take Anne and her mother back to Dallas? His action was doubly stupid, not only because of the risk involved after his earlier offense but also because it would hardly be easy to explain to Anne's already hostile mother how he had so quickly obtained a second car.

As it was, he was not able to take the two women home because they had already left when he returned to the farm at San Augustine. Clyde therefore started to drive back into Dallas by himself in the stolen car. While he was still not far from San Augustine, another car slowed up and stopped close beside him and Clyde panicked again. He jumped out of the car, hid in a ditch, and then ran on; as he looked back he saw that the car, which he had mistaken for a police vehicle, was full of drunken blacks. But he had lost his nerve and, leaving the stolen car by the side of the road, hitchhiked back to Dallas.

His theft of the car was not discovered by the police, nor was he punished for the incident with the rented car. It is therefore difficult to see why his sister should suggest that the incident with the rented car at San Augustine was the primary cause of his criminal career. Indeed, it is very difficult to accept Nell's account of her brother's behavior at this time. There is, for example, independent testimony from a neighbor that in 1926 he was a member of the Root Square Gang: "The gang was a bunch of young kids just starting out as thieves. They would steal automobile tires, sell them and get drunk and hopped up with the money. A little later the gang ventured into burglary."

The superintendent of the Dallas City Police recalled that he tried to prevent Clyde's youthful descent into crime: "I thought that a bit of good talking would make him see light and turn from the path of crime toward which his actions were leading. But even then Clyde was a tough, unresponsive and stubborn character who believed every policeman to be his mortal enemy."

Clyde Barrow was, in fact, developing strong antisocial tendencies and exhibiting behavior that psychologists classify as psychopathic. No doubt such behavior could be interpreted in terms of some intricate flaws in his brain pharmacology. Modern psychiatry looks for an explanation in the childhood of the psychopath, and an almost universal postulate is that of early parental neglect. The neglected child early realizes the absence of parental attentions and because of this can fail to develop "moral controls." Without conscience the child psychopath is essentially asocial; he cannot regulate his aggression and is led to purposeless, impulsive action; emotional frustration leads to intensified desires uninhibited by conscience or emotional attachment.

Parental neglect is more frequent in poor families struggling to exist in difficult economic conditions. Clyde would seem to have been a classic case: born of poor white parents who were exhausted by their labors, on an isolated farm with barely enough to eat; left as a baby to the inexpert cares of an elder sister and nearly perishing from several childish accidents; rarely corrected and never punished; repeatedly packed off to various relations to fend as best he could. The move from the ramshackle farm at Telico to the squalid streets of West Dallas was hardly improvement, and by adolescence Clyde Barrow was a failure at school and had taken his first steps in petty crimes.

When he was arrested with his elder brother Buck on a charge of stealing turkeys just before Christmas 1926, Nell again tried to excuse her younger brother: It was all the fault of Buck, "who was notorious for stealing." Nell complained that the police "began classing the Barrow boys together," despite the fact that Clyde was again released and Buck was sent to jail for a week. She later maintained that this treatment made Clyde "resentful of the law and disgusted with their methods." However, although tough in their methods, the police had not pressed charges against Clyde Barrow during 1926, and it is difficult to accept Nell Cowan's contention that Clyde Barrow's criminality was entirely a consequence of early police harassment. Her attitude seems to be an example of the criminal values of the Bog and of the family solidarity that even when they were children in the farmstead at Telico meant that they presented a united front whatever the rights and wrongs of the matter.

Certainly Anne's family was very unhappy at her relationship with Clyde Barrow, despite Nell Cowan's boast that "the most respectable and educated people were his friends," for Anne's parents brought sufficient pressure to bear on their daughter to end her affair with Clyde Barrow.

Shortly afterward, Clyde fell in love for a second time, with someone Nell describes as "a beautiful girl named Gladys." Clyde had the name GLADYS tattooed on one arm, the other being already occupied by the name ANNE. He met Gladys while on a visit to the booming oil town of Wichita Falls, 120 miles northwest of Dallas. It seems to have been a very intense love affair; when he returned from Wichita Falls he announced that he was already married to the beautiful Gladys.

Clyde and Gladys set up house in rented rooms on Liberty Street and invited Nell over to meet the new Mrs. Barrow. She was forced to admit that Gladys was "a likeable person, very slim and pretty," but felt their relationship would be difficult.

The network of small towns in Texas that Bonnie and Clyde most frequented

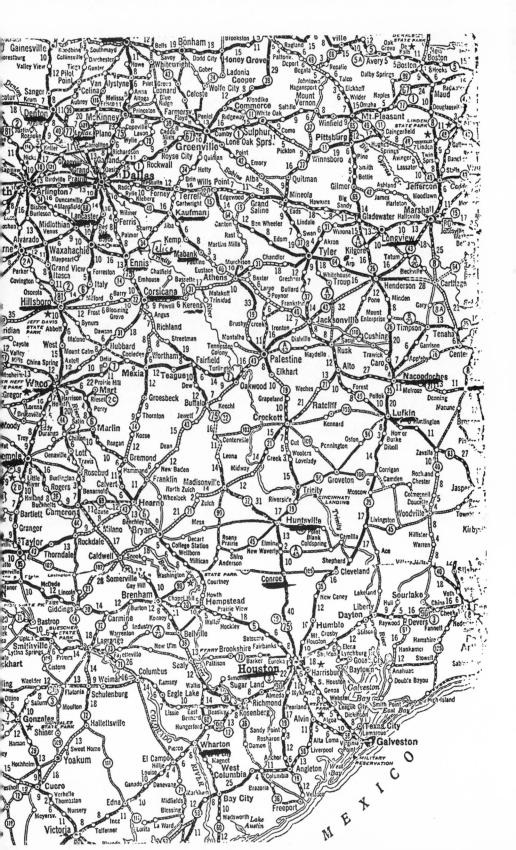

In particular, Nell was worried that Gladys's tastes would be too expensive for Clyde Barrow's wages. They were. When Gladys did not get the things she wanted, she could be very disagreeable, and as a result, Clyde became unsettled and dissatisfied with his earnings.

Nell Cowan was able to witness their relationship at first hand, for her own marriage had broken up and she moved in with Clyde and Gladys. It must have been a difficult situation, for she had to observe constant disputes and quarrels as Gladys complained about Clyde's low wages, about his previous relationship with Anne, about Anne's tattooed name, and about their lack of a car.

While Nell was staying on Liberty Street, Clyde stole a car in Oklahoma that he drove back and hid in a garage in West Dallas. Nell visited him at the garage while he was working on the car. She did not at once realize that the car was stolen and could not understand why he was filing away the engine number and removing the paint from the bodywork with alkali. When she accused him of having stolen the car, Clyde laughed at her, and, in Nell's words, "we had a big row about it . . . I refused to speak to him and his face was blazing with anger."

Nell Cowan left the apartment after this and moved in with her mother. A few weeks later Gladys also left Clyde Barrow and went back to Wichita Falls. Nell then discovered that Gladys and Clyde had not been married at all.

After these setbacks Clyde gave up his job and moved in with a friend "who seemed to be a nice boy," according to the doting Nell. Once again she was mistaken, because the friend was a hardened young criminal with a police record. One of their first joint ventures was to rob a drugstore at Oak Cliff on the southern outskirts of Dallas. After this Clyde and his friend joined up with Buck Barrow and a lad from Houston but were arrested on the suspicion that they were planning to hold up a lumber company in Dallas. The four were released on bail and moved for the night into Mrs. Barrow's house, where Nell was also staying. The next morning the police called again at the house. As soon as they heard them talking to Mrs. Barrow, the four men scattered: the Houston boy hid under the house, Buck made for the back door but fell down and sprained his ankle, and Clyde and his friend ran outside with the police firing after them. However, the police bullets brought them to a halt, and they walked back slowly to the house. Nell remembered that Clyde was crying as he came back into Mrs. Barrow's kitchen and told her that he hated the police station and could not face the prospect of returning there.

Nell Cowan was touched by Clyde's tears and accompanied him, rounding on the police for harrying her eighteen-year-old brother. The police seem to have been patient and good-natured: they told Nell that they were interested in Clyde's car, a yellow Buick that was parked outside the house. Determined to protect Clyde, Nell claimed that the car was her own, but it emerged that the police were interested in it because it had been seen in the vicinity of several robberies, in Luftkin and Hillsboro.

According to Nell, it took the police some time to convince her that her younger brother was now a habitual criminal. She eventually left the police station with the unenviable prospect of telling her mother of Clyde Barrow's descent into a life of safecracking, store robbery, and car stealing, although Mrs. Barrow must by this time have had a good idea of her younger son's activities.

The police could not, however, have possessed conclusive evidence, for, much to Nell's surprise, her brother and his friends were released from custody a few days later. It did not take them long to get into trouble again, for in October, 1929 Clyde, together with Buck Barrow and two other men, traveled 105 miles to the northwest to Henrietta, a small town gathered around its redbrick courthouse, and stole a car. They then drove down to the brick-manufacturing town of Denton, thirty miles from Dallas, broke into a garage, carried out the safe, loaded it into the stolen car, and drove off. Clyde Barrow was at the wheel, and this was their undoing, for he was reckless. They soon attracted the attention of a police car, which gave chase, frightened Clyde into driving even more dangerously, and eventually forced him to hit a curb. This broke the front axle and threw Clyde out of the car. According to Nell, when "he hit the ground he kept on running." As he ran, he heard shots and a scream of panic from his brother. Clyde afterward said he thought that Buck Barrow had been killed, but he still kept on running. He spent the night hiding in the alleyways of Denton and next day found his way back to Dallas. Nell said that Clyde "was a pretty scared boy when he got in."

The Barrow family read in the newspapers of Buck's arrest and of the flesh wound that he had sustained. One of the other men had also been arrested, but the rest of them had not been identified: Clyde Barrow had got away again.

Buck Barrow was tried and sentenced to five years in the state penitentiary in Huntsville; the other man was jailed for ten years. Nell was relieved that "Buck had taken all the blame for the affair and done everything he could to keep Clyde clear from complicity in the Denton matter."

Clyde seems to have lain low after the Denton debacle. He can hardly have been pleased with himself, for his adventures had been singularly unsuccessful, but to Nell he was still "just a normal boy, full of fun, lovable, fond of a good time." And when he walked into the kitchen of the girl with the broken arm in West Dallas on a cold day in January, 1930, Bonnie Parker saw not an unsuccessful petty crook with jug ears but a handsome and desirable man. To Clyde, Bonnie must have appeared as attractive as she was to Nell Cowan: "an adorable little thing, more like a doll than a girl. She had yellow hair that kinked all over her head like a baby's, the loveliest skin I've ever seen without a blemish on it, a regular cupid's bow of a mouth, and blue, blue eyes." What's more, "she had dimples that showed constantly when she talked, and she was so tiny, she was only four feet ten inches tall, and weighed between eighty-five and ninety pounds. Her hands took a number five glove, and her feet a number three shoe. She was so full of the joy of living, she seemed to dance over the ground instead of walking; she always had a comeback for any wisecrack; her sense of humor was applied to herself as well as to the other fellow; she worked hard, lived at home, stayed in nights and never ran around; and, she simply adored and worshipped her mother." In Nell's loving eyes, "Bonnie Parker was the answer to a sister's prayer for a wife for a best loved brother."

As Nell had hoped, Bonnie "overlooked" Clyde's past out of "a sympathy and a compassion that is evident only when a woman loves a man with all her heart and soul." However, this angelic girl had already had a husband who was a criminal and, despite Nell's belief that "she never ran around," probably knew a thing or two about the low life of West Dallas.

Mrs. Parker, who was at first unaware of Clyde's exciting past, was much taken with the young man: "He certainly was a likeable boy, very handsome, with his dark wavy hair, dancing brown eyes . . . he had what they call charm, I think." Anne's mother might have disagreed.

4

Lonesome Blues

THE REALITY OF Clyde's first meeting with Bonnie Parker differs greatly from most of the popular versions of this event. For some unexplained reason, many newspaper and magazine articles set the encounter in Kansas City where Bonnie was supposed to have had a job in a café. Always she is represented as a tough, brassy blonde—very different from the generous little waitress who so charmed Ted Hinton and was gratefully accepted by Clyde's sister—and, usually, that first fateful meeting takes place in the café, as in this 1945 magazine version:

> Bonnie then rushed over, fluffed her soft yellow hair, roughed up her lips, then walked to the big front window to wipe away its steam. . . . Looking out the window into the cold gray morning of this February day, she saw a spare-built young fellow, wearing shoddy clothing, heavy shoes, his coat collar turned up, a cap pulled down over his eyes. He was reading the sign, "Home Cooked Foods." Seeing her, he grinned and came in.

In this version Bonnie quickly recognizes the prison pallor of the customer but is not deterred; indeed, she regards it as a positive asset, for what she has in mind:

It was a crazy notion to imagine that a young man with no more evident prosperity than this one, could lift her from the position of a lowly waitress to that of a woman of means. But Bonnie had definite ideas how this transformation could be brought about—ideas she had gathered from past associates. This fellow's bold, strong face told her he had qualifications she could use.

The theme of the vulgar scheming seductress was also used in an early attempt by J. Edgar Hoover specifically to counteract the dangerous appeal of Bonnie and Clyde in the first of his anticrime films, *Persons in Hiding*, released in 1939. In this portrayal, a glamorous female, Dorothy Bronsen (played by Patricia Morison), is a thoroughly bad lot, who from their first meeting sets to work to convert a small-time criminal, Freddie Martin, into a big-time crook. The same basic theme was later used in the 1958 film, *The Bonnie Parker Story*, where she is again a brassy blonde waitress who heaves the sizzling contents of a frying pan over "Guy Darrow" at their first, café, meeting but quickly succumbs after his promises of big money: "You and me, fifty-fifty. 'Cause, honey, I am goin' places."

In Arthur Penn's film version of the legendary first meeting, the ravishing Faye Dunaway is first spied, partially clothed, at her bedroom window, as she watches Warren Beatty attempt to steal her mother's car. In the ensuing encounter the young waitress does not get to work (where, like her predecessors Patricia Morison and Dorothy Provine, she is pursued by lustful truck drivers) but quixotically throws in her lot with Clyde after he shows her his gun and later holds out the rosy prospect of her walking into the dining room of the Adolphus Hotel in Dallas "wearing a nice silk dress."

It is improbable that the real Bonnie had any ideas of a profitable criminal partnership at her first meeting with Clyde Barrow in her friend's house in Dallas in January, 1930. She responded to him as would many a lonely young woman after meeting a man who greatly attracted her: she took him home to mother. She came back to Dallas for that purpose, bringing Clyde Barrow with her. According to Mrs. Parker,

Clyde intended to leave Dallas the following morning. As he stayed late that night, she invited him to spend the night on the living room couch.

Mrs. Parker said later that she did not know Clyde was a wanted man (some of his robberies in Waco and Sherman had by this time come to light), but had she known this, she would "have sent him out of the house before daylight"—not, it should be understood, to get a criminal out of the way but to save him from arrest. As it was, she allowed him to sleep on, letting her son Hubert and son-in-law Fred get off to work.

When the police arrived, Clyde was still in bed. One of the officers woke him up, according to Mrs. Parker, with a humorous reference to his brother: "If you've got any rabbit in you, you'll run like a Buck." Clyde Barrow replied, "Buddy, I'd sure run if I could."

While Clyde was dressing, Mrs. Parker had her hands full with Bonnie: "I thought she was going crazy. She screamed and cried, beat her hands on the walls, begged the officers not to take him." After Clyde and the policemen had gone, Mrs. Parker recalled, "Bonnie stopped crying and just sat down like the end of the world had come." When Mrs. Parker left for work, her daughter was "pathetic and helpless looking, with tears rolling down her cheeks, crying silently."

BONNIE PARKER VISITED Clyde Barrow whenever she could while he was awaiting trial in Dallas. She was still shattered by the loss of her lover and must have been quite a trial for her mother: "She'd ask over and over if there wasn't a chance that he might be freed of the charges. If he could just get out of this, she said, he'd never do anything else wrong—she knew it—she knew it!"

In her anguish, Bonnie sought the company of Clyde's mother; it comforted her to be with a relative of her so recently acquired lover. She also wrote him letters, telling of her love for him and of her hopes for a secure future for them both: "And honey, if you get out o.k., please don't ever do anything to get locked up again. If you ever do, I'll get me a railroad ticket fifty miles long and let them tear off an inch every thousand miles, because I never did want to love you and I didn't even try. You just made me. Now, I don't know what to do." Her letters to Clyde Barrow continued when he was taken off to Denton (where it was decided that there was insufficient evidence for him to be put on trial) and to Waco, where he was taken as a suspect in several robberies in that town. There he was tried for five car thefts and two burglaries and was given a two-year sentence on one charge and a twelve-year suspended sentence on the others: he was to be held in the penitentiary in Huntsville.

The recurring theme of Bonnie Parker's letters to Clyde Barrow at this time is her constant loneliness interlaced with expressions of her love for him together with small items of news, details of her day-to-day life and of her hopes for their future. Another letter tells of her despair when she went to the Dallas jail to find that Clyde Barrow had been taken by the Denton police: "I was so blue and mad and discouraged, I just had to cry. I had Maybelline on my eyes and it began to stream down my face ... I laid my head down on the steering wheel and sure did boohoo." She felt suicidal and contemplated crashing her car or even hanging herself.

Bonnie was determined to get to Denton to visit her lover and had planned to take Clyde's mother with her but didn't meet her on time and found that Mrs. Barrow had gone on by bus. On the way up to Denton, the silencer fell off the car, which worried Bonnie in case she would be in trouble for making so much noise. She ran out of gas and had to "walk for two miles in the rain to get some more," a failure which increased the misery of her loneliness.

So many things could hurt her at this time. Gene Austin singing "Lonesome Railroad Blues" on her Majestic Radiola overwhelmed her with nostalgia for her Clyde. It was always raining. She was irritated by a rumor that she was to be divorced from Roy Thornton. She had sprained her wrist. Her only comfort was the prospect of her life with Clyde Barrow when he was released from jail, like a distant golden day glimpsed from within a long dark tunnel. She hoped that Clyde would then lead a normal life with her: "I want you to be a man, honey, and not a thug. I know you are good and I know you can make good." She wanted to show him that "this outside world is a swell place, and we are young and should be happy like other boys and girls instead of being like we are." These entirely conventional attitudes are very different from those attributed to her in legend in which she is early corrupted, or corrupts, in a desire for material wealth (as, for example, in the films *Persons in Hiding, The Bonnie Parker Story,* or *Bonnie and Clyde*) or excites her lover for the sensual thrill of violence (as did the heroine in *Gun Crazy* and the Bonnie Parker of some pulp magazine articles).

Before Clyde Barrow was moved to Waco for his trial, Bonnie Parker left her home to stay with her cousin Mary, who had recently married and was living in Waco, a rapidly growing town on the Brazos River, seventy-five miles south of Dallas. Clyde's mother went with her, to stay one night and the following day there, while Bonnie stayed on in Waco and was able to visit Clyde regularly, sometimes twice a day.

Bonnie's cousin went with Bonnie on her visits to the Waco jail. According to Mrs. Parker, cousin Mary was much taken with him: "She thought he was the most charming and likeable fellow she'd ever met." The charming and likeable fellow had, however, devised a plan to escape in which he involved his lover.

To succeed, the plan required the use of a gun. Clyde discovered that a fellow prisoner had one hidden in his home in East Waco but did not want his mother or sister to smuggle in the gun in case they should be caught and get into trouble. Clyde Barrow, however, had no such scruples and suggested that Bonnie Parker should bring it to them. Despite Bonnie's recently expressed wish for Clyde to lead a normal, honest life, she readily agreed—evidently her desire for Clyde had overcome her romantic notions of his making good and of their being "happy like other boys and girls"—an example of the uncanny and well-documented power that psychopaths can exert over the women they attract.

As the mother and sister of his friend were both out working, Clyde decided that Bonnie should get into their house during the day, take the gun, and bring it to him when she next visited the forbidding jail, with its castellated clock tower and tall narrow windows. A map of the house was drawn for Bonnie, telling her where the key could be found and where the gun and ammunition were hidden.

Cousin Mary accompanied Bonnie to the house in East Waco on March 11, 1930. She says that she thought Bonnie was merely going to fetch some clothes for Clyde's friend and was very surprised when Bonnie took the hidden key and entered the house. By her own account Mary was even more surprised, and very frightened, when she learned the real purpose of their visit: "I never was so scared in my whole life. My feet were like ice and my knees like water. I just knew policemen were all around the house, waiting to pounce on us when we came out. I begged Bonnie to leave, but she said no sir, she wasn't budging till she found that gun."

Bonnie could not find the gun in the hiding place that had been described to her and began to ransack the house. Despite her initial scruples Cousin Mary also joined in the search: "We turned that house topsy-turvy before we found it [the gun] in the window seat, and the place was in such a unholy mess that there was a big story in the papers next day about its being ransacked." There was, however, no mention of the gun in the newspaper story.

Cousin Mary was still in a great fright when they left the ransacked house. She recalls that "Bonnie wasn't scared, though. She put on two belts, one under her dress to hold her slip tight to her body, and another on top. She slipped that horrible gun between her breasts in the pocket the two belts made."

The two women drove straight back to the Waco jail. As Bonnie had already paid one visit to Clyde that day, the jailer in charge said that she could not stay long during this second visit.

Cousin Mary waited with considerable apprehension as Bonnie went up to meet Clyde, but she soon returned and the two women left without speaking. As they drove home, Bonnie told her that it had gone well and that Clyde now had the gun—a shiny Colt .32 revolver.

Fortunately for them, Mary's husband was away from home, and they pulled down the window blinds and locked the doors; the two women waited until it was dark, when Mary made some supper for them. They were both frightened and worried that Clyde Barrow or his friend might use the gun they had supplied. They slept little. In the morning they bought a newspaper and read that Clyde Barrow and two other prisoners had escaped using a handgun.

According to Cousin Mary, Bonnie cried with relief when she read the story but neither of the women could relax despite their lack of sleep the previous night. Bonnie talked continuously about her Clyde: "He wasn't a bad boy ... he just hadn't a chance. If he got out of this mess and safely away, she'd get a divorce, go to him, and marry him. They would go to some far-off place and everything would be all right. Clyde wasn't ever going to do anything to get into trouble again. He had promised her and she knew he meant it, because he loved her!"

The two women spent another restless night. At half past nine they were frightened to hear footsteps outside the house and even more scared when there was a loud pounding on the door. From a window of the unlit house they saw two men sitting on the cold pavement, where they waited for more than two hours before departing. As it turned out, the men were friends of Mrs. Parker and had been asked by her to bring Bonnie home in a truck that they were driving. The two women were convinced that the police had discovered Bonnie's part in the escape and were now searching for her.

To avoid using a bus or train, which they feared would be watched by the police, Mary drove her cousin out on the road to Dallas and left Bonnie to hitchhike home. Cousin Mary said that she "certainly was a forlorn looking little thing, starting off down the road alone in the cold gray dawn."

According to her mother, Bonnie did not at first tell her about Clyde's escape or of her part in it when she returned home. She noticed that her daughter was on edge and that she anxiously scanned the newspapers. There was no news of her lover's recapture, for Clyde Barrow had got to Nokomis, Illinois, from where he sent a telegram to Bonnie telling her that he was safe and praising her part in the escape from Waco Jail.

Bonnie was thrilled by Clyde's flattery and, according to her mother (who now seemed to know about the escape), probably saw herself as a successor to the famous woman bandit Belle Starr.

BONNIE'S ELATION WAS short-lived, for Clyde Barrow was recaptured only one week after his escape. With characteristic incompetence he and his fellow fugitives had been caught by the police in Middleton, Ohio, where they had burgled a dry-cleaning firm and the offices of the Baltimore and Ohio Railroad. The three of them refused to give their names to the police, but their identities were soon revealed from the fingerprints and they were returned to the Waco jail. Once again, Bonnie was devastated. Her mother recalls that she "cried constantly" and again sought consolation in writing to her lover.

She seems, nevertheless, to have had some misunderstanding with Clyde (who was evidently suffering pangs of jealousy at this time) as he revealed in a letter written to her from his prison cell:

> I just read your sweet letter, and I sure was glad to get it for I am awfully lonesome and blue. Why did you say you didn't know whether I would accept it or not? Now, honey, you know darn well I didn't mean what I said in my last letter. I'm just jealous of you and can't help it. And why shouldn't I be? If I was as sweet to you as you are to me, you would be jealous too.

Two days after writing his letter, Clyde Barrow was transferred from the Waco jail to the state penitentiary to serve a sentence of fourteen years' imprisonment.

5

THE
WALLS

THE STATE PENITENTIARY, known as the Walls to the criminal fraternity, was fifty-four miles south of Dallas in the pleasant leafy town of Huntsville. The prison had a grim and sordid reputation, for behind its ornate, Spanish-style façade the prisoners lived in crowded, insanitary conditions. The antiquated prison hospital was infested with insects; some prisoners had to sleep on concrete floors with only a single blanket for covering; the meals were monotonous and badly prepared from spoiled foodstuffs supplied by unscrupulous wholesalers. Even the forty prison guards were forced to live in a single room with only two broken chairs and one lavatory.

In early 1930 the penitentiary contained about 5,000 convicts in the main prison at Huntsville and in the eleven prison farms, which had a combined area of nearly 80,000 acres. The conditions on the farms were even worse than in the main prison, and the newly appointed governor believed that "the slave camps" of olden times could not have been more insanitary. At Camp Two, located on flat land, there was no drainage, the sewerage stood in the open flat. Everywhere was filth and garbage—and in consequence a set of disgruntled and rebellious prisoners."

Not surprisingly, escape attempts were frequent, and during that year 302 prisoners had broken out. Clyde Barrow's brother Buck was one of these: He had escaped on March 8, 1930, just three days before Clyde had walked out of the Waco Jail.

Fortunately for Clyde, the new prison governor, Lee Simmons, was appointed only days before the young criminal was taken to Huntsville. Simmons was a tough, determined man who immediately initiated a series of drastic reforms that transformed the life of the prison. He ordered a two-story wooden building to be erected to accommodate 200 convicts; he moved large numbers out to the prison farms to relieve the crowding in the main prison and started a vigorous gardening scheme that within sixty days was providing fresh fruit and vegetables for the prisoners. Simmons also began to soften the harsh discipline of the prison, where brutal whippings were commonplace and the convicts were continually abused and insulted. He instructed the prison guards: "From this time on, every prisoner is some mother's son, some woman's husband, some sister's brother. I expect you to treat them as human beings."

The morale at the Huntsville penitentiary improved under the new regime, but discipline was still rigorously enforced; and Lee Simmons successfully resisted an attempt by a legislative committee to abolish the "bat," a twenty-four-inch-long and four-inch-wide leather strap that was still used to punish the inmates. He was also quite prepared for escaping or mutinous prisoners to be shot down by the prison guards.

CLYDE BARROW WAS not taken directly to Huntsville to serve his fourteen-year sentence but was kept in the Waco Jail, apprehensively awaiting the arrival of Bud Russell, the chief transfer agent of the Texas prison system. Russell, a large, kindly man, was known affectionately as Uncle Bud by the Texas underworld. Bonnie Parker certainly knew about Uncle Bud, for Clyde referred to him several times in his letters to her while he was waiting in the Waco Jail.

Uncle Bud eventually called for Clyde on April 21, 1930. Clyde was chained by the neck to the other criminal passengers and driven (in the "one-way wagon") a hundred miles southeast, on a warm spring day, to the state penitentiary under the watchful eye of the man who boasted that he had transported 115,000 persons into captivity during his forty years in the Texas prison service.

After admission to the main prison, a frightened and anxious Clyde Barrow (now convict number 63527) was moved to one of the prison farms, in Eastham, some forty miles north of Huntsville. This was one of the larger farms, about 13,000 acres in extent, and, because of its isolation (it was five miles from the nearest main road), was used to accommodate the more dangerous convicts.

Barrow was set to work in the fields in a gang, with fifteen other prisoners, working under the supervision of a mounted guard who was armed with a bat, a shotgun, and an automatic pistol. Also on hand was one of Governor Simmons's innovations, the specially selected "long-arm man" or "backfield man": a proficient marksman, armed with a Winchester rifle, who, according to Simmons's instructions, "had no duty except to stay well clear of the convicts and to be in the background ready with his Winchester in case of excitement."

The work was hard and monotonous. Although he had labored in the fields as a boy, it had not been like this, and since he had left the country, Clyde had become unused to farm work. It was particularly trying in the summer heat, especially in September when the convicts harvested the cotton crop in the cruel glare of the Texas sun.

The discipline was strict and, despite Governor Simmons's reforms, sometimes brutal. Illegal whippings still occasionally occurred. Clyde's gang was made to run the two miles to and from their work, and the bat could be vigorously applied for any transgression. According to Nell Cowan, Clyde was beaten for complaining that the "pace set for chopping cotton was too fast for him" and again when he was accused of passing a note to his sister during a visit to the Eastham prison farm. Such treatment must have been particularly painful for a young man who as a boy had never been disciplined by his parents and had always been spoiled and petted by his older sister.

The working conditions and discipline led to occasional mutinies during the early part of Lee Simmons's governorship of the Huntsville penitentiary. A squad of men who had been sent out to cut wood for timber and fuel turned on the captors but were prevented from escaping by a particularly determined guard. When Simmons arrived on the scene, he found the wounded guard sitting down: "The wood squad lay on the ground in front of him, some of them dead, some of them wounded, but all of them quiet, counted and accounted for."

Another gang refused to pick cotton in the September heat or to work under a "dog sergeant" whom they accused of causing the death of two of their number. This revolt was quelled only by the personal intervention of Lee Simmons, who later revealed that he was quite prepared to use guards armed with pitchforks to drive men to their work.

There were also occasional fights between prisoners. Nell Cowan recalls that Clyde was upset by an incident in which "he saw a 'lifer' knife a young boy to death before his eyes one night," and she believed that this and other brutal aspects of prison life "ate into Clyde's mind."

This was also the view of Ralph Fults, who at the age of nineteen was a companion of Clyde's at Huntsville. He said that Barrow's whole attitude to life was changed by his prison experiences, which led to a fierce resentment of authority and a bitter hatred of law officers. Clyde's bitterness became like a coil of steel within him, a force that would be instantly sprung by uniformed authority. Fults recalled, years later, that Clyde Barrow's only objective was to gain his parole and then, in what at the time must have seemed pure fantasy, to form a gang to raid the hated Eastham prison farm and release as many prisoners as possible from what he saw as their brutal degradation.

Clyde's misery at this time must also have been increased by an apparent change in Bonnie's attitude to him. By the summer of 1930 she seemed to have recovered from the shock and loneliness of their parting, just as she had done when Roy Thornton left her. Her mother says that by this time Bonnie had stopped writing to Clyde Barrow, but in the winter of 1930 they were corresponding again: On December 11, in a letter in which he addressed her as his wife (prisoners were only allowed to write to their relatives), he expressed surprise that she should write to him at all.

Whatever differences there were between Bonnie Parker and Clyde Barrow at this time, his adoring sister remained loyal to him, and she visited him whenever she could, though prison rules allowed only one hour a month. Like Bonnie when Clyde was in the Waco jail, Nell Cowan tried to plan for the future: "I tried not to think of what might be happening to Clyde... and spent my efforts in trying to have a job waiting for him when he did get out. I was determined that Clyde should be a man, as Bonnie had said, and not a thug." Nell was, in fact, hoping to get a job for her brother through the influence of a friend in Worcester, Massachusetts.

One piece of good news Nell could give him was that their lazy, easygoing brother Buck had met and married "a splendid, gentle, good country girl named Blanche Caldwell." The marriage took place on July 1, 1931, in McCurtain County, just over the Texas border, where Buck Barrow was still in hiding. Blanche was apparently unaware that she had married an escaped convict, but her husband confessed to her after a few weeks of marriage. When she had recovered from the shock, Blanche Barrow started a campaign (in which she persevered) to convert Buck to an honest life and, according to Nell, "prevailed on him to come home and talk things over with his folks." Her hopes were identical with those of Bonnie and Nell for Clyde Barrow: she too "wanted a man for a husband, not one who must sneak and hide."

Clyde eventually learned that his new sister-in-law had succeeded in the first stage of her task and that his brother had agreed to surrender himself to the authorities at the Huntsville penitentiary. After the Christmas festivities were over, Buck Barrow drove up to the ornate main building of the prison and, no doubt to the astonishment of the prison officials, gave himself up on December 27, 1931.

It is unlikely that Clyde Barrow shared the enthusiasm of his sister and sister-in-law for his brother's unexpected act of honesty; according to Nell, Clyde was in a state of "despondency, despair and utter hopelessness with life." In an attempt to get a transfer from the Eastham farm, Barrow became, in the words of Lee Simmons, "one of those who early in my administration appeared in the records as a victim of self-mutilation." He persuaded a fellow convict to chop off two toes from his foot, with an axe, but it did not get him what he wanted, for the determined Lee Simmons saw to it that the young convict stayed on at the Eastham farm.

Ironically, while Clyde Barrow was recovering from his terrible injury, he learned that his case had been under consideration, that he had been given parole and was shortly to be released from prison.

CLYDE BARROW'S SELF-MUTILATION, which vividly illustrates the extent of his desperation and bitter unhappiness at this time, became an element in the cinema legend of Bonnie and Clyde. In Fritz Lang's film, *You Only Live Once*, Eddie (played by Henry Fonda) is a truck driver who is wrongly accused of murder during a bank robbery and is sentenced to death. Like Clyde he mutilates himself, in this case by slitting his wrist, and, again borrowing from reality, arranges for his young wife to smuggle a gun into the prison hospital. Eddie too is pardoned but, before he learns of this, shoots the prison doctor and then the chaplain who try to bar his way. His escape, which is also reminiscent of a later incident in the life of Clyde Barrow, is given a nightmarish quality: the prison yard is choked with fog, pierced by moving searchlight beams and blaring loudspeaker voices. Fritz Lang used these incidents to portray with great sympathy the desperate plight of a victim of terrible injustice (a "three-time loser") who is forced into the life of a hunted fugitive with the woman he loves. In Arthur Penn's explicit 1967 portrayal of Clyde Barrow, his self-mutilation is only indirectly referred to as he cheerfully hobbles along with the newly acquired Bonnie and is used to build up the character of a tough young criminal, an essentially antiauthoritarian figure, in his fight against repressive authority.

The real Clyde Barrow left the Huntsville penitentiary on February 2, 1932—a very different person from the youth of two years earlier. He returned home on crutches to a rapturous welcome from his sister.

Nell Cowan recalls that one of their first acts was to take Clyde downtown and buy him "a complete outfit, except shirt and gloves." Nell was particularly concerned that he should *not* have a silk shirt and kid gloves, for she considered these totally unsuitable for what she evidently hoped would be her reformed brother. "Nobody," Nell argued, "but bootleggers and gangsters wear silk shirts. Nice people just don't go in for them, that's all." But that was exactly the sort of image that Clyde Barrow sought. "I'm going to have a silk shirt," he announced, and as of old, his generous and long-suffering sister walked around with him until they had located the desired silk shirt. Nell regarded her brother's longing for a silk shirt as a bad omen. She told her sister, "I don't like that silk shirt business at all," and with characteristic disregard for his recent criminal past, considered that it was "not like the Clyde I used to know."

When Clyde had emerged from his bath, Nell and her sister returned to the theme that seemed common to the women in the Barrow brothers' lives: "What you ought to do now is to get a job and a good girl and get married and settled down." Clyde appeared to have immediate plans only for the second of his sisters' pieces of advice; he set off at once to visit Bonnie Parker. He seemed to be in some doubts as to his reception, for Nell remembers him saying, "I'm going to doll up now and go over there and see if Bonnie will speak to me. Maybe not. No decent girl would, I suppose."

When he arrived on his crutches at the Parker house, Clyde found Bonnie sitting in the living room with another boyfriend. Mrs. Parker was in the kitchen but was strategically placed to witness her daughter's reaction. "The instant she looked up and saw Clyde, it was like he'd never been away at all. She jumped up and ran to him where he stood, looking at the two of them, sort of uncertain and defiant, and she went right into Clyde's arms." According to Mrs. Parker, the other boyfriend then left.

Mrs. Parker must have been worried at the turn of events;

she called to Clyde to come to the kitchen, where he received some familiar advice. "Listen, Clyde," Mrs. Parker said, "if you want to go with Bonnie, that's all right with me. But I want you to get a job first and prove to me that everything is going to be all right." While this good advice was being given, Mrs. Parker recalled her daughter was "hanging around his neck, perfectly radiant, like a fire had been turned on inside of her." Clyde reassured Mrs. Parker by telling her of the job that his sister had got him in Massachusetts. Bonnie's mother was evidently impressed: "Maybe you'd get to like it up there. And surely that's far off enough that the law wouldn't be knowing you every time you stuck your head out of the door."

Clyde Barrow remained in Dallas for the rest of an unseasonably warm February, spending most of his time with Bonnie at the Parker house. By the end of the month his mutilated toes had recovered enough for him to be able to walk without crutches, and in early March he departed for his job with a construction company at Worcester, Massachusetts. Mrs. Parker recalls that Bonnie was very happy, despite the prospect of further loneliness with which she was by now very familiar.

Things did not go well in Worcester. After Clyde had been away a week, Nell Cowan received a letter from her friend to say that Clyde was restless and could not settle down to his work; after two weeks Clyde threw up the job and on March 17 or 18 returned to Dallas. He told his sister that he was unable to settle down to work and, in her words, "that he lived in daily and hourly fear of arrest and that the horror of prison was always with him." He also told her that he needed to be close to Bonnie and his family even though he realized, as Nell pointed out, that his life would be difficult in Texas with his known criminal record. By then Clyde Barrow was trapped in his psychopathy and could no longer endure the restrictions of normal life: He had an urgent need for immediate excitement and was willing to sacrifice everything for fleeting desires; he was impulsive and had no stable values; like a child he was entirely absorbed in his own needs and with unthinking cruelty would devastate the lives of many people, of total strangers and of those who loved him.

SHORTLY AFTER CLYDE Barrow's return, Bonnie Parker told her mother that she had taken a job in Houston: She was to be a demonstrator of cosmetic products. The Depression was still hard in Texas at that time, jobs were difficult to find, and Mrs. Parker was, therefore, not too surprised that her daughter was to leave Dallas for the first time in her life. She was very surprised indeed, however, when two days later she learned that her daughter was in jail in Kaufman, a small country town clustering around a quiet square of shops only some twenty miles southeast of Dallas.

6

MUD,
MULES,
AND
TEARS

EMMA PARKER FOUND a very crestfallen daughter awaiting her when she walked through a white wooden porch into
the two-storied sandstone jail in Kaufman on a day in late
March, 1932. Bonnie burst into tears when she saw her mother.
She was locked in a cell next to a "crazy negro woman" and was
overawed and frightened; Mrs. Parker said long afterward
that "death would have been much easier" than seeing her
daughter in such a place.

Bonnie admitted to her mother that she had not taken the job
at Houston but instead had joined Clyde Barrow—she did not
say where. He and his young jail companion, Ralph Fults, had
"planned a robbery"—again she did not say where. Typically
(for Clyde Barrow seems to have been still a most incompetent
criminal) the plan misfired. According to Emma Parker's
account, they were surprised during the attempt and were
lucky to escape in a car that they had stolen for the purpose.
Hotly pursued by the police, they drove wildly along small dirt
roads until eventually the car stuck in the mud and they were
forced to flee on foot across some neighboring fields. In a
farcical scene (far removed from the romantic American
legend they were eventually to acquire but certainly in the
spirit of Steno's Italian film parody) they chased, caught, and

mounted some mules in a desperate attempt to escape from their pursuers, who by now were near enough to fire at them. True to their mulish natures, the animals refused to budge, and the fugitives were forced to take to their heels again amid flying police bullets. They eventually stumbled into a muddy ditch where they remained panting and scared. Fortunately, their abrupt descent into the ditch threw the police off the trail, and after a time, Clyde Barrow was able to carry his bedraggled, barefooted partner, who had lost her shoes in the mud, to an empty building (a church, according to Emma Parker, a barn, according to Ralph Fults's recollection) that he had noticed. There he left Bonnie in the gathering dusk while he went looking for a car to steal.

Bonnie Parker crouched in the darkness, listening anxiously to the night sounds outside the empty building. Once she heard the voices of the searching police officers, but to her surprise and relief, they did not look inside. Hours passed, and still Clyde did not return. Eventually Bonnie decided to leave, imagining that Clyde had been caught. Bonnie told her mother that she had intended to hitchhike back to Dallas, but the police caught sight of her as she was trudging down the road, and she was arrested. The police had also caught the dejected Ralph Fults as he too tried to escape from the district. There was no sign of Clyde Barrow. Once again he had abandoned his companions after a bungled crime, but he was safe, for Bonnie Parker and Ralph Fults refused to reveal the identity of their confederate to the police.

BONNIE SEEMS TO have perked up quite quickly after the immediate shock of her incarceration had worn off. She also seems to have exercised her charms on the jailer and his wife, for Emma Parker remembers that they "were very nice to her" and even allowed her to "sit on the lawn in the evenings and romp with their children."

According to her mother, Bonnie Parker also did something rather unexpected in a young woman of her background and associations: she wrote the first draft of a poem. It was to be completed in very different circumstances and was destined to be printed in newspapers and magazines throughout America.

She called her poem "The Story of Suicide Sal." Apart from a little metrical clumsiness, it is an extremely well-written example of an American popular tradition. Can it have been composed by the same person who wrote the mawkish letters to Clyde Barrow during his spells in jail? Mrs. Parker always maintained that the poem was written by her daughter, and she kept the cheap exercise book with the poem written out in Bonnie's hand. Perhaps her daughter possessed a genuine literary gift (as Bonnie's cousin Bess said she did as a child); if she wrote "Suicide Sal," she certainly understood the rhythms of the Western ballad and made skillful use of them. It is possible that a newspaperman may have put a professional polish on Bonnie's early ideas, but there is no evidence for this.

"The Story of Suicide Sal" is a narrative poem written in the style of the late nineteenth- and early twentieth-century ballads that were printed in local newspapers, recited in homes, bars, and theaters, and published in dime books and cheap magazines. Bonnie Parker would have been familiar with the genre. She was also an assiduous moviegoer and could have adapted the imagery of Hollywood for her description of the corruption and abandonment of Sal by her criminal lover.

The subject of the poem was strikingly relevant to Bonnie's predicament as she languished in the Kaufman jail in the spring of 1932. Its writer was clearly fascinated by criminal slang and by the life of the professional criminal even though she had been so ignominiously abandoned by her lover in their first crime. This fascination is particularly baffling when compared with Bonnie's previous exhortations to Clyde "to make good" and "to be a man . . . and not a thug!"

How could Bonnie Parker have plunged so suddenly into the criminal life? Most probably the descent was not so abrupt as it might appear from her letters and her family's picture of her earlier innocence and goodness. She had been brought up in one of the roughest parts of Dallas; she had been married to one criminal and been the friend of others. Above all, she was deeply in love with a man whom she knew she could never reform. She had spent the previous weeks in his company. Without doubt he would have described to her his tough prison companions, their way of life, their slang, and their fantasies of spectacular criminal success. Only in this way could he counteract the memory of the degradation to which he had been subjected: the hard discipline and beatings with the bat, the long hours of menial farm labor, and the contempt of the prison guards. Her theatrical and exhibitionist side would have responded to her lover's talk. If she could not reform him, then she could at least see herself as an associate in glorious criminal adventures in the tradition of Jesse James, Billy the Kid, and especially Belle Starr—the legendary figures from the recent Texas past.

The form of her poem is exactly in the tradition of the contemporary ballads celebrating the criminal psychopaths who had become the folk heroes of the American mid- and southwest. Perhaps Bonnie Parker was corrupted by cheap literature.

After the absurdity and failure of Bonnie's first robbery with her lover, what else was there to sustain her but fantasy? At least she could glorify her degradation and see herself in the romantic role of the wronged, golden-hearted Suicide Sal: a singularly appropriate image for the generous little waitress from Marco's Café.

At the same time she could also enjoy the alternative role as she protested to her long-suffering mother her desire to "go straight" and lead a good, honest life. This role had the additional advantage that it not only helped her immediate situation (by convincing the jailers of her essential goodness) but might also impress the jury that was about to consider her case in the tall brick courthouse that stood in the center of the sleepy town square at Kaufman.

The Story of Suicide Sal

We each of us have a good "alibi"
For being down here in the "joint";
But few of them really are justified
If you get right down to the point.

You've heard of a woman's glory
Being spent on a "downright cur,"
Still you can't always judge the story
As true, being told by her.

As long as I've stayed on this "island,"
And heard "confidence tales" from each "gal,"
Only one seemed interesting and truthful—
The story of "Suicide Sal."

Now "Sal" was a gal of rare beauty,
Though her features were coarse and tough;
She never once faltered from duty
To play on the "up and up."

"Sal" told me this tale on the evening
Before she was turned out "free,"
And I'll do my best to relate it
Just as she told it to me:

I was born on a ranch in Wyoming;
Not treated like Helen of Troy;
I was taught that "rods were rulers"
And "ranked" as a greasy cowboy.

Then I left my old home for the city
To play in its mad dizzy whirl,
Not knowing how little of pity
It holds for a country girl.

There I fell for "the line" of a "henchman,"
A "professional killer" from "Chi";
I couldn't help loving him madly;
For him even now I would die.

One year we were desperately happy;
Our "ill gotten gains" we spent free;
I was taught the ways of the "underworld";
Jack was just like a "god" to me.

I got on the "F.B.A." payroll
To get the "inside lay" of the "job";
The bank was "turning big money"!
It looked like a "cinch for the "mob."

Eighty grand without even a "rumble"—
Jack was last with the "loot" in the door,
When the "teller" dead-aimed a revolver
From where they forced him to lie on the floor.

I knew I had only a moment—
He would surely get Jack as he ran;
So I "staged" a "big fade out" beside him
And knocked the forty-five out of his hand.

They "rapped me down big" at the station,
And informed me that I'd get the blame
For the "dramatic stunt" pulled on the "teller"
Looked to them too much like a "game."

The "police" called it a "frame-up,"
Said it was an "inside job,"
But I steadily denied any knowledge
Or dealings with "underworld mobs."

The "gang" hired a couple of lawyers,
The best "fixers" in any man's town,
But it takes more than lawyers and money
When Uncle Sam starts "shaking you down."

I was charged as a "scion of gangland"
And tried for my wages of sin;
The "dirty dozen" found me guilty—
From five to fifty years in the pen.

I took the "rap" like good people,
And never one "squawk" did I make.
Jack "dropped himself" on the promise
That we make a "sensational break."

Well, to shorten a sad lengthy story,
Five years have gone over my head
Without even so much as a letter—
At first I thought he was dead.

But not long ago I discovered
From a gal in the joint named Lyle,
That Jack and his "moll" had "got over"
And were living in true "gangster style."

If he had returned to me sometime,
Though he hadn't a cent to give,
I'd forget all this hell that he's caused me,
And love him as long as I live.

But there's no chance of his ever coming,
For he and his moll have no fears
But that I will die in this prison,
Or "flatten" this fifty years.

Tomorrow I'll be on the "outside"
And I'll "drop myself" on it today:
I'll "bump 'em" if they give me the "hotsquat"
On this island out here in the bay. . . .

The iron doors swung wide next morning
For a gruesome woman of waste,
Who at last had a chance to "fix it."
Murder showed in her cynical face.

Not long ago I read in the paper
That a gal on the East Side got "hot,"
And when the smoke finally retreated,
Two of gangdom were found "on the spot."

It related the colorful story
Of a "jilted gangster gal."
Two days later, a "sub-gun" ended
The story of "Suicide Sal."

—*Bonnie Parker*

7

"THAT HILLSBORO THING"

THREE DAYS AFTER Bonnie Parker was locked in the Kaufman jail, the lover who had left her to be caught had recovered his nerve sufficiently to attempt another criminal venture: the robbery of the Sims Oil Company in Dallas. A month later Clyde Barrow was again involved in crime. His accomplice was a short, fair-haired young man—an extrovert and talkative jail companion, Raymond Hamilton. The crime took place on a warm spring night in Hillsboro, a quiet, straggling little town situated on the main highway to Austin, forty-five miles south of Dallas. Their victim was a sixty-one-year-old businessman, John N. Bucher, a respected citizen of the town, where he had been in business for more than thirty years. He was a member of the First Baptist Church of Hillsboro, a pioneer motorist, and an excellent mechanic. Butcher was a man of parts, for he combined the running of a filling station with a prosperous jewelry business and a general store where he lived with his wife, Madora.

Shortly after midnight on April 27, 1932, John Bucher heard a man's voice calling to him from somewhere outside the filling station. He spoke to the caller from an upstairs window and was told that the man wanted to buy some guitar strings from his store. Despite the late hour, Mr. Bucher went downstairs, with a revolver prudently stuck in his belt, turned on the lights in the store, opened the front door, and let in his nocturnal customer.

The customer followed Bucher to the back of the store (where the guitar strings were kept in a glass showcase) and, after selecting what he required, walked back to the front of the store with its owner. As the purchaser of the guitar strings handed over a ten-dollar note, a second stranger entered the store, through the opened front door.

John Bucher did not have money to change the banknote and called to his wife to come downstairs to open the safe for him. Madora Bucher unlocked the safe and, turning, opened the door. As she turned, she saw one of the customers aim a revolver and fire a single shot at her husband. The bullet passed right through John Bucher's body, piercing his heart. He died instantly. The revolver in his belt fell to the floor. With surprising adroitness and great courage, Madora Bucher snatched it up, but the gunman forced her to place it on the counter. One of the intruders stepped over John Bucher's body and took fifteen dollars in cash and a number of diamond rings (worth about $2,500) from the open safe. The bandits then ran from the store and vanished into the night. Madora Bucher afterward recalled that she heard no sound of a car drive up or leave the property.

The police arrived on the scene within minutes of receiving Madora Bucher's telephone message. Every police officer in the district was alerted, and the sheriff organized a search of the immediate countryside during the hours of night that still remained. He was confident that his men would get John Bucher's murderers and announced in the local newspaper that "the pair would be placed under arrest within the next few days." But he was wrong, for it was not until May 9, with John Bucher already buried in the Ridge Park Cemetery, that the *Hillsboro Evening Mirror* carried the news that the Hillsboro police were "seeking two men, that are said to have police records, and since the murder have not been seen by officers in any section of the state."

SO CLYDE BARROW had been involved in another bungled crime. Unable even to rob an elderly man efficiently, one or other of the young criminals had panicked and turned what would have been just another inquiry about a petty robbery into a full-scale murder hunt.

Faced with the results of his own incompetence, Clyde Barrow did what he had done on many previous occasions when he got into trouble: he ran home to his family—to the long-suffering mother who had never punished him for any childish crimes and the adoring sister who excused his weaknesses and thought him handsome and charming.

Nell Cowan found him at her mother's home when she called there two days after the murder. Mrs. Barrow told her daughter that Clyde was "hiding behind the house." Clyde at first denied to his sister that he had been involved in what she called "that Hillsboro thing" but eventually blurted out, "I told those dumb eggs not to use any gun play—and I beat it the minute I heard the bullets popping." He then admitted that he had taken part in the robbery but had not fired the shot that killed John Bucher.

Clyde told Nell that he had gone to the Buchers' store "to look over the joint," some time before the robbery. On this visit he recognized Mrs. Bucher (who, he claimed, had lived in West Dallas), and she had recognized him. This story seems improbable, because Madora Bucher was a Hillsboro woman who had married John Bucher in 1902, a few years after the death of his first wife, and had lived with him ever since in Hillsboro. Possibly Nell concocted the story of Mrs. Bucher's familiarity with Clyde Barrow in West Dallas to explain her subsequent identification of him from police photographs, but whatever the truth of the matter, Nell Cowan believed her brother when he said that he had not entered the store during the robbery and had not shot John Bucher. According to him, he remained in the getaway car. When he heard shots he drove away, leaving his companions (he claimed that there were two accomplices) to look after themselves—it must be admitted, a very typical Barrow escape strategy.

Although at the time there were no reports of a woman being involved in the affair, subsequent accounts of the Hillsboro robbery and murder added Bonnie Parker to the scenario. The Drapers, for example, in a twenty-five-page pamphlet published in 1945 *(The Blood-Soaked Career of Bonnie Parker. How Bandit Clyde Barrow and His Cigar-smoking Moll Fought It out with the Law)*, have her prominently involved in the proceedings: "Bonnie drew her pistol and pointed it at the old man. "You stick up your hands!" she cried. "This is a real hold-up. We mean business." . . . Bonnie struck Mrs. Bucher down with the butt end of her gun. They ran to the car where Raymond Hamilton was waiting, laughed loud and long as they counted the money. Bonnie shoved the diamonds into her bosom to remind her, she said, of their first successful hold-up together." Even the rather more scholarly account of Myron J. Quimby* states categorically that "Clyde Barrow, Bonnie Parker and Raymond Hamilton held up the grocery store in Hillsboro, Texas."

There was no mention in contemporary newspaper reports of a woman being involved in the Hillsboro robbery and murder, for at the time Bonnie Parker was in the Kaufman jail. Neither was Bonnie involved in the next crime that has been attributed to Clyde Barrow: the robbery of the Magnolia Service Station at the timber town of Lufkin on May 5, 1932. This was a more professionally executed affair, in which the manager of the service station was kidnapped, along with the manager of the Gulf Service Station a few blocks down the road that was also successfully robbed. The two managers, who were released in the forested outskirts of Lufkin, later identified one of the robbers as Clyde Barrow.

Nell Cowan was outraged at this identification, for her brother told her that he was not involved in the robberies in Lufkin: "We believed Clyde when he said he didn't do a certain robbery or murder. . . . Why should he lie to us? What was one

---

*Contained in a book dealing with the lives of several of America's notable criminals, *The Devil's Emissaries* (1969).

more robbery more or less during a spring and summer that was filled, not only with robberies, but murders?"

MEANWHILE EMMA PARKER was making efforts to secure the release of her daughter from the Kaufman jail. On the advice of the jailer's kindly wife, Mrs. Parker had decided not to apply for bail for her daughter, principally because she could not raise the money to do so, but also to give her daughter the opportunity to "think matters over."

Bonnie Parker appeared before the grand jury in Kaufman on June 17. The evidence against her was not strong, and she managed to convince the jury of her contrition. She was consequently released from custody.

When she returned home, her mother noticed that "she was soberer, more quiet, and a great deal older than the Bonnie who left home three months before." Emma Parker "talked the situation over" with her daughter, concluding with the rather obvious advice, "If Clyde's going to keep on the way he's been going, you're going to have to stay away from him." Bonnie agreed, assured her mother that she would have nothing more to do with Clyde Barrow, and abruptly left the room—to "have a good cry," Mrs. Parker suspected.

Bonnie stayed with her mother until late June 1932. She was having no success in finding a job and was clearly unsettled and unhappy. One hot evening Emma Parker returned from work to find that her daughter had again left home. This time Bonnie had gone to Wichita Falls, 170 miles northwest of Dallas, to try for a job in a newly opened café there. At that time Wichita Falls had changed from a ranch town into a booming oil center and was famous for its saloons, bars, and cafés that had earned for it the nickname of Whiskeytaw Falls. Mrs. Parker was very worried about her daughter working in the town but was consoled by a postcard from Bonnie telling her about the new job.

BONNIE PARKER WAS, indeed, in Wichita Falls, and was working in one of the cafés there. What her mother did not know was that her daughter had joined Clyde Barrow, who was living there in a rented cottage with Raymond Hamilton. The two men were resting up and planning their next venture: the robbery of the Neuhoff Packing Company in Dallas, for which they had already begun to make preparations, including the mapping of their escape route.

Barrow and Hamilton drove back to Dallas with Bonnie Parker at the end of July and left her at the Barrow home in West Dallas. As they drove away in boiling summer heat at noon on July 31, Clyde called to his lover, "Listen over the radio, honey, and see if we make our get-away." Bonnie replied, "Don't say things like that, Clyde. It's a jinx."

To Bonnie's relief she soon heard the news on the radio that the Neuhoff Packing Company had been robbed and that the bandits had escaped. She then knew what to expect, for Barrow and Hamilton had told her that they would drive back through the city and along the Industrial Boulevard (the highway that divided the poor white area of the Bog from downtown Dallas) to pick her up and then head eastward toward the town of Grand Prairie, where they had selected an abandoned farmhouse several miles from the town for their hideaway.

Five days later, Clyde drove Bonnie and Raymond back to Dallas. The two men dropped her at her mother's home and then left to drive for eighty miles across rolling prairie country north of Dallas and over the state border into Oklahoma, out of reach of the Texas Police.

8

STRINGTOWN
FOLLIES

CLYDE BARROW AND Raymond Hamilton crossed the Red River on August 5, 1932, and drove northward into the hilly country of southern Oklahoma. They were in a car they had stolen earlier in the day at Corsicana (some forty miles southeast of Dallas) so that their journey must have been roundabout and tiring in the summer heat.

Barrow and Hamilton had picked up a friend; they had been drinking heavily, and Hamilton, in particular, was in an excited state. Cruising along a quiet country road that hot Friday night, some fifty miles into Oklahoma, they saw lights and heard music in full swing at a little country place called Stringtown in Atoka County. Hamilton wanted to stop and join in the fun, for he loved to dance. Emma Parker was outraged when she learned of this later. As she told Bonnie, "If Raymond just had to dance, he could have turned on the radio in the car and got out by the side of the road and hopped up and down by himself." But this was not what Hamilton had in mind at all, for he and the others wanted to join in the excitement of a country dance where they could see shirt-sleeved men and women in summer dresses jigging away in the open air on a square-dancing floor with a banister around it and a small gate at one end to admit the dancers. Four high school kids were vigorously scraping and twanging away (on a violin, banjo, and two guitars) in an open-sided canvas pavilion at one side of the dancing floor. At about nine o'clock one of the guitar players, Duke Ellis, noticed a car containing the three men drive in from the gathering darkness and park close to the lighted dance floor. The men remained in the car, drinking from a whiskey bottle, talking and watching the dancing before one of them got out and joined in the dancing, leaving Clyde and Raymond in the car. According to Duke Ellis "they were having a high ole' time."

Also watching the proceedings were the local sheriff and his deputy, who were becoming very suspicious of the occupants of the parked car. Sheriff Maxwell walked slowly and deliberately over to the vehicle, followed by Deputy Moore, and leaned down to speak. There was no spoken reply—only a burst of gunfire. Sheriff Maxwell fell to the ground with bullet wounds in his chest, side, arms, wrist, and leg. And then all was pandemonium: the engine roared and the car hurtled forward across the grass, amid shouts and screams and a fresh explosion of gunshots as the wounded sheriff raised himself on an elbow and fired at the departing car.

The car careered on to the road, then crashed and overturned into a railway culvert. Two figures scrambled out and were immediately on their feet, firing back in the direction of the lighted dance floor, which was now a scene of considerable panic. Everyone was running and shouting. Duke Ellis fled into a nearby garage by pushing aside a loose plank in the wall, followed by another musician who had managed to soak his shirt in engine oil and was convinced that it was blood from a serious flesh wound. His friend tried to jump across a ditch but landed astride a barbed wire fence. Another man, trying to get his two young sons to safety, was shot in the shoulder. Deputy Gene Moore dropped dead with a bullet through his heart while some of the dancers picked up the fallen officers' guns and fired back into the darkness.

The pandemonium continued for about five minutes, by which time Hamilton had collected up the remaining ammunition and, with Clyde following, crawled along the culvert underneath the railway line on to another road. As they hesitated on the roadside, a passing car stopped and the driver, a kindly Stringtown man, asked if they needed help. Clyde responded to his courtesy by ramming a revolver into the driver's ribs, forcing him back into his car. The fugitives packed into the car with its frightened owner. Undeterred by his recent accident, Clyde Barrow continued his reckless course. Fifteen miles along the road, the car was brought to an abrupt halt by the loss of one of the wheels. Hamilton was thrown out, uninjured, and his accomplice managed to scramble free, leaving their hostage behind in his disabled vehicle.

Barrow and his companion ran to a nearby farmhouse and, according to Emma Parker's account, told the farmer, "We've had a wreck. A fellow down there is badly hurt and we've got to get him to a doctor, quick. Have you got a car?" The farmer's nephew backed his car down from the farmhouse, but he too was jabbed in the ribs with a gun for his trouble and ordered to drive west along a small road through the Jackfork Mountains. After a few miles Clyde took the wheel and drove on to the small township of Clayton, some forty miles from Stringtown. There they stole yet another car, abandoned their hostage, and drove south into Texas, crossing the Red River. They reached Grapevine on the northeast outskirts of Dallas, where they abandoned the car.

Thus ended the journey which was originally intended to take the men across the state line into the sanctuary of Oklahoma. As with so many of Clyde's criminal enterprises, it was a pathetic failure, for all that the pair of them had done was to arouse the Oklahoma police for no criminal profit whatsoever.

The shooting of the two country sheriffs at Stringtown bore the characteristic Barrow hallmark—panic. More professional criminals would have disarmed the sheriffs, who were not, after all, carrying their weapons in their hands. Even that undersized psychopath, Baby Face Nelson, could control a streetful of onlookers, including police officers, during a bank robbery. An expert gangster such as John Dillinger would have made the sheriffs drop their weapons and would, no doubt, have executed a well-organized getaway with some of the Stringtown dancers hanging on to the car running boards as hostages. Clyde Barrow and his companions could only shoot wildly at two unsuspecting country policemen and then crash two cars in their inglorious flight. They had, of course, been drinking this time, but Barrow's behavior in Stringtown was essentially similar to that on previous occasions—when he fled from the carful of drunken blacks, mistaking them for the police during the affair of the overdue rented car in San Augustine or when he abandoned Bonnie Parker in the deserted building near Kaufman or when he panicked during the robbery and murder of the elderly storekeeper in Hillsboro.

Emma Parker was particularly outraged by the business in Stringtown. "The entire affair was utterly without justification or logic.... They weren't staging a hold-up and caught and forced to fight for their lives. In fact, there was no excuse for them being where they were in the first place." One wonders what that much-more-formidable criminal matriarch, Ma Barker (at that time organizing her family gang with ruthless discipline and efficiency) would have made of the affair.

Luckily for Clyde Barrow and his compatriots, the Oklahoma Police did not, at first, know who they were or where they had gone. The *Indian Citizen Democrat*, the Atoka newspaper, reported that "posses of local officers and citizens chased the desperadoes all night and the greater portion of the day. The bloodhounds were brought from McAlester as it was thought they might take to the hills on foot but the dogs were useless as matters worked out." Also: "The entire force of the State Bureau of Identification, with the exception of one man, came down from Oklahoma City."

The Atoka newspaper later reported that two of the fugitives had been "positively" identified. "One of them is Clyde Barrow, wanted for murder of L. [*sic*] Bucher, a merchant of Hill county, Texas, and Raymond Hamilton, pal of Barrow and wanted for hijacking and other crimes."

SOME TIME AFTER the Stringtown shooting that strange human alchemy began its transformation of reality. Inevitably, Bonnie Parker is introduced into the proceedings. First, there were stories that a stranger, a young woman in a red dress, had been seen dancing on the night of August 5, 1932. She must, of course, have been Bonnie Parker. Then Clyde and Raymond Hamilton are given a prominent part in the jollifications. According to the Drapers' account, Bonnie danced "first with Clyde and then with Raymond, whirling around in her bright red dress—and easily the prettiest girl in the place." A dispute arises, and the local sheriff appears on the scene, taking the side of a local lad whose advances have been rejected by Bonnie. Only then do "the boys [Barrow and Hamilton] . . . answer with a volley of gunfire."

Now this late version (which is, surprisingly, also detailed in the ghosted biography of the lawman Ted Hinton) is very far from reality. Two surviving eyewitnesses (Ralph "Duke" Ellis and John Winters of Stringtown, Oklahoma) make no mention of Bonnie Parker, and according to Ellis (who was very well placed to see), neither Clyde Barrow nor Raymond Hamilton went on to the dance floor that night. The contemporary account of the affair, published in the *Indian Citizen Democrat* of Atoka, does not mention that the men had a female companion with them at the dance. Emma Parker said that Bonnie was staying with her in Dallas on August 5, 1932.

These transformations are very characteristic of the early growth of legend. For the purposes of storytelling it is necessary to involve the romantic female in the proceedings. This is analogous to the incorporation of fictional Maid Marian into the legend of the Outlaw of Sherwood. She does not appear in the tales of Robin Hood and Little John until the sixteenth century—two hundred years after the first extant versions.* The storytellers also change the emphasis so that "the boys" now take part in the merriment and in so doing become involved in a dispute that is none of their making. Sheriff Maxwell is certainly not the wicked Sheriff of Nottingham but nevertheless is clearly on the wrong side and, in this sense, gets what is coming to him.

---

*See J. C. Holt, *Robin Hood* (1982).

Bonnie Parker is not, however, an innocent Maid Marian figure. She is a hellcat more like another local female outlaw from an earlier generation, Belle Starr, as in this pulp magazine version of the Stringtown affair: "Bonnie jumped out on the ground, half drunk and crazy mad. 'Not us you great big fools.' She started clawing and kicking the officers. Then, standing back, she shouted, 'Let's run 'em off boys. Let 'em have it.'"

THE REAL BONNIE Parker, at home in Dallas, rose early on the morning after the Stringtown shootings. Her mother recalled that she eagerly seized and searched through the newspapers on that Saturday morning in August 1932, but whatever she had expected to see, it cannot have been the news of the pointless murder at Stringtown by three Dallas men. She must have suspected that Clyde might be one of them, but never could she have imagined that her name would one day be linked with these events in Atoka County, Oklahoma.

That evening Bonnie sat with her mother on the porch of their house, relaxing in the coolness after the heat of the August day. Bonnie had told Emma Parker that she would be returning to Wichita Falls the following morning and that she had booked a taxi to call for her at five o'clock to take her to the bus station.

Mrs. Parker recalls that a car, driven by a young man she had not seen before, stopped in front of their house. Bonnie ran down to the car, talked to the driver for some minutes, and then walked back to her mother. She told her that she had been offered a lift to Wichita Falls and would be leaving at once. With characteristic generosity she gave her mother the money that she had kept for her bus fare, snatched up her handbag, kissed her mother good-bye, and drove off with the stranger.

The driver of the car was a friend of Clyde Barrow's who had been sent by him to collect her. He drove her back to the abandoned farmhouse near Grand Prairie, where they had been living before Clyde and his companions left on their futile journey into Oklahoma.

While staying in the farmhouse, Bonnie did not make any

attempt to see her mother. Clyde, on the other hand, made regular visits to his family. Mrs. Barrow relayed the messages from her son to his sister, Nell Cowan, so that she too could come along. There was apparently a family code to cover this eventuality; when Mrs. Barrow told Nell that she was "cooking red beans for dinner" it meant that "the kids would be in."

A few days after Clyde returned to his hideout in Grand Prairie, Nell Cowan drove to her mother's home in Dallas. She sat in the summer darkness waiting in her car for the arrival of her adored brother.

At a little after ten o'clock she decided that he was not coming and, very disappointed, started to drive away just as a car came up dangerously close behind her, as though to force her off the road. Nell, now thoroughly alarmed, increased her speed, only to be nearly driven off the road a second time by the strange car. She could now see that the driver had startlingly red hair and was signaling her to pull over, but again she continued to accelerate. The two cars raced along together for some seconds, and then she heard a familiar voice shouting at her, "For God's sake, Sis, you dumb egg!"

Only then did Nell recognize the driver as her brother, Clyde, and pull off the road; sitting beside him in the car was Bonnie Parker. Nell climbed out of her car and went over to talk to her brother. She recalls that as she attempted to stand on the running board of his car, he pushed her away. Her first thought was that he did not want her fingerprints on the car, but Clyde laughed and told her that he was only worried that she would be muddied by the dirt that clung to the car, for they had been driving over muddy side roads to avoid police attention.

Clyde Barrow had never failed to charm his sister, and she can seldom have seen her brother in a happier temper. He told Nell that he had asked Bonnie to dye his hair but that she had blistered his scalp in the attempt, and Nell could see that his hair was now a conspicuous and very unnatural red. Clyde seems to have been delighted at this meeting with his favorite sister. He made jokes and said that he would like to wear a woman's blonde wig as a disguise. Bonnie, on the other hand, was tired and dispirited, failed to laugh at her lover's jokes, and told his sister, "Nothing's very funny the way I'm feeling tonight."

Clyde admitted that he had been involved in the shooting at Stringtown and told Nell that he did not know who had killed the deputy sheriff, as both he and Raymond Hamilton had fired simultaneously. Nell began to cry when she heard him admit this, for she had previously refused to believe that her brother had been involved in the murder. Her tears were not for the victims or their families but for her younger brother, who she now knew without doubt would be a hunted murderer. She even suggested that he should give himself up, for he might "just get a sentence," but Clyde mocked her, saying that he "would get the chair" if he were caught and that he would prefer to have a little while longer with Bonnie and then "Out— like Lottie's eye."

When Nell asked where the two fugitives would go, Clyde answered with the words that she remembered long afterward, "Driving, just driving from now till they get us. Kansas, Missouri, Oklahoma, Mexico—Texas, always Texas where we were born!"

9

THE
LOST
DINNER

BONNIE PARKER HAD now deliberately and irrevocably committed herself to the life of a hunted criminal. Her decision to share her life with Clyde Barrow seems to have arisen from two primary and possibly linked causes: her genuine love for him and her fascination with criminals and criminality.

It is difficult, at first sight, to divine why she should love so intensely a man who had become what she had once said she despised: "a cheap and vicious thug." But to call him that was just to affix a label. To her he was still the high-spirited boy she thought so handsome and desirable—only he now had a history of swift impulsive acts of violence.

The ability of some violent antisocial men to elicit strong love and to dominate the women who offer it is a trait that is well known to criminal psychologists. Perhaps the most extreme example in modern times is that of the Moors Murderers. Like Bonnie Parker, Myra Hindley was a popular and happy-go-lucky young woman. She was apparently normal, honest, and extremely fond of young children. Yet she fell deeply in love with a petty thief with some very unpleasant habits who influenced her to such an extent that she procured young children for him and joined in his torture and murder of them.

Bonnie Parker was clearly dominated by Clyde Barrow. He

91

altered her whole attitude to life as effectively as the young fanatics of the Symbionese Liberation Army kidnapped and turned heiress Patty Hearst into a gun-toting bank robber more than thirty years later.*

This is very far from the relationship depicted in some versions of the legend of Bonnie and Clyde. In several written accounts and films it is the woman who dominates—rather like Maid Marian taking over from Robin Hood. Thus in *Gun Crazy* the Bonnie and Clyde figures (Annie and Bart) establish a very unequal relationship: Annie (portrayed by Peggy Cummins, wearing a Bonnie beret) is a sharpshooter in a sideshow who persuades Bart to abandon the fairground for a life of violent crime to satisfy her sensual pleasure in weaponry even though he is repelled by the prospect of killing. Critics of *film noir* attributed great significance to this implied phallic symbolism. Dorothy Provine's Bonnie in *The Bonnie Parker Story* also turns into a bossy gun-toting wildcat and, despite much initial bravado by "Guy Darrow," finds him less than adequate sexually, as does Faye Dunaway's Bonnie, who comments quite specifically on his limitations when he fails to come up to expectations. "Your advertising is just dandy. Folk'd just never guess you don't have a thing to sell." Despite his sexual failures, Warren Beatty's Clyde is a tough character and is certainly not dominated by Bonnie.

The representation of the celluloid Clyde as a violent man who can initiate but not sustain a full sexual relationship is plausible, for psychologists recognize that the male psychopath will frequently be at first regarded by women as a romantic and virile lover. This is generally a false image. ("None of the psychopaths personally observed have impressed me as having

---

*William Sargant has shown, in the *Battle for the Mind* (1957), how in conditions of emotional stress people's ideologies and loyalties can be very dramatically changed. Such abrupt changes can be long-lasting or even irreversible. The stress can be deliberately imposed (as in the brainwashed Patty Hearst) or can occur in the course of ordinary human affairs. Sargant cites the example of Arthur Koestler's quixotic conversion to Communism at a time of deep unhappiness. Bonnie Parker, desperately lonely and unhappy when she met Clyde Barrow, would have been psychologically vulnerable.

particularly strong sex cravings even in this uncomplicated and poverty stricken sense." H. Cleckley, *The Mask of Sanity,* 1976.) Clyde Barrow was evidently an undemonstrative lover. Emma Parker once laid great stress on the fact that she never saw Clyde kiss her daughter "more than three times"; a companion who spent some time in his company noticed Clyde's instant aversion to a particularly sexy brunette who came briefly into their lives; another long acquaintance remarked that "Clyde had a mistrust of any woman except Bonnie."

Whatever his sexual limitations Clyde Barrow had plainly kindled something in Bonnie's quick impressionable nature that made her see criminals not as sordid clowns but as glamorous adventurers. In just this way earlier psychopathic killers such as Jesse James and Billy the Kid had been transformed in the eyes of ordinary people by the heroic myth of the Western outlaw. All that was necessary was to disregard the victims; the people Clyde left bleeding to death in the road were, after all, not of Bonnie's kind—they were just guardians of an affluence that she could not share. Perhaps the violence and weaponry of criminal violence also stirred deeper, physical levels of her love for Clyde as it did for some of her Hollywood counterparts.

DESPITE HIS INITIAL shortcomings as a professional criminal, Clyde Barrow had by this time developed considerable driving skill. He could not only quickly read approaching danger signs and react with lightning speed, but he possessed great stamina; on occasions he could drive continuously for many hundreds of miles in a single day. He had also begun to build up an intricately detailed knowledge of the roads of Texas and the surrounding states that would stand him and his companions in good stead in the future.

Of all the vehicles that he stole and drove for so many thousands of miles, Clyde Barrow favored Ford V-8s. These tall black cars with their narrow, rakish bonnets and large shining radiator grills were arguably the most reliable ones on the roads of America in the early 1930s. They were ruggedly built, with rod brakes and strong springs and could be driven with relative comfort, not only along dirt roads but even across open countryside and plowed fields. Most importantly, the Ford V-8s of the period were fast, traveling up at to seventy in second and ninety miles an hour in third gear. What is more they were nimble, responding quickly to a flick of the steering wheel and holding the road superbly while cornering. They were also well upholstered, quieter to drive in then many modern vehicles, and although narrow-bodied, with a rather cramped front seat, there was plenty of legroom in the backseat of the four-doored version—an important advantage when sleeping in the car. The V-8s of the time were, in addition, well ventilated—another useful feature in the days of hot engines and in the heat of the Texas summer.

The reliability and speed of Clyde Barrow's favorite cars, together with his considerable driving skills, enabled him invariably to outstrip pursuing lawmen. The police were handicapped, for they were usually equipped with less-powerful six-cylinder cars, often Plymouths and Chevrolets, that were no match for the V-8s. Two years later, when he had achieved national notoriety, Clyde was apparently moved to express his gratitude to the creator of the V-8, for the Ford Company at Detroit received a letter (signed "Clyde Champion Barrow") congratulating them on the quality of their product.

The Barrow and Parker families took pride in Clyde's driving abilities. There was, after all, little else about him of which they could boast. Emma Parker, in particular, extolled his and Bonnie's skill at the wheel—"Their daring escapes, their breathtaking speed, the boldness with which they came and went, were becoming legends up and down the land." She too was impressed by his topographical knowledge. "He came to know all the roads in Texas, Oklahoma, Louisiana, Arkansas, New Mexico, and Missouri. Not only the main roads, but all the side roads and little country lanes. His mind was a photostatic copy of the intricate windings where he could rush in and hide, elude capture, fade into the landscape and become lost to sight."

Clyde Barrow's ceaseless driving, which carried him for some hundreds of thousands of miles fast and aimlessly across the

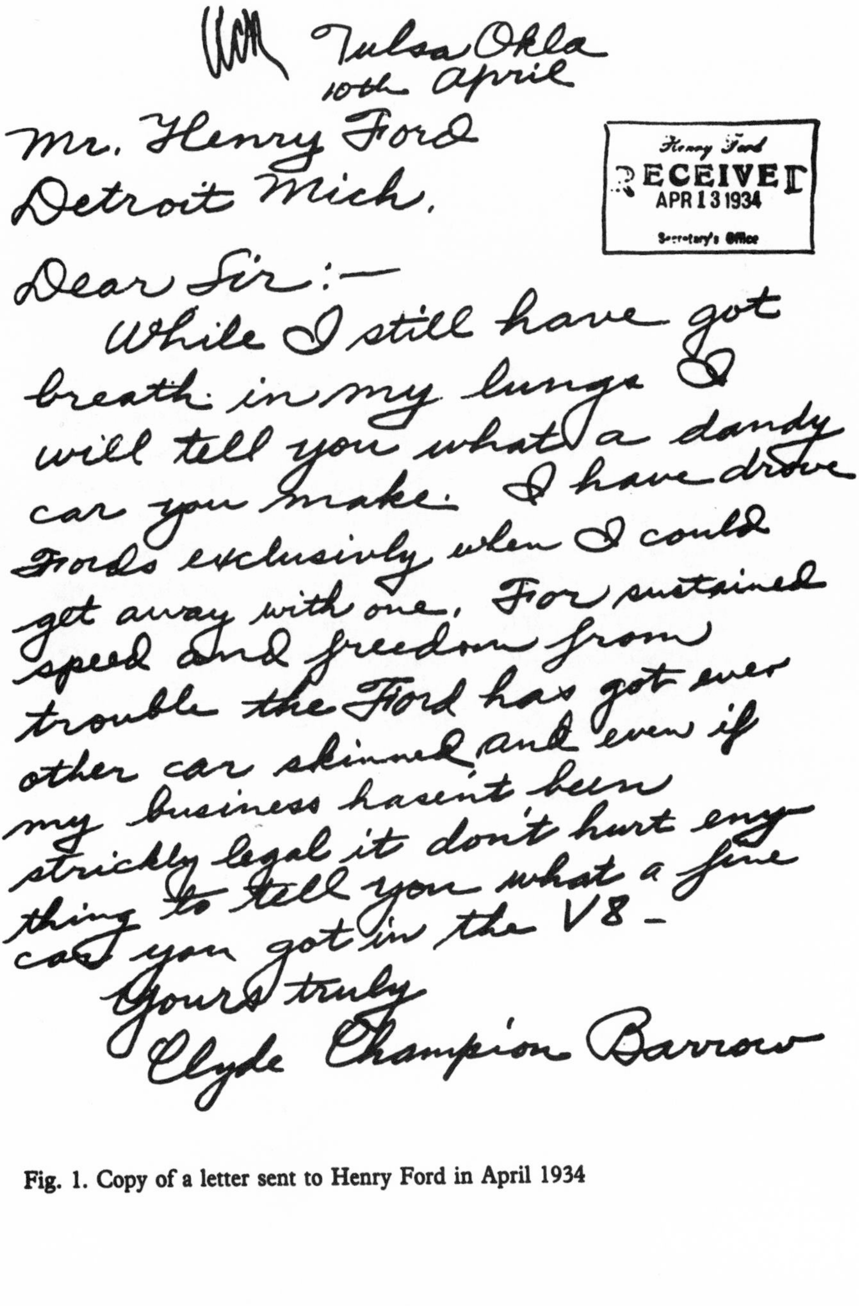

Tulsa Okla
10th April

Mr. Henry Ford
Detroit Mich.

Dear Sir:—

While I still have got breath in my lungs I will tell you what a dandy car you make. I have drove Fords exclusivly when I could get away with one. For sustained speed and freedom from trouble the Ford has got ever other car skinned and even if my business hasent been strickly legal it don't hurt eny thing to tell you what a fine car you got in the V8 —

Yours truly
Clyde Champion Barrow

RECEIVED
APR 13 1934
Secretary's Office

Fig. 1. Copy of a letter sent to Henry Ford in April 1934

United States, was as much an aspect of his disturbed psychopathic nature as was his thoughtless aggression. It was also an
effective escape strategy and became central to the legend of
Bonnie and Clyde: like an amalgam of the stories of the outlaws
of Sherwood and Dick Turpin's ride to York. It was a constantly repeated theme of the Hollywood films: from the sad,
beautiful face of the young Henry Ford with Sylvia Sidney at
his side seen through the windscreen of a rain-soaked automobile in their endless drive down muddy country roads to the
distant shots of Warren Beatty's lurching Ford V-8 careering
across sunlit grassland closely menaced by two pursuing police
cars.

Perhaps the most spectacular of Clyde Barrow's feats of
driving occurred after the fugitives abandoned their rural
hideout near Grand Prairie in the intolerable mid-August heat
of 1932. Their destination was the little town of Carlsbad, some
few hundred miles to the west. Bonnie's aunt (her mother's
sister) lived on a farm near Carlsbad, and the fugitives sought
sanctuary there in the vain hope that they would not be spotted
in that quiet corner of New Mexico. However, an observant
sheriff noted the number of their stolen car, and they were
forced to an unexpectedly abrupt departure (taking the sheriff
of Carlsbad along as hostage), leaving Bonnie's unsuspecting
Aunt Millie picking vegetables in the garden for their Sunday
dinner.

The three of them headed toward Texas. They drove southeast and then turned east, passing through a hot landscape of
long mountain valleys and high plateaus, and then down into a
country of plains and small hills to the old Spanish city of San
Antonio. It was a drive of more than four hundred miles, but
they arrived at San Antonio by the late afternoon of Sunday,
when they released their hostage.

They continued in a southwesterly direction across flat
wooded countryside and by the following morning had reached
the busy town of Victoria, only a few miles from the coast of the
Gulf of Mexico. In Victoria they replaced their stolen car by
another—a Ford V-8 sedan—and, shortly afterward stole a
Ford coupe, which Clyde drove, leaving Hamilton with the V-8

sedan. Unfortunately for the fugitives the police soon learned
of their car stealing and, what's more, guessed their likely
direction of travel. The two cars were now traveling northeast,
across the flat coastal plain on the road toward Houston.

The police had laid an ambush at the bridge that spanned the
Colorado River at Wharton, a small town shaded by moss-
draped oaks. The plan was to trap the fugitives by blocking the
eastern end and then closing the western end of the bridge
after they had driven well into the middle. But the ambush
misfired badly, for the waiting police had no idea that two cars
were now involved and were confused when they saw a sedan
closely following the coupe driven by Clyde. Furthermore,
Clyde glimpsed the police as he approached the open western
end of the bridge. He braked, swung the coupe around, and
accelerated back along the road by which they had come. The
policemen dispatched a hail of bullets at the retreating car.
Hamilton miraculously also managed to swing around the car
he was driving and race away amid flying bullets.

Just down the road the two cars stopped. Clyde and Bonnie
leaped from the Ford coupe and jumped into the other car.
Hamilton gave up his place and Clyde, the better driver, took
over the wheel of the sedan. He swung the sedan back on to the
road, rammed down the accelerator, and hurtled forward at
such speed that pursuing police were left behind and unable to
catch the fugitives.

SHORTLY AFTER THE dramatic escape from the Colorado
bridge in Wharton, Raymond Hamilton announced that he
wished to go to Michigan to stay with his father, who now lived
in Bay City on Lake Huron. A certain amount of tension might
have built up between Hamilton and his two confederates at
this time. Perhaps that is why Hamilton had stolen the second
car near Victoria rather than share the Ford coupe. He was an
excitable and garrulous little man who might well have got on
his companions' nerves when they were confined with him for
hours and days on end. It later transpired that he also had his
own ambitions to engage in more profitable robberies.

According to Emma Parker, Clyde agreed to drive him for

more than a thousand miles to Michigan. She said that they left on September 1, 1932, immediately after the Wharton bridge incident, and headed northward from the flat coastal plain through the Texas prairies and across the middle-western states to Indiana and then north into Michigan. When they reached Bay City Hamilton decided that he would stay with his father, and so after a few days, his two companions left and headed back toward Texas. They drove through Indiana, Illinois, Missouri, and into Kansas, presumably paying the expenses by robbing filling stations and country stores, reaching Kansas City toward the end of October. "The two kids played around awhile," Mrs. Parker recalled, "going to shows, eating at the best restaurants, having their nails done, buying some clothes. Bonnie got a permanent, too." But, according to Nell Cowan, the social round in Kansas City began to pall for Bonnie, and she and Clyde returned to Dallas on October 31.

This family account of Bonnie and Clyde's activities during September and October 1932 differs considerably from the police version of the events at that time. The Dallas police, for example, attributed the robbery of a bank in Cedar Hill, south of Dallas, on October 8 to Clyde Barrow and Raymond Hamilton. It was only after this robbery (in which $1,401 was stolen) that Hamilton decided to leave for Bay City. Police reconstruction of events indicates that Hamilton picked up another criminal friend, Gene O'Dare, and traveled by railway to Michigan.

The official version is far more convincing, for good evidence was later obtained that showed that Clyde Barrow and Bonnie Parker were still in Texas at the time. On October 11 they were, in fact, driving through the small but rapidly growing town of Sherman, forty-five miles north of Dallas, when they spotted a general store that looked eminently suited for one of the wayside robberies by which they sustained themselves.

Published accounts of their robbery of the store vary considerably. According to some, Bonnie Parker entered the store with Clyde Barrow and asked for a loaf of bread and a can of salmon. She then offered the cashier a five-dollar bill. As he opened the till to give her change, she pulled a revolver from her purse and ordered him to put up his hands. According to another, probably more reliable, version, Clyde Barrow entered the shop by himself, leaving Bonnie hiding in the car. Barrow ordered bologna sausage and cheese. While these items were being cut for him, he suddenly produced a revolver and demanded money.

Whatever the truth of the preliminaries, all accounts agree about the entry into the proceedings of a tall, lean man, a former cowboy named Howard Hall. He was determined that his shop should not be robbed and threatened the robber (in the second version) with a meat cleaver. Clyde Barrow fired at Hall, wounding him dreadfully in the chest. The ex-cowboy slumped to the ground as Barrow (and Bonnie Parker, according to the first version) ran from the shop, jumped into the car, and drove off.

The shocked staff of the store carried Howard Hall across the road to St. Vincent's Hospital, which was situated on the other side of the street. But Hall's wounds were fatal. He died almost as soon as he entered the hospital. The total profit from the murder of the elderly grocer was about twenty-eight dollars in cash and a few items of grocery.

Despite the description and subsequent identification by two employees at the store, Clyde later denied that he and Bonnie were involved in the robbery and murder in Sherman on October 11, 1932. As we have seen, their families also accepted the story that he and his lover were still in Kansas City on that day. Nell Cowan complained that "every robbery, hold-up, or murder committed in the South was attributed to Clyde and Bonnie, no matter if they were a thousand miles away when it happened." She accepted her brother's denial because she reasoned that as he had carried out and admitted to so many crimes, he would have nothing to gain by lying about the murder of Howard Hall or for that matter of John Bucher, which he also denied committing. In one sense he would have had the most important reason of all for denying his involvement in these murders: it preserved the heroic image of the daredevil who only killed his uniformed hunters in self-defense. The murder of two shopkeepers would have reduced him to the level of a vicious thief.

Yet that is what he was. As the Dallas newspapers were later able to report, his fingerprints were found in Hall's grocery store in Sherman, and thirty-six years later, the incident would be reenacted by Warren Beatty and Faye Dunaway—but with the omission of murder, which would have adversely affected the essentially romantic image of Bonnie and Clyde in Arthur Penn's film.

IT WAS AFTER the robbery and murder in Sherman that Bonnie began to be overwhelmed by homesickness and the need to see her mother once again. Like Roy Thornton before him, Clyde had had to come to terms with his lover's intense need for her mother. He told Nell Cowan, "She'll start crying and simply float me out of the car when she wants her mama, so I just put on a bathing suit and drive her in." He drove her home in late October 1932.

The two fugitives announced their return to Dallas by throwing a bottle into Mrs. Barrow's garden as they drove past her house. The bottle was used as a signal that they had returned but dare not call because there were people around at the time. In the bottle was a message giving a rendezvous for a family meeting. The Barrow family duly turned up and heard of the recent adventures of the fugitives and their high living in Kansas City. Emma Parker was not present because she was working. Nell Cowan recalled that "Bonnie moped around all the afternoon because she couldn't see her mama. She announced that she was going to go down on Lamar Street, where her mother lived, just as soon as it was dark." Despite the risk, Clyde dropped Bonnie at her mother's house and circled the block while she ran in. The meeting lasted five minutes, long enough for Bonnie to kiss her mother and tell her that she was well before the young couple drove off into the security of the dark Texas countryside.

10

MURDER
IN THE
BOG

LIKE RAYMOND HAMILTON, both the fugitives had a strong and continuing need for their home territory and their families—especially Clyde for his sister Nell and Bonnie for her mother. In this respect they exactly conformed to a traditional pattern of criminal behavior. The outlaw murderers of an earlier generation, such as the James brothers, often took great risks to visit and stay with their families. Even that most formidable and professional of gangsters, John Dillinger, felt strong desires to return to Mooresville, Indiana, to stay with the father to whom he had never been particularly close as a child or a youth.

Eric Hobsbawm, in his study of archaic forms of social movement in the nineteenth and twentieth centuries, recognized this aspect of criminal behavior as a strong tradition in European peasant banditry: "The extent to which the ordinary bandit is tied to his territory—generally that of his birth and 'his' people—is very impressive." Such dependency has obvious practical reasons, for the traditional bandit frequently relied on his family and his village for his supplies. The South Calabrian outlaws, as Hobsbawm describes them, were "lone wolves . . . individuals living on the margin of their villages, attached to them by threads of kin or support, kept from them by enmities and the police."

Bonnie and Clyde were free from immediate dependency on their kin due to the mobility conferred by the automobile, much as their immediate predecessors (the Western outlaws) relied on the horse and the newly constructed railroads. Even so, they were still psychologically dependent on their homes and their families. To them it was also important that they were still accepted by the community in which they had grown up. Bonnie Parker expressed this in a second ballad poem that she later wrote:

> From Irving to West Dallas viaduct
> Is known as the Great Divide,
> Where the women are kin,
> And the men are men,
> And they won't "stool" on Bonnie and Clyde.

These lines reflect the bandit's deep psychological need to know that somewhere there is a sanctuary for him. The horseback outlaws who were Bonnie and Clyde's immediate criminal predecessors, such as Cherokee Bill and Jim French, could escape into the Cookson Hills of southeastern Oklahoma, safe from betrayal by local inhabitants. As another ballad records, the Cookson Hills could still shelter a gangster of the machine-gun age, Pretty Boy Floyd.

> And Pretty Boy found a welcome
> At many a farmer's door.

Like much of the subject matter of balladeers, myth far exceeded reality. In the case of Bonnie and Clyde, the Dallas sanctuary that was so important to them was hardly a secure haven, for they could visit it only briefly and secretly and in so doing exposed themselves to the traditional bandit danger: betrayal and capture.

RAYMOND HAMILTON'S WISH to visit his father soon led to his betrayal and capture in Bay City. During his holiday in

Michigan, Hamilton, very much a ladies man, was attracted to a good-looking young waitress. Typically, he could not resist bragging to her of the money that he had and, what is more, how he had obtained it. Unfortunately for him the waitress had another boyfriend who was a police officer. She told him of Hamilton's boasting about the crimes he had committed in Texas. The Bay City Police arranged for his arrest in a most convenient way, from their point of view. It happened on December 6 when Hamilton and Gene O'Dare had taken the waitress and another girl to a roller-skating rink: The two men were arrested with their skates on, a most difficult situation in which to escape from the police. It was the second time that Hamilton's lively social life had got him into serious trouble.

The two criminals were taken to Texas for trial. Gene O'Dare was convicted of various crimes committed around Dallas. Raymond Hamilton was tried in a Dallas district court. He pleaded not guilty, but offered no defense. He was found guilty of taking part in the robbery of the Cedar Hill Bank with Clyde Barrow, for which he was sentenced to thirty years' imprisonment. He was also sentenced to an additional twenty-five years for his involvement in the robbery of the Neuhoff Packing Company. And that was only the beginning of Hamilton's trials, for they continued through the summer, by which time he had accumulated the grand total of 263 years' imprisonment. Hamilton was transferred to the Huntsville penitentiary on August 8, 1933.

Clyde Barrow was appalled when he learned of his former confederate's capture. He is reputed to have sworn that he would rescue Hamilton from Huntsville within the year. He also managed to attract fresh recruits to replace Hamilton: two young hoodlums who no doubt imagined that Clyde and Bonnie were successful criminals whose considerable profits they would share.

The four of them drove northeast to Missouri and established themselves in a cabin at a tourist camp about ten miles from the small town of Carthage. After some minor thieving and an inept robbing of a bank in Oranago, Missouri, which yielded a grand total of $115, the two recruits took themselves off—the prospect of Clyde Barrow as their gang leader being more than they could stomach.

Left to themselves, Clyde Barrow and Bonnie Parker attempted another bank robbery to augment their dwindling supply of cash. Clyde's sister describes how he "made elaborate scouting plans, looking over the situation, and finally selected a little bank in a small town in Missouri." His plan was that Bonnie should stay by the car to guard the door while he burst into the bank. Once inside, Barrow found only an elderly man, sitting by himself in a corner, who was surprisingly unimpressed by the gun that was thrust at him: He told the would-be robber that the bank had closed four days previously.

The desertion of his two recruits was a considerable setback for Clyde. He needed another confederate for the purely practical business of robbery as well as to provide some semblance of a gang for him to lead. By early December he was back in West Dallas taking on a fresh recruit for the Barrow Gang: a sixteen-year-old volunteer by the name of William Daniel Jones. Jones had known the Barrows since 1922 when, as a child of six, he and his family had camped alongside them on the damp grass with their few shabby possessions under the arches of the Houston Street Viaduct. As a stocky, round-faced boy (invariably known as W.D.), Jones had hero-worshiped the teenage Clyde Barrow. On December 1, 1932 he appeared unexpectedly at Emma Parker's house, where she found him on her return from work on a cold, dark winter's evening. W.D. informed Bonnie's mother that he had arranged to meet Clyde at her house and that he intended to become the next member of the Barrow gang. He told his childhood hero when he arrived on the scene that he was an accomplished car thief (he had some practice) and argued that as he was in and out of jail all the time he "might as well get something out of it."

Jones later gave a very different and distinctly dubious account of his recruitment to the Barrow gang. Both would differ from the film version in which Warren Beatty's young accomplice, "C.W. Moss" (who was, in fact, a combination of Raymond Hamilton, W. D. Jones, and a later criminal accomplice), is first encountered as an attendant at a wayside garage, a rather comical figure with a large cap and cherubic cheeks.

He quickly clears a blocked fuel line in Clyde's four-cylinder Ford coupe, belches, and after some embarrassment learns who his famous customers are. Faye Dunaway, who has been shrewdly eyeing him, announces, "Well, I'm Miss Bonnie Parker and this here is Mr. Clyde Barrow. We . . . rob . . . banks." C. W. is completely overcome by this unexpected revelation, capers about in amazement, and hammers his fist on a wooden post. He is quickly persuaded to join Arthur Penn's Bonnie and Clyde, and stealing some banknotes from the garage till to show his true mettle before climbing in the rumble seat, he is driven off at great velocity to the sound of lively hillbilly music.

With a macabre sense of timing, Clyde Barrow chose Christmas day 1932 to test his young apprentice. That afternoon they were driving through the deserted streets of Temple, a vigorous and businesslike community 120 miles south of Dallas, when they noticed what looked like a brand new car standing outside a house in South 13th Street. The car had just been bought by a twenty-seven-year-old salesman who worked for Strasburger Stores in Temple. Doyle Johnson was celebrating Christmas with his and his wife's families and was enjoying an afternoon nap after eating Christmas dinner. Outside, in the cold empty street, W. D. Jones jumped from his car and ran to Mr. Johnson's vehicle, which was unlocked and, what's more, had the ignition key in place. But, despite his boasted expertise, Jones could not start the car. Clyde Barrow ran to help him, and the two men began to push Doyle Johnson's car in an effort to get it started. While this was happening, Johnson's wife, his father-in-law (Henry Krauser) and brother-in-law (Clarence Krauser) emerged from the house to find out what was going on. When the thieves saw them approaching they scrambled into the car, which they had just managed to start. Henry Krauser shouted in alarm, while Clarence Krauser ran up to the side of the car yelling at the occupants. At this, the two men jumped from the car with drawn revolvers. Clarence Krauser bobbed behind a tree, while his father and sister ran back to the house. Barrow and Jones then got back into Johnson's car and again tried to drive away.

Now it was Doyle Johnson, woken from his after-dinner nap

by his mother, who ran from the house up to his car. A gun was thrust at him by Jones. As Johnson tried to grab the gun, a shot was fired, the bullet ricocheting off the car bumper. Clyde Barrow then let off his .45 revolver: the bullet struck Doyle Johnson on the side of the neck and passed downward into his spinal cord.

As the fatally wounded salesman slumped to the ground, Barrow and Jones drove away. Before long they abandoned the car, leaving the doors conspicuously wide open, and were picked up by Bonnie Parker in the stolen black coupe in which they had driven up to the Johnson house shortly before 2:30 P.M. on that quiet Christmas afternoon.

The events on South 13th Street completed the corruption of the sixteen-year-old apprentice who had been made to assist in the casual murder of a man woken from his after-dinner nap on Christmas Day. The incident recalled Bonnie and Clyde's first inglorious criminal venture when they attempted to escape from a bungled robbery by mounting two mules, failed, and then fell into a drainage ditch before Clyde abandoned Bonnie in an empty building. Their macabre Christmas Day failure is, in fact, more compatible with the exploits of the pudgy, ineffectual Clyde as portrayed by Paolo Villaggio in the Italian film parody than the more sober accounts of the legend of Bonnie and Clyde. ·

Even the long-suffering Emma Parker, whose affections for her daughter and her lover were undiminished by their crimes, seems not to have been able to stomach the fact that the murder of Doyle Johnson occurred on Christmas Day. In her account of the proceedings she very firmly, and totally unconvincingly, states that the killing occurred on December 5, 1932.

THE TEMPLE POLICE at first had no idea of the identity of Doyle Johnson's murderers. On December 29 the *Temple Daily Telegram* reported that two suspects who had been held in Houston had been cleared. Two days later it was reported that two ex-convicts had been picked up in Madill, Oklahoma, but again they could not be implicated in the murder in Temple. On Janury 5 the *Telegram* announced that the investigator working on the crime had returned from Fort Worth with photographs of the suspects. "These photographs were identified by many persons who saw two men and a girl in a 1932 model Ford coupé traveling west of Temple at a high rate of speed." Finally on January 7 the newspaper carried banner headlines and a report linking the killing of Doyle Johnson with the murder of a deputy sheriff in Fort Worth (on the previous night) with "Clyde Darrow [sic]" and on January 8 that a "state-wide search for Odell Chambless and Clyde Barrow got under way after the killing of Deputy Sheriff Malcolm Davis in a gun battle at a house in west Dallas Saturday morning."

What had happened was that the police had captured a young man who had been involved in a bank robbery during the Christmas holiday in Grapevine (then a small town twenty miles northwest of Dallas, but now engulfed by the Dallas–Fort Worth International Airport). He revealed to the police that another young hoodlum, Odell Chambless, had taken part in the robbery of the Home Bank. He also hinted that Chambless was a friend of Clyde Barrow and might try to contact him in West Dallas, possibly at the home of Raymond Hamilton's sister, Mrs. Lillian McBride, who lived at 507 County Avenue, close to the Barrow family gas station and store.

Accordingly, several law officers, with Sheriff Bradberry in charge, arrived at the home of Lillian McBride on the evening of January 6, 1933. With him was the investigator from Temple and Malcolm Davis, a deputy from Tarrant County, and two other officers who were investigating the Grapevine bank robbery. There they learned from her older sister that Mrs. McBride was not at home. She was actually visiting Raymond Hamilton at Huntsville, taking him—at Clyde Barrow's instigation—a radio, the sound of which was intended to mask the noise of the sawing of the bars of Hamilton's cell. Bradberry decided they would wait, leaving Davis standing in the brick porch while he entered the house with the other officers to wait in the living room. Later Bradberry asked that the lights might be extinguished but agreed to Mrs. Fairris's request that the small red light in the room in which her child was sleeping should remain on.

At about midnight the officers heard a car approaching along the cold dark street. It slowed in front of the house and then drove away. At this point, Bradberry commanded that the red light be turned out, for he suspected that it could be a warning signal. No sooner was this done than the car returned. In it were two men and a woman. The driver was Clyde Barrow. He left the car and walked toward the house. Bradberry ordered Mrs. Fairris to go to the front door, open it, and let Barrow in. She opened the door but, as she did so, called, according to one account, "Oh, no don't shoot—think of my babies."

Barrow reacted instantly by firing a shotgun (which he had been carrying unobtrusively) at Fred Bradberry whom he had spotted standing in the window of the darkened living room. Hearing the shot, Malcolm Davis ran around to the front of the house but did not notice the dark figure standing on the porch and was blasted with a second charge from the shotgun. Shots were also fired at the windows of the house from the car as it abruptly drove away, leaving Clyde Barrow to run into the night.

Malcolm Davis died before his colleagues could get him to hospital.

The police strongly suspected that the other man, who had remained in the car and fired at the officers in the McBride house, was Odell Chambless and that he had also been involved in the Christmas Day murder of Doyle Johnson. On January 18, Odell Chambless surrendered himself to the no doubt surprised Dallas police, claiming that he had not been involved in either of the incidents and that at the time of the murder of Malcolm Davis he had been in California and only subsequently hitchhiked back to Dallas. Two days later the Texas newspapers reported that Chambless had established his alibi and was left to face only the lesser charge of the Grapevine bank robbery.

The identity of Clyde Barrow's male accomplice was still a mystery, for the police had not at this time realized that W. D. Jones was on the scene. The hunt for Clyde Barrow was intensifying. He had begun to acquire national notoriety. As Emma

Parker boasted; "Clyde and Bonnie were making themselves famous or infamous, depending on the viewpoint. Their daring escapes, their breath-taking speed, the boldness with which they came and went, were becoming legends up and down the land. Pretty Boy Floyd was crowded into oblivion; Machine Gun Kelly was an also-ran. Bonnie and Clyde had the center of the stage and were to keep it till they died."

11

RED BEANS, SOLITAIRE, AND BULLETS

IMMEDIATELY AFTER BLASTING away at Malcolm Davis on the night of January 6, Clyde Barrow turned back into the protective darkness, the sound of the explosion still ringing in his ears. As he did so, he saw the car driven by Bonnie Parker accelerate away from him down the straight dirt road between the rows of painted wooden houses. She had been drinking that night and was confused by the unexpected firing and shouting from Lillian McBride's darkened house. Bonnie imagined in her panic that Clyde had been captured, had run away or been killed, but she recovered herself and began cautiously to circle the block until, to her enormous relief, she saw Clyde's familiar figure running toward the car through an alleyway between the clapboard houses in the next street. Bonnie moved over to give him the wheel as Clyde scrambled into the car and accelerated through the empty streets of West Dallas, leaving by a side road and low viaduct across flat boggy grassland—a favorite escape route, the "back door." He then swerved on to the Industrial Boulevard, piercing the darkness with the lonely glow of the car lights to head northeast toward Missouri.

Bonnie sat trembling, white faced and silent at his side as Barrow hurtled the car along dark, straight roads. Neither of them knew what had happened at the shooting, whether anyone had been wounded or killed by Barrow's two blasts from his shotgun. At last Bonnie spoke in a small voice saying that she would not go to see her mother (as she had planned) and would very likely never see her again.

Later, at one of their clandestine meetings, Nell Cowan asked her brother how he felt that night with the knowledge that he might have killed yet another man: "Like I always felt—sick inside, sick and cold and weak—and a sort of dull wishing that I'd never been born."

Clyde Barrow drove through that winter night and by a cold bleak dawn had reached eastern Oklahoma, where he rented a cabin in a secluded tourist camp. But the trio soon took to the road again. In late January they were in Missouri, where they captured a motorcycle policeman who had pursued their reckless speeding. They bundled the surprised policeman on to the floor at the back of the car, where he was forced to remain with W. D.'s feet on his back and a gun pointing at his head. They drove the terrified lawman on a circuitous route around southeast Missouri before abandoning him on a lonely country road.

The Parker and Barrow families were greatly entertained by this incident when they read about it in the newspapers and later received a firsthand account from Bonnie and Clyde. Nell Cowan recorded, with some satisfaction, that "the officer was as mad as a wet hen, and aware that his plight was rather ridiculous."

BY MARCH, 1933 the Barrow family had something else to celebrate: Clyde's brother Buck was to be pardoned and released from the Huntsville penitentiary. Mrs. Barrow and Buck's wife, Blanche, had pleaded to some effect on Buck's behalf, a plea that was assisted by the prisoner's excellent behavior and by the fact that he had, in any case, surrendered himself at the penitentiary two years earlier.

Buck Barrow emerged from prison on March 22; his family had great hopes for him as he returned on that cool spring day. Nell Cowan saw him as a "changed man," his wife Blanche was thrilled at his promises to try for a job and build a home for her, and Buck's other sister gave him some money that she had saved to enable him to buy a motor car. It was planned that he and Blanche would use the car, a secondhand Ford sedan, to drive to see Blanche's family at their farm in Missouri; it was also even mentioned as a possibility that the reformed Buck might work on the farm—a most unexpected proposal, for he had never had a job before and even the loyal Nell was forced to admit, "He didn't know how to do any sort of skilled labor, and he just wasn't attracted to work, anyway."

There was only one snag: Buck Barrow had expressed the strong desire to meet his younger brother Clyde. He told Nell Cowan that he had worried about Clyde constantly while he was in prison. One of Buck's jobs had been to clean out the "death house," and every time he swept around the electric chair he imagined his younger brother sitting in it; he even dreamed of Clyde being brought into that grim building.

At first sight there is little reason to doubt the Barrow family's account of Buck Barrow's motives at this time. It seems improbable that Buck's desire to meet his brother had any other basis than that of a brotherly reunion, an occasion on which Buck might try to persuade his younger brother to surrender himself to the law authorities in the hope of receiving some clemency. It is difficult to imagine that Buck Barrow had deliberately decided to throw away all the benefits of his recent good behavior by joining his young brother and Bonnie Parker in a life of violent crime.

Whatever were Buck's true motives, his wife was bitterly opposed to the planned meeting, for, as Nell Cowan gratefully recognized, Blanche Barrow "was a good country girl, timid, shy and rather quiet." Nell suspected that if Blanche had known Buck Barrow was an escaped convict she would never have married him.

Despite Blanche's opposition, the arrangements went forward. Nell Cowan was involved in communicating to Buck one of the secret messages that the Barrows and the Parkers were becoming expert at intercepting and interpreting. Buck and Blanche were to meet Clyde and Bonnie and W. D. Jones outside Fort Smith, Arkansas, and then the party would drive on to Joplin, Missouri, which, besides being the busy center of many local lead and zinc mines, was traditionally one of the "safe" cities for gangsters at this time. Blanche wept for two whole days before she and her husband left West Dallas for Arkansas.

As appointed, the two couples eventually arrived in a quiet, tree-lined road in the Freeman Grove residential district of Joplin, where Clyde Barrow had booked an apartment at the rear of a solid, limestone-built house on the corner of 34th Street and Oakridge Drive by posing as Mr. W. J. Callahan, a visiting civil engineer from Minnesota. The apartment at 3347½ 34th Street consisted of a comfortable living room, two bedrooms, a bathroom, and kitchen and had the advantage that there was a double garage beneath it, which could conceal stolen cars and from which a rapid escape could be made. In his role as Mr. Callahan, Clyde had also rented another garage at 3339 Oakridge Drive. Three cars were parked in the garages: a Ford V-8 and a Ford coupe in the apartment garage and in the Oakridge garage Buck's Ford sedan. The first two had been stolen.

THE REUNION WAS a great success—very much in the spirit if not the detail of the Warren Beatty-Faye Dunaway gathering depicted in *Bonnie and Clyde* in 1968. Clyde Barrow and Bonnie Parker were regaled with much-desired family news and they no doubt told of their recent adventures with W. D. Jones. They sent their laundry out, and in Nell Cowan's words, "the two girls mended and darned." Bonnie wrote and did some of the cooking, especially of red beans and cabbage, one of her favorite dishes. Blanche played with the pet dog that she had brought along while the men relaxed, reading magazines, talking, and playing card games.

This easy family life continued, behind drawn curtains, for about two weeks before funds started running low; they were, in fact, down to their last eight dollars when Clyde and W. D. decided that they would soon have to seek out suitable places to rob. The neighbors were becoming distinctly uneasy about the newly arrived Mr. Callahan and his family. For one thing, they had noticed an alarming quantity of guns and ammunition being carried into the apartment together with a surprisingly large number of car license plates. The police were informed, and two state highway patrolmen were set to watch Mr. Callahan and his companions. After three days they were convinced that the apartment was occupied by criminals, probably bootleggers or local burglars, and three Joplin law officers were called in. The reputed immunity of criminals in Joplin at that time evidently did not extend to the lower orders of the profession.

CLYDE BARROW AND W. D. Jones left on their projected scouting expedition on the afternoon of Thursday, April 13. According to Nell Cowan's account of the proceedings, they told Bonnie but not Buck and Blanche Barrow what they were going to do. The two scouts were not away for long, however, for Clyde sensed danger and, according to W. D. Jones's later account, turned the car around and headed back for the apartment. When they returned, they garaged the car and started to shut the doors. Upstairs Bonnie Parker was cooking cabbage and red beans; Blanche was playing solitaire; Buck Barrow and the dog were asleep.

The police arrived moments later, at about 4:00 P.M. They came in two cars. As they drove up to the apartment, the officers glimpsed a man standing by the garage doors. One of the detectives drove his car up to the garage and then yelled at his colleague to get inside before the door could be closed. A burly policeman leaped from the car and moved toward the white-painted garage doors. As he did so, Clyde Barrow pushed a shotgun around one of the doors and fired point-blank at the man: the blast blew him almost in two.

As he fired, Clyde called up to the apartment, "It's the law, Bonnie." Almost at once there came the sound of gunfire from upstairs as Bonnie Parker, apparently in negligee and house slippers, and W. D. Jones fired at the police with powerful automatic rifles.

Bonnie later told Clyde's sister that her most vivid memories of the gun battle "was the fact that she could smell her precious red beans burning, hear Blanche screaming and running, and the dog barking wildly." Blanche had, in fact, completely lost her head; she ran down the stairs of the apartment and out into the yard, screaming, with her pet dog yapping at her heels. The police were apparently so surprised at her unexpected appearance that no shots were fired at her as she fled along the neighboring street.

By this time another detective had run from his car, which was parked in the street. As he came up to the garage, Clyde fired his shotgun, virtually detaching the fifty-three-year-old man's right arm from his body. At this disastrous turn of events one of the policemen sprinted to a nearby house to telephone for reinforcements, while the other detective ran around the side of the house to try to enter it from the back. This left one policemen in front of the apartment, and he only had one round left in his gun. As he moved backward to reload, he tripped and fell. Thinking that the man was shot and the way now clear, Clyde Barrow called W. D. Jones to come to him in front of the garage, but as he appeared, the recumbent constable fired his last bullet, slightly wounding Jones in the head, and then bolted for safety.

As Clyde flung open the garage doors, Bonnie and Buck dived into one of the cars. Clyde climbed into the driving seat and only then noticed blood on his shirt from a wound in his chest. Turning to Bonnie, he asked her to dig out the embedded bullet, which he could feel; Bonnie whipped out a hairpin and quickly dug out the flattened bullet, which had ricocheted to cause a superficial flesh wound.

The wound seems to have maddened Clyde, for he clambered out of the car, carrying a machine-gun according to one account and a shotgun according to another. "For God's sake, come back and get in the car," Bonnie yelled. "Not until I get the rat that shot me," Clyde Barrow replied. He blasted away in the general direction of the detective, who had now reappeared from the back of the house but who quickly ducked behind a wall unharmed. When Clyde's rage subsided sufficiently for him to be persuaded to get back in the car, they still could not get the car away, for the drive was blocked by one of the police cars. W. D. Jones ran to the obstructing vehicle, released the hand brake, and gave it a shove that was sufficient to send it rolling down the sloping drive and crashing into a tree. He or Buck or Clyde (depending on the account) also rolled away the corpse of the policeman and the body of the wounded detective.

Bonnie Parker later told Clyde's sister that she had "never lived through such hell. Every minute seemed like it would be our last. Clyde was wounded. W. D.'s head was spouting blood, Blanche was gone, and the shells were still spatting, and snarling at us." Eventually, "still firing with one hand, Clyde Barrow slipped under the wheel and we roared down the driveway. W. D. was taking care of his side of the car with another machine gun. I tugged at Clyde's shoulder and pointed. 'Blanche went this way,' I yelled above the din."

Bonnie was right, for they found Blanche, two blocks away: "She was still running and sobbing, her face was white as chalk and her eyes popping out with fright. The little dog was in her arms." Blanche was still clutching the playing cards—it took thirty minutes to pry them from her hand.

Clyde drove "like an insane man." He headed west, driving for nearly four hundred miles right across Oklahoma and into Texas. After eight hours they reached Amarillo, where they bought some medicines for W. D. Jones's wounds.

SO ENDED THE strange family reunion in Joplin, Missouri. Behind them they had left another corpse, a dying man, and more grieving parents, children, and wives. Constable Wes Harryman was forty-one and had been the father of five children; he had no salary (only such fees as he could collect) and a small family farm. After his death Mrs. Harryman had to sell the farm, and Harryman's eldest son, Claude, who was then twenty, was forced to work to support the whole family, and it was not until all the Harryman children had grown up that he could marry and take over a farm in Saginaw, Missouri—all a result of the Barrow reunion in Joplin in April 1933.

Detective Harry McGinnis died at eleven o'clock that night (in St. John's Hospital, Joplin) from the fearful wounds that had been inflicted upon him. McGinnis was a widower (his first wife had been killed two years earlier in a motor car accident) and had planned to marry his fiancée, Nellie Gager, in only three weeks' time. He also left an eighty-one-year-old widowed mother to mourn her affable, middle-aged son.

Buck and Blanche's lives were also ruined by their visit to Joplin. Nell Cowan maintained that Buck Barrow really was reformed when he left Huntsville and had visited his younger brother primarily to persuade him to renounce violent crime. If this were the case, then Clyde was guilty of leading his innocent brother to destruction. Had Buck Barrow really visited Joplin to convert his younger brother? Bonnie told Buck's sister that she saw him carrying a gun during the Joplin battle, and an eyewitness said that he used "a sawed-off shotgun." Then there is the extraordinary intensity of Blanche Barrow's reaction, in Dallas, to Buck's proposed reunion with Clyde. If this were to have been a temporary visit, it is difficult to see why someone associated with the Barrow family, with its extensive criminal contacts and regular meetings with Bonnie and Clyde, should have behaved in such a hysterical manner at the prospect of a single reforming visit. It seems much more likely that Blanche knew that her husband intended to join his brother to form what had long been Clyde's ambition: the Barrow Gang.

12

SNAKE-EYED KILLER, CIGAR-SMOKING MOLL

THE JOPLIN POLICE had few doubts as to the identity of the murderers of Wes Harryman and Harry McGinnis. Not only was Clyde Barrow suspected, but his brother's involvement was revealed by, among other things, the marriage certificate found in Blanche's handbag. The Joplin newspaper had also landed a scoop that would do more than anything else to establish the legend of Bonnie and Clyde. "A mass of clippings and writings in the bag indicated that the killer's [Clyde's] wife was a lover of morbid and gangster poetry. In fact she was composing such a poem, entitled 'Suicide Sal,' when the shooting started, for the unfinished poem, with pen and ink near by, was found on a writing table in the apartment. In the poem she told of being the 'pal of a killer' and of her love for him, despite the reckless life she was leading." Bonnie Parker must have been putting the finishing touches to the poem, which her mother said she started in the Kaufman jail, as did her fictional counterpart, Faye Dunaway, in the romantic Hollywood re-creation of the Joplin massacre.

Also in the apartment were two rolls of camera film. The developed pictures showed Bonnie Parker, Clyde Barrow, and W. D. Jones in a variety of poses: Bonnie leaning against the back of a car looking pensively at the camera with a pair of large revolvers thrust into her belt; Bonnie threatening Clyde Barrow with a shotgun that looked enormous in her tiny hands; Clyde standing with W. D. Jones; and—the picture that became most famous of all—Bonnie with one foot on a car bumper, a revolver in her hand and a huge cigar in her mouth. The pictures, which appeared first in the *Joplin Globe* two days after the shooting, were quickly published in newspapers and magazines throughout the country and were also used in the thousands of police notices and circulars that were printed.

Bonnie Parker would soon be known to millions of American newspaper readers as the "cigar-smoking gun moll" and Clyde Barrow as "the snake-eyed killer." Bonnie and her family were infuriated by her cigar-smoking image, for she had, in fact, merely borrowed the cigar from Buck to pose for the photograph. Clyde became so angry about the repeated publication of the photograph* and the references to her cigar smoking that he wrote to the owners of the *Fort Worth Star Telegram* on the matter threatening that he and Bonnie would be "coming after him" (the owner) if his newspaper did not desist.

The identity of the mysterious third man in the photographs puzzled the Joplin police, but when two Dallas deputies arrived at Joplin, they were able to confirm that the stocky, round-faced young man with neatly parted hair was the West Dallas teenager W. D. Jones.

CLYDE BARROW AND Bonnie Parker were now becoming nationally known criminals. Their faces appeared in newspaper photographs and on police leaflets and posters through Texas, Missouri, Kansas, and Oklahoma. From this time on every chance encounter with ordinary people was fraught with danger; they could no longer run the risk of booking into hotels, apartments, or tourist camps; even the purchase, and certainly the theft, of food, gas, and other necessary supplies exposed them to risk of identification and capture; visits to their fam-

---

*The story that the cigar was painted over a rose that she was holding in her mouth by a frivolous newspaper photographer seems to have no foundation.

ilies in West Dallas more than ever carried the risk of betrayal and police ambush. The *Dallas Herald* announced beneath banner headlines that "Under instructions to shoot to kill officers throughout North Texas were grimly determined to end the crimson careers of the Barrow brothers, should they attempt to reach any of their hideouts in this vicinity."

As the spring of 1933 advanced and the weather improved, so the five fugitives adopted a restless, nomadic life: camping in secluded country places and driving, always driving, in stolen cars along quiet country roads. They still kept in touch with their families. Like conventional tourists they sent a regular stream of letters back to West Dallas telling of their travels and trials. Nell Cowan recalled that "there was never any telling where a letter would be postmarked": New Mexico, Kansas, Louisiana, Missouri, Texas, Oklahoma, even Iowa and Illinois. At their nightly camps they would sleep by turns, so that there was always someone, armed and awake, to guard against surprise attack from out of the surrounding darkness or dawn mists.

This nomadic life must have been uncomfortable, especially for the two women of the party. Personal hygiene seems to have been a particular problem, for there was no possibility of even the occasional hot bath or shower—a distressing lack for people cooped up together in cars for long periods. However, they would soap themselves down and rinse themselves in the water of country streams, which still retained the icy winter cold, and run back to the relative warmth of the car, blue and shivering. The Barrow brothers and W. D. Jones were forced to shave in cold water and only occasionally ran the risk of having their hair cut in barbershops in small country towns.

Clyde Barrow, in particular, seems to have been fastidious about his appearance and insisted that his suits were cleaned and pressed and his shirts and underwear laundered. To do this they were forced to leave their soiled garments at carefully selected laundries; Blanche Barrow carried out the deliveries and collections, for her photograph had not been circulated by the police or printed in newspapers. The collection of their laundry was potentially the most dangerous part of the operation, and they would very carefully reconnoiter beforehand. Nell Cowan (never at a loss to find something to praise in her criminal relations) was proud that "such was their standard of cleanliness that they placed themselves in this danger week after week, in order to be decently clothed."

Their clothes were clearly important status symbols for the Barrow brothers and W. D. Jones. Although no more than petty robbers, who found themselves in their present situation due to their own criminal incompetence, they still affected the image of the successful gangster leaders with their smart suits, silk shirts and ties, wide-brimmed hats, and snappy shoes. Bonnie seems to have been busy at this time in modifying one of Clyde's suits to enable him to carry a sawn-off shotgun down his right trouser leg. The gun was revealed when required by flinging back the coat and opening a zip fastener on the trouser leg.

Their food was purchased at small shops in quiet country towns or from wayside stores and gas stations. Again it was most likely Blanche who did the shopping, with the others armed and on the alert for any sign of trouble. Cooking was difficult, for the smoke from fires could have attracted attention, and at this time they lived largely on a diet of cold or hastily warmed pork and beans, cheese and biscuits, and canned meats. Bonnie was certainly deprived of red beans and cabbage and Clyde of his favorite drink, hot chocolate, although Bonnie devised a substitute for him made from canned milk, which lacked the "whipped cream and oceans of marshmallows" for which he craved.

LIVING IN SUCH confined and difficult circumstances must have produced considerable strains among the curious quintet: a multiple murderer and unsuccessful thief, his weak-willed, ex-convict brother, a sixteen-year-old apprentice to crime, a timid, hysterical wife, and an excitable eighty-five-pound woman with bizarre tastes and romantic criminal notions.

Blanche later told her sister-in-law, Nell, of a row that blew up between Clyde and his lover at this time. "They started fighting about something—then I don't remember what, it was such a little thing—and the row grew and grew till Clyde told her to shut up." At this, Bonnie insisted that the car be stopped so that she could get out and hitchhike back to Dallas and mother. She gathered her belongings into a paper bag and, according to Blanche's account, got out of the car and marched off down the dusty road clutching the bag with Clyde following behind in the car and then getting out in an attempt to make it up. Bonnie would have none of it: she turned, still furious, into a cornfield where Clyde followed her up and down the rows of corn until he caught up with her. They continued quarreling until, in Blanche's words, "he picked her up and brought her back, kicking and scratching and crying. The paper sack was torn and her clothes were scattered from one cornstalk to another." Clyde held the tiny, struggling woman in the car until her protests subsided and reconciliation was achieved, while the helpful Buck collected all Bonnie's scattered belongings from the cornfield.

Nell Cowan portrays this disagreement merely as a lovers' passing tiff in which her debonair young brother used his strong masculine charms to win back his lover, but it seems more likely that it resulted from the tensions that built up between the fugitives at this time. W. D. Jones was to claim that a very peculiar relationship existed within the group, a relationship very different from the rather carefree atmosphere (reminiscent of Robin Hood and his merry men in Sherwood Forest) that Nell Cowan and two Hollywood films tried unconvincingly to portray.

Bonnie found the feeding arrangements particularly difficult to bear. She missed her cooked red beans. On one occasion Bonnie detected the smell of her favorite food being cooked in a farmhouse on one of the quiet country roads that were their hiding places and insisted that they should try to share this delicious rustic feast. Blanche was dispatched to ask the farmer's wife if she would sell some of the cooking beans and corn bread: the woman was persuaded to part with the meal for what was then the princely sum of two dollars.

Although the fugitives were avoiding public attention, they were forced to resort to occasional robberies. These must have been anxious times for the two women. Nell Cowan relates how on one occasion the Barrow brothers and their young apprentice left Bonnie and Blanche all one night in a parked car on a deserted road while they went, unsuccessfully as it turned out, to attempt some extortion. After the men had left, there was a spectacular storm and downpour and Bonnie Parker, who was terrified of thunder and lightning, had an attack of hysterics. Blanche Barrow later told her sister-in-law that Bonnie "covered her ears, put her head between her knees, moaned and prayed, and begged for Clyde or her mama." Blanche claimed, with understandable relish, that Bonnie "behaved much worse than I did in the Joplin battle. She got down on the backseat at last and made me pile up all the pillows and blankets on her head, and then she wanted me to sit on top of them! I never heard such goings on as Bonnie did that night."

13

OKABENA
HOLDUP

DESPITE THEIR ATTEMPTS to disappear quietly from public view, the fugitives were forced to go on robbing, not only for money to buy supplies, but also to replace the stolen car that Clyde Barrow had virtually worn out with his ceaseless driving. Two weeks after the Joplin murder, they stole a car at Ruston, a small town in the north of Louisiana not far from the Arkansas border, and kidnapped the angry owner, a young undertaker and his fiancée who had been sitting on a swing in a porch of a boardinghouse enjoying the warm spring sunshine. The frightened hostages were eventually released after hours of driving along lonely country roads.

Nell Cowan regarded it as a merry adventure (as did the makers of *Bonnie and Clyde*, who incorporated the incident into the film), rather like the Sherwood Forest outlaw's capture of a greedy bishop. In reality it was more revealing of Clyde Barrow's vindictive nature: He resented any show of resistance on the part of his victims, and his behavior in terrorizing the hostages for several hours during the protracted car ride is more reminiscent of the sadistic pleasures of his boyhood than of a merry outlaw hero.

By the time that the police learned of the kidnapping in Ruston, Louisiana, they were a thousand miles north, at the small town of Okabena in Minnesota, and money was running short. Their robbery of the First State Bank, one of the few prominent buildings in the dusty Main Street of Okabena, was at first quite professionally executed, but unfortunately for them the raid was so obvious that, in Clyde Barrow's words, "everyone in town seemed to know about the holdup before we did, and there was a regular reception committee waiting for us when we came out, everybody shooting right and left." Among the reception committee was an ancient local hero who attempted to impede their escape by heaving a large log in front of their getaway car. Clyde had to swerve dangerously to avoid the log and was exceedingly cross because Bonnie had disobeyed his order to shoot the man. "Why honey," Bonnie excused herself, "I wasn't going to kill that nice old man. He was white headed."

The robbery in Okabena provided the Barrow Gang with much-needed funds, and they were able to continue their bizarre nomadic life without the frequent risks associated with their usual petty wayside thieving.

Their ceaseless driving through the spring of 1933 appears, at first sight, to be a novel phenomenon: a result of the ready availability of fast mass-produced cars, which enabled criminals for the first time to escape rapidly from the scene of their crimes and to be hundreds of miles away within a few hours. But this was really not the case, for the peripatetic life of the Barrow Gang at this time was essentially similar to that of their historical predecessors the Western horseback outlaws.

Cole Younger, for example, once made a round trip of a thousand miles to see Myra Belle Shirley (later to become known as Belle Starr) and their daughter Pearl Younger. All that separated the movements of the James-Younger and the Barrow Gangs was their speed—the difference between the distance that a horse could travel in a day as compared with that of a 1930s automobile. This difference very roughly corresponds to the duration of the outlawries of the two gangs: two years for the Barrows as compared with a decade for the James-Younger Gang.

During their outlawry the horseback gangs were estimated

to have murdered ten men as compared with the twelve slain by Clyde Barrow and his confederates with their more modern weapons. Like Barrow, Jesse James was a psychopathic killer and was capable of putting a bullet through the head of an unarmed bank cashier for no real purpose and without any sign of remorse. Also like the Barrow Gang, the James and the Younger brothers showed great attachment to their families and often traveled long distances and ran considerable risks to visit them.

There is, however, one marked divergence between the behavior of the horseback gangs of the 1870s and the Barrow Gang in the 1930s: the effectiveness of their criminal enterprises. The largest sum that the Barrow Gang stole was probably the $2,500 taken from the Okabena bank as compared, for example, with the $57,000 taken by the James-Younger Gang from their first robbery of the bank at Liberty, Missouri, in 1866. It has been estimated that in their twenty bank robberies the James-Younger Gang probably stole a total of about half a million dollars.

Clyde Barrow and his curious collection of confederates were very ineffective when judged by the only valid criterion of robbery: profitability.

SOON AFTER THE bank robbery in Okabena, the fugitives laid plans for a meeting with their families. Bonnie Parker's need for her mother was becoming desperate, and the bank robbery had provided them with fresh funds and something for the men to boast about.

It was decided that Blanche Barrow, as the only member of the gang who could not be recognized, should make her way alone to West Dallas. She traveled to Dallas by bus on a Wednesday in late May 1933 and then took a taxi to the Barrow house.

Nell Cowan was delighted to see her gentle sister-in-law again and to hear the news of her two brothers and Bonnie. Blanche told the Parkers and the Barrows of the plans for the family meeting. The fugitives had selected a lonely country road near the small college town of Commerce, some forty

miles northwest of Dallas, at a place where a bridge crossed a
ravine. The news was soon flashed around the family by the
usual message about having "red beans for supper."

Blanche Barrow must have enjoyed eating cooked food again
and bathing and washing in hot water and the luxury of sleeping in a bed. She also took the opportunity of doing some
shopping. Her sister-in-law recalls that she "went into town
and shopped for some riding boots and breeches." Nell thought
that she looked very nice and trim in them.

Such was the excitement among the Barrows and Parkers at
the prospect of the longed-for meeting that when they arrived
the women found that they had forgotten to prepare any food to
take with them. It had rained heavily during the night, and the
road was unpleasantly muddy. The cars were parked on the
bridge over the ravine, and the five fugitives sat in them talking with their families. Occasionally, Clyde Barrow would
have to back his car along the bridge and out of sight when
approaching cars were spotted in the distance.

Months later Nell Cowan said, "I don't think there was ever a
visit filled with so much happiness and sorrow. We had lived
through a million hells since we last met. . . . It was a great deal
like visiting those in prison condemned to die. We knew that
death was coming eventually, as surely as the sun rose. But we
could not know when."

The meeting could not have been but heartbreaking for the
two mothers, torn between their immediate enjoyment of the
occasion and the awful prospects for their children. Nell
Cowan said that Emma Parker and Cumie Barrow had aged
dreadfully in the past year: both were prematurely gray and
their nerves were "ragged." It must have been particularly
painful for Mrs. Barrow to hear her son describe his murders,
for only a few weeks before she had defied newspaper reporters
and the Dallas Police with her belief in her sons' innocence. The
Associated Press reported on April 14, "The mother of Clyde
and Buck has refused, in spite of a long record of crime by her
sons, to believe the accusations of police and firmly maintains
that they are "being framed."

According to Nell Cowan's account of the meeting in the cars on the lonely bridge in May 1933, Clyde was very upset at his involvement in his brother's plight. He maintained that Buck should have run out of the apartment, like Blanche, with his hands held up in surrender. But Buck replied that "things happened too fast for me to figure that out you don't think too good at a time like that": a confession that epitomized the tragedy of the Barrow brothers, for their predicament resulted chiefly from "not thinking too good." Clyde Barrow had exhibited his impulsive stupidity in the unnecessary murders of defenseless shopkeepers, of Doyle Johnson, and, most of all, of the senseless shooting of the deputy sheriff at the Stringtown dance the previous summer. Buck Barrow had foolishly taken his nervous young wife for a prolonged stay with a wanted murderer, despite her desperate and hysterical protests. He had carried a gun during the shooting and may have used it and had afterward taken part in a bank robbery.

Whatever his motives were in joining Clyde and Bonnie, the effects were the same, for as Buck recognized, the police would not believe his story that he had not fired a shot during the Joplin shooting. Very probably, as Buck told his relations as they sat in a car on that damp May day, "I'd get the chair."

Bonnie Parker also talked to her mother about her terrifying future as they took a short walk together along the muddy road during the meeting on the bridge. Emma Parker tried to persuade her daughter to surrender herself to the police; she argued that Bonnie would get only a prison sentence, which, although unpleasant, would be better than the certainty of death from police bullets. Bonnie Parker would have none of it. "Clyde's name is up, mama. He'll be killed sooner or later, because he's never going to give up." She told her mother that she loved him and would stay with him to the end. "When he dies, I want to die anyway."

THE INTENSITY OF Bonnie's love for the multiple murderer whose life she chose to share was the vital ingredient that transformed the sordidness of their lives and, more than anything else, contributed to the growth of the legend of Bonnie and Clyde. However, it is difficult to believe, at this stage at least, that Clyde Barrow could have genuinely loved Bonnie, for he was self-centered in a peculiarly thorough way and probably possessed only limited capacity for real love and affection. He was, for example, capable of lying repeatedly to his mother and to his favorite sister, and even the adoring Nell managed to portray him, against the grain, as an unreliable cadger. ("What positive feelings appear during the psychopath's interpersonal relations give a strong impression of being self-love." H. Cleckley, *The Mask of Sanity*, 1976.)

Clyde Barrow's ability to elicit the love and protective impulses of the women in his life is also a well-documented attribute of the psychopathic male. In case after case psychologists have observed the astonishing power that nearly all psychopaths have to win and bind the devotion of women. This quality goes some way to explain Bonnie's love for him and the amazing tolerance that Nell Cowan, Emma Parker, and the long-suffering Cumie Barrow showed toward his inadequacies and viciousness.

Certainly Clyde could exercise considerable charm despite his looks. His sister found him fascinating, and Bonnie appears to have fallen in love with him at first sight. This is the unconscious strategy of the psychopathic charmer. ("Alert and friendly in his attitude, he is easy to talk with and seems to have many genuine interests. There is nothing at all odd or queer about him, and in every respect he tends to embody the concept of a well adjusted, happy person." *Ibid.*) Typically, the relationship cannot develop into a normal sexual one but is sustained by strong female protective instincts. Women seem to have wanted to mother Clyde Barrow. It is as though their intuition detected the vulnerable infant concealed beneath the false maturity of the psychopathic killer. As the philosopher Thomas Hobbes recognized, "The wicked man is but the child grown strong." Bonnie had very strong maternal instincts, and it was these that sustained the love that she gave so completely to Clyde.

All the fugitives were now inexorably trapped, as a consequence of the criminal standards and attitudes which all the party that met on the bridge in May 1933 understood and accepted. Theirs was a poor society that strongly encouraged the virtues of loyalty, generosity, shrewdness, and love. But these values were flawed by a traditional acceptance of violence and deceit to create an ugly pattern. Clyde Barrow, helpless in his psychopathy, provided the impetus that would lead inevitably to their destruction.

14

THE PIGGLY WIGGLY ROBBERS

AFTER THE FAMILY meeting, the Barrow Gang split up, Buck and Blanche Barrow driving off to visit her parents on their farm in Missouri. The others continued their nomadic existence. In early June they were racing across the high plains of the Texas Panhandle toward a disaster that would transform the relationship between Bonnie and Clyde. They were close to the border with Oklahoma when it happened. Approaching a bridge across the Salt Fork River, Clyde noticed too late that it was closed for repairs, swerved at the last moment, and crashed down a steep embankment. He was thrown free by the impact and managed to drag W. D., with some guns, from the car, but Bonnie was trapped, screaming hysterically as the car suddenly exploded into flames. W. D. Jones afterward said that Clyde became "like an insane person," desperately trying to pull Bonnie from the blazing car as she begged him to shoot her, so great was her agony and fear.

Bonnie was saved by the arrival of two farmers who ran up to help pull the car to one side and release the badly burned woman. They carried her, in agony, to the nearby farmhouse, where the farmer's wife laid Bonnie on a bed and, in the soft light of a paraffin lamp, dabbed her legs, arms, and chest with damp baking soda and bathed her face with Mentholatum. She told Clyde that they must telephone for an ambulance, but he refused immediately, for they dared not run the risk of almost certain recognition. His refusal aroused the woman's suspicions, but she kept on tending the dreadfully burned skin of the tiny, frightened woman, while Clyde went off to look for a suitable car to steal and to collect their guns that were still scattered on the ground. Clyde returned to Bonnie's bedside, where he sat, anxious and worried, watched by the still shaken W. D., a small menacing figure at the edge of the lamplight. Then there was a knock at the farmhouse door, the latch was lifted, and the door began slowly to open. The silence was shattered by a deafening explosion, followed by a scream as a young woman—the farmer's daughter-in-law—staggered into the room, her hand shattered by Jones's shotgun blast. Now all was pandemonium: the farmer ran to his daughter-in-law, crouching over her and cursing his captors as Bonnie staggered across the room through the open front door into the dark yard, followed by Clyde and W. D. Jones.

While all this was happening, two figures were quietly approaching the closed back door of the farmhouse. The sheriff and the Wellington town marshal had been summoned by a telephone call from the other farmer who had unobtrusively slipped away to call for police assistance. The two men cautiously pushed open the back door and tiptoed toward the open front door—to find themselves looking directly into the muzzles of the guns held by Clyde Barrow and W. D. Jones. The surprised officers were ordered to drop their weapons, were quickly secured by the wrists with their own handcuffs and then pushed into their own parked car: one in the back with Bonnie, the other uncomfortably sandwiched between Clyde and W. D. in the front seat.

Clyde drove across the Texas border and then north for twenty miles toward the tiny town of Erick, in Oklahoma, where they had already arranged a reunion of the Barrow Gang on a little-used country road. The journey was agonizing for Bonnie with her terrible, untended burns. The captive marshal was so moved by her plight that he tried, as best he could, to support and cushion her pain-racked body. Before

2 TEXAS DESPERADOES KIDNAP TWO OFFICERS

Woman Companion Injured as Car Is Wrecked—Farm Family Terrorized; One Is Shot.

WELLINGTON, Texas, June 11 (Æ).—Two machine-gunning motorists today terrorized a farm family, kidnapped two officers and escaped with an injured woman companion after their automobile plunged over a road embankment.

Sheriff Dick Corey and City Marshal Paul Hardy, kidnapped in the Sheriff's motor car, were driven to near Erick, Okla., and left wired to a tree. They identified the gunmen as Clyde Barrow, Dallas (Texas) desperado, and Icy Barrow, his brother.

Steve Pritchard, a farmer, was threatened by two submachine guns when he went to the assistance of the motorists after the crash late last night.

At the insistence of the men, he bore the injured woman to his home to administer first aid, but pleaded that he be permitted to call a physician.

"We can't afford it," said one of the men.

Pritchard's daughter-in-law, Mrs. Jack Pritchard, was shot in the hand when she knocked at the door of the house. The gunmen punctured the tires of Pritchard's car with bullets.

While one of the men returned to the wrecked coupé to get a rifle, Lonzo Carter, who lives with the Pritchards, slipped away to the home of a neighbor and telephoned officers.

Both the terrorists were on guard when Sheriff Corey and Marshal Hardy arrived. They surprised the officers in the darkness, bound them with their own handcuffs and, taking the injured woman with them, made off in Corey's car.

The officers said they were tied up near Erick early today with barbed wire cut from a fence. They freed themselves thirty minutes later and notified officers at Sayre, Okla., but the trail of the gunmen was lost on a highway leading toward Pampa, Texas.

The Barrow brothers are wanted for the slaying of two officers in a gun fight near Joplin, Mo., recently.

Fig. 2 By June 1933 the exploits of the Barrow Gang were being regularly reported even in such sober journals as the *New York Times*

they reached Erick, Clyde turned into a quiet country road and stopped the car. The two handcuffed law officers were ordered from the car and tied to a convenient oak tree with lengths of rusty barbed wire wrenched from an adjacent fence.

While this operation was in progress, Buck and Blanche Barrow appeared. Poor Blanche, who must have dreaded this reunion with her criminal relations, was appalled by Bonnie's burns and quickly climbed into the back of the car to comfort her and do what she could to ease her pain. Buck Barrow walked over to the oak tree and watched the law officers being wired up. According to Nell Cowan's account, he casually asked his brother: "Are you going to kill 'em, Clyde?" The answer came: "No, I've had them with me so long I'm beginning to like them."

THE REUNION OF the Barrow Gang occurred in desperate circumstances, which none of them could have foreseen. Once again they were being closely pursued, but now they had a badly burned woman on their hands with no means of salving her wounds or acquiring drugs to dull her pain. They carefully eased Bonnie into Buck Barrow's car and, with Clyde at the wheel, headed away from Texas across the flat landscape of Oklahoma toward the Arkansas border.

Clyde's sister considered this one of his greatest feats of driving. "He became like an insane man. He had only one thought: Bonnie. Her burns had never been dressed, and it was imperative that they be attended at once if she were to live."

Bonnie was in great pain and delirious. They hid in a tourist camp in Fort Smith, where Clyde remained constantly at her bedside (as Nell Cowan described), "holding her hand, talking to her, pleading with her to live, putting pillows to ease her, trying to get her to take nourishment, lifting her up and down as if she were a baby." But his tiny lover was visibly declining and, after a week, a doctor, whom they had taken the great risk of calling in, suggested that her mother should be sent for as he feared that Bonnie had not long to live. Clyde made a quick decision: He would have to drive to Dallas to collect Bonnie's sister, Billie, who was living with her mother while her husband was in jail, to nurse his lover back from the very edge of death. He left Fort Smith at noon on June 19 and arrived in Dallas at about eight o'clock that evening, picked up Billie at a secluded spot to the north of the city, and by dawn was back in Fort Smith.

Even the hard-bitten Billie was shocked at the sight of her sister, who did not recognize her. Bonnie regained consciousness three days later, recognized Billie, and from that moment began slowly to recover. She must have been a trying patient: excitable and demanding, insisting that her bandages be changed every few hours to bring some relief from her pain. Clyde stayed with her night and day for a whole week, never leaving her bedside for longer than five minutes at a time. He was totally wrapped up in this tiny injured creature. It was as though love for Bonnie had begun to grow within him: Never again was he to abandon her, however great the danger, and indeed he behaved from then on with courage and resourcefulness in his protection of her.*

Surprisingly, Bonnie's ordeal after the car crash at Wellington did not become a prominent feature of her legend. Even in the 1967 film (the closest approximation to reality) Bonnie was not subjected to the horrible burning of her flesh. Perhaps it is an essential ingredient that the outlaw heroine retains her full beauty to the end.

IT WAS LEFT to Buck and W. D. to carry out the necessary robberies to replenish their dwindling funds during the time of Bonnie's recovery in Fort Smith. On June 23 the two men drove out of the tourist camp and headed north. After some fifty miles they spotted a suitable place to rob: the Piggly Wiggly Stores in the small town of Fayetteville. Characteristically, it was a bungled affair: The car registration number was recorded, their direction of travel observed, and detailed descriptions made of the robbers. This information was tele-

---

*It is absurd to maintain that the psychopath's incapacity for abject love is absolute, that is to say that he is capable of affection in literally no degree." H. Cleckley, *The Mask of Sanity* (1976).

phoned to Alma, a town at the road junction to Fort Smith toward which they were speeding.

The town marshal, Henry Humphrey, was very interested to hear of the approaching bandits because they sounded remarkably like two villains who on the previous day had robbed the bank at Alma and, what is more, had tied him to a pillar, threatening to kill him if any attempt at resistance were made by the bank employees.* Humphrey accordingly set up a strategic roadblock and then, together with his deputy, patiently awaited the arrival of the Piggly Wiggly bandits. At about half past six on that warm summer evening, the marshal spotted a car in the distance that as it drew closer he realized belonged to a friend of his who was slowing down to find out what all the fuss was about. But behind his friend's car Marshal Humphrey saw another vehicle approaching fast. The marshal waved to his friend to move through the roadblock, but before he could do so the second car, which was now braking hard, smashed into the back of the first one.

Accounts vary as to the events that followed. According to one version, the enraged driver of the first car attempted to attack the offending vehicle with a large rock. In another he was trapped beneath his own overturned vehicle. But all accounts agree about the subsequent happenings: Marshal Humphrey walked toward the second car, followed by his deputy, and called for the occupants to get out. They emerged with drawn weapons and shot him. The deputy retreated to a nearby farm to reload his gun, while the two robbers drove off in the murdered marshal's car.

Buck Barrow and W. D. Jones were now in considerable trouble, for the whole countryside was soon alive with searching posses, some of whose efforts resembled the antics of the Keystone Kops. One enterprising deputy sheriff commandeered a hearse belonging to a local undertaker and filled it

---

*The local police credited Clyde Barrow and W. D. Jones with this very professional robbery, which yielded $3,600. It is difficult to believe that the two men would have bothered to carry out a petty shop holdup on the following day if they had already netted several thousand dollars.

with a number of officers, all heavily armed and disguised as undertakers' assistants. The operation was intended to trap the two criminals, who, it was earlier reported, had been attempting to purloin such a vehicle. The hearse, accompanied by several carloads of lawmen, drove madly along country roads in the hope of picking up the criminals, one or both of whom were assumed to be injured. The only suspicious character they found was a local botanist whom they surprised in the midst of his field studies. However, on their way back the officers in the decoy hearse were surprised by another one that shot past them at high speed. They gave chase, and the two hearses careered along narrow country roads for ten miles. The driver of the second hearse was, in fact, a shopkeeper who had borrowed the vehicle to transport a load of overalls. He was convinced that he was being pursued by a party of dangerous bandits who had hijacked a hearse for the purpose of robbing him.

DESPITE THE FUROR caused by the murder of Marshal Humphrey, Buck and W. D. eventually found their way back to the tourist camp at Fort Smith by the simple stratagem of hitching a ride with a friendly farmer who was driving a truckload of vegetables into town. But the fugitives knew they were now in great danger and that it would be only a matter of time before they would hear a warning shout and see blue-clad figures moving outside their cabins.

It was then that Clyde Barrow left Bonnie's bedside to resume the leadership of his motley gang. They would have to leave in two stages, for they now had only one car. First he would take the three women away while his brother and W. D. Jones packed their baggage and tidied the cabins. The car had no backseat and so Billie would sit beside Clyde with Bonnie on her lap. Poor, long-suffering Blanche was to be stowed away in the rumble seat, hidden beneath some bedding.

They left the next morning, heading for a lonely hilltop that Clyde had selected for a temporary hideaway. It must have been a particularly trying journey for him. Not only did he have Bonnie, still racked with pain, and the querulous Blanche to contend with, but he also had three punctures to cope with on the way.

Clyde left the three apprehensive women on the hilltop and then drove back to collect Buck and W. D. That evening they were once again together in a makeshift camp, with Bonnie propped on their precious store of bedding, enjoying the freshness of the summer night after their days of confinement in the stuffy heat of the Fort Smith cabins.

They slept for three nights in their lonely hideaway. On the second day Clyde drove off with W. D. Jones (leaving Buck to guard the women) first to steal another, larger car and if possible to get more weapons and ammunition. They succeeded in both of their objectives. In Enid, in northern Oklahoma, they took the local doctor's car (in which, very conveniently, he had left a bag of medical supplies) and also increased their arsenal by breaking into the National Guard Armory and taking several Browning Automatic Rifles and a quantity of ammunition. These were deadly additions to their weaponry that would shortly stand them in good stead, for the bullets fired from these military rifles were powerful enough to penetrate armor plating.

Clyde's next objective was to get Bonnie's sister safely back to Dallas, and on the night of Sunday June 26, the Barrow Gang drove south to drop Billie north of Dallas in the town of Sherman. From there Billie took a train to Dallas, while the others turned north and drove in pleasant summer weather for more than three hundred miles up through Oklahoma and across high wheat plains to the town of Great Bend in central Kansas, a daunting journey for a badly burned woman.

Again the fugitives took the risk of booking into a tourist camp, for Bonnie still needed somewhere more comfortable than a makeshift camp in which to rest and recuperate. Clyde acted as her nurse, gently tending her wounds as often as she demanded. It was a bizarre role for a multiple murderer, tending a highly strung patient, exacting in her demands and prone to recurring fits of crossness.

15

THE
HUNTERS
PREPARE

IN 1933, 12,000 murders were recorded in the United States, 3,000 kidnappings, and 50,000 robberies. There were a number of causes. The years of prohibition had led to a proliferation of bootlegging by criminals who prospered from the manufacture and sale of illegal liquor and from a multiplicity of protection rackets. Then the repeal of the Eighteenth Amendment (which reestablished the legality of liquor trading) deprived the criminal fraternity of a major source of income and led to a dramatic increase in other enterprises, especially bank robberies and kidnappings, as the villains of the bootlegging era sought new ways to maintain themselves. This tendency was accentuated by the Great Depression, which threw 13 million people into unemployment and great hardship, especially in the country and towns of the Midwest.

Like Clyde Barrow and Bonnie Parker, a good proportion of the gangsters of the early 1930s were products of the villages and small towns of the Mid- and southwest who had drifted into the cities during the Depression. John Dillinger was reared in Mooresville, Indiana; Kathryn Thorne, the brains behind George ("Machine Gun") Kelly, was born in Saltillo, Mississippi, and moved to the small Texas town of Coleman; Charles ("Pretty Boy") Floyd spent his childhood on a small farm near

Akins, close to the Cookson Hills of Oklahoma; the formidable Kate ("Ma") Barker brought up her disagreeable family on a tumbledown farm near Aurora, Missouri.

By 1933 the newspapers of America were filled with the doings of these gangsters. The as yet unsolved kidnapping and murder of the Lindbergh baby had shocked the nation, as did the increasing number and extent of the bank robberies. The Barker-Karpis Gang had not long before lifted $240,000 from the Cloud County Bank in Concordia, Kansas. News of the Kansas City Massacre in the summer of 1933 (in which four law officers were gunned down in front of the city railway station) caused public concern and was announced on the same day as the kidnapping of the St. Paul businessman William Hamm, Jr. Shortly after, the equally spectacular kidnapping of another businessman, Charles F. Urschel of Oklahoma City, was made by Machine Gun Kelly and his confederates, which yielded a ransom of $200,000.

The agencies of law enforcement were ill prepared to cope with this state of affairs. The new breed of gangsters was well armed and regularly used machine-guns. They benefited from the recent development of mass-produced, fast cars in which they could easily escape from the scene of their crimes along state highways and into an intricate maze of country roads. They were assisted by havens that were provided not only by their families but by safe cities and towns such as St. Paul, Minnesota, Hot Springs, Arkansas, and Joplin, Missouri, where the local law authorities had established an unholy alliance with the underworld.

More than anything the gangsters of the 1930s were assisted by archaic laws that prevented the police of a particular city from pursuing their quarry into the surrounding country. Beyond the city limits escaping criminals became the concern of the county and state authorities. Liaison between the law authorities—city, county, and state—was frequently poor, especially in the days before the general use of radio communication by the police. The common strategy adopted by fleeing gangsters of crossing into adjacent states was a very effective means of escape.

Fig. 3 Comment by the *Dallas Morning News*, of 21st May 1934, on the need to amend the laws which prevented pursuit of criminals across state lines

Furthermore, the law-enforcement agencies themselves were often ramshackle affairs. Dillinger's biographer, John Toland, summarized the situation: "County officials were . . . helpless. Most of them had no training in law-enforcement and some were completely incompetent. And the state police, with few exceptions, were little more than paper organizations." Ordinary police officers at that time were usually ill equipped for contest with armed gangsters: "They had few machine guns, their cars were old and often broke down during pursuit; they were undermined and underpaid, often left to buy their own guns and provide their own transportation. In addition, police chiefs were frequently changed by new political administrations at the cost of efficiency and morale."

It is easy to see how, under these circumstances, Clyde Barrow and his companions could so easily and repeatedly escape from pursuing law officers. Yet reforms were being made that would lead to more effective crime prevention and that would eventually destroy Bonnie and Clyde.

The Division of Investigation, under the direction of the young J. Edgar Hoover, was to emerge two years later as the Federal Bureau of Investigation. Hoover's special agents were an elite, consisting of trained, educated men usually of considerable daring and courage. But in 1933 there were fewer than three hundred G-men. At this time they too were hampered by various obsolete laws that restricted their freedom of action in the various states in which they sought out the most dangerous criminals.

Changes were also taking place in state, county, and city police forces. In Texas at the end of 1932 R. A. ("Smoot") Schmid had been elected sheriff of Dallas County and immediately initiated changes to improve law enforcement. Schmid was a bulky, oval-faced man who stood six feet four inches tall and took size thirteen shoes—which gave him his other nickname: Big Foot. One of Schmid's first reforms was to recruit a number of new deputies among whom was a tall, reserved man called Ted Hinton, the son of a railroad worker. Hinton, then twenty-nine years old, had been brought up near Dallas and, in his own words, "was on the street early among the rough

CLYDE BARROW
BONNIE PARKER
JOHN DILLINGER

REWARD
$1,000.00

With full knowledge of the records of Clyde Barrow, Bonnie Parker and John Dillinger, we are prepared to pay immediately, the sum of One Thousand Dollars, *$1,000.00 to each or all of the above named persons if, as and when they appear in person at* either our Dallas, Ft. Worth or San Antonio Stores and find a single flaw in any of our Certified Perfect Diamonds. Shaw Jewelry Co., Texas' Greatest Jewelers.

•

Fig. 4 Bonnie and Clyde even provided copy for the ad-men of the time

element of the town." As a boy he knew the Barrow family, had been a customer of Bonnie's in his favorite Dallas café, and like Clyde had been a Western Union messenger in Dallas. When he was about eleven or twelve, Ted Hinton had caught Smoot Schmid's eye, and it was Schmid who helped the boy to buy the bicycle that was essential for his youthful delivery duties. Sheriff Schmid chose Ted Hinton for one of his deputies because he knew that Hinton had an unrivaled knowledge of the rough life of the Bog and, what is more, was tough and resourceful.

Another of the fifty-seven deputies who lined up on January 1, 1933, to be sworn in was Bob Alcorn. Like Ted Hinton, Alcorn was a powerful and determined young man and an excellent shot with a rifle. He had started his career as a motor mechanic but had later become a deputy in the previous administration. Sheriff Schmid was so impressed with Alcorn that he asked him to stay on and serve for another term.

Sheriff Schmid was not mistaken in his assessment of Bob Alcorn and Ted Hinton, for both these men were to play a critical part in the hunting and destruction of Bonnie and Clyde.

16

RED CROWN AMBUSH

THE FIVE FUGITIVES hiding in a cabin at the Great Bend tourist camp were becoming progressively more isolated from the everyday life of the people around them. They were like a nest of scorpions, kept together by strong instinctive needs and attachments, striking savagely at anyone who resisted their parasitic criminal demands. Their victims were not only the uniformed representatives of authority but such ordinary people as the kindly farmer's daughter-in-law in Wellington whose hand they had mutilated in a single vicious defensive reflex.

Confined day after day behind drawn curtains or crammed into stolen cars, their view of such normal people as they saw must have become increasingly unreal. Their real human contacts were limited to their remote families, to frequent letters and postcards, and rare, hazardous visits to West Dallas.

By mid-July Bonnie's burns had healed sufficiently for the fugitives to think of leaving Kansas, although she still could not walk by herself and had to be lifted into the backseat of the car. Her leg seemed to be permanently bent, and her face and arms were swathed in bandages.

In intense summer heat they headed northwest across a flat landscape of ripening wheat and into Iowa, to Fort Dodge.

There they made a temporary camp and on July 18 executed a succession of characteristic crimes, holding up three gas stations. With their funds replenished, the gang left behind the inevitable hue and cry that accompanied their modest robberies and headed for Missouri. By ten o'clock that night they reached the small township of Platte City, lying just west of the main highway that ran down to Kansas City.

After carefully reconnoitering the neighborhood, Clyde Barrow selected the Red Crown Tavern for the gang to rest that night. It was most suitable for their purposes: It lay at the intersection of two highways (giving excellent alternatives for rapid escape) and possessed a separate motel behind the hotel. The fugitives booked two single-storied, brick-built cabins for the night. Each had a separate door and single window at the front. Between the cabins were two wide garages in one of which the stolen car could be safely concealed.

The Red Crown Tavern was renowned locally for its food, especially its fried chicken, and in 1933 was also a popular meeting place for teenage dancers. But the Barrow Gang could not enjoy fried chicken or dancing on that hot July night; instead the long-suffering Blanche Barrow was dispatched across the road to the Slim's Castle, a combined restaurant and gas station, where she bought beer and sandwiches and carried them back to the motel cabins.

The following morning Blanche was again sent out shopping, this time to Platte City, while W. D. Jones strolled over to Slim's Castle, telling its owner that he was Jack Sherman (an alias often used by the Barrow Gang) and bought more sandwiches and cold drinks. Later on, Blanche went into the main building of the Red Crown Tavern, settled the bill, booked the cottages for another night, and paid ten dollars for five large dinners and soft drinks.

All these comings and goings attracted attention in the small rural community. An employee of the Red Crown Tavern had noticed the visitors; so had the nephew of the manager, who told his uncle of his suspicions. They telephoned the tavern's owner, Emmett Breen, who soon appeared on the scene to take a look at the guests. He recalls that he saw three of them (whom he later identified as Blanche, Bonnie, and Clyde) sitting, surprisingly, in full view in the hotel dining room. Breen said, "They sure didn't look like dangerous criminals to me." Nevertheless, he decided to telephone the sheriff of Platte City, who appeared in the early evening, together with a captain of the state highway patrol. They managed to get a man into one of the motel garages and were able to confirm that the car ensconced there was stolen but still could not be certain that the recent arrivals were, in fact, the much publicized and greatly feared Barrow Gang.

Emmett Breen was most anxious that the sheriff and his men should not take any action while the hotel was full of customers. It was thus agreed that the raid should be delayed until later that night when the diners and dancers had departed.

Meanwhile, Clyde Barrow had decided that his patient required some additional medicines for her burns. He slipped out of one of the motel cabins, walked on to the highway, and hitchhiked into the small town to buy further supplies from the local drugstore. Arriving at dusk (about eight o'clock at that time of year), Barrow unknowingly entered the drugstore on the heels of the Platte City prosecutor, D. R. Clevenger, who commented on the unusual police activity around the Red Crown Tavern, made his purchase, and then left without realizing that the customer in the blue open-necked shirt was the cause of all the fuss.

Clyde Barrow made his way back, and at about nine o'clock watching policemen saw the lights go out, first in one cabin, then in the other. In the warm summer darkness, the police moved into position, surrounding the silent, unlit cottages. But the order for the raid was not given as there were still too many customers around. The police were also expecting the arrival of further reinforcements: an armored car and steel protective shields, lent (at the suggestion of Clyde's fellow shopper at the drugstore) by the Kansas City sheriff.

At eleven o'clock the raid was eventually started. Emmett Breen watched from a doorway at the back of the main building; across the road in Slim's Castle, Kermit Crawford was also looking. He recalls that the armored car moved forward and stopped in front of the white-painted doors of the motel garages. Sheriff Coffey stepped forward holding a steel shield in front of him; behind him walked his teenage son, who had come along to see the fun, deliberately disregarding his father's instructions to keep out of sight.

All was peaceful inside the two redbrick cabins. According to Nell Cowan, who later received a firsthand account of the events, "Bonnie had been put to bed and was asleep. Clyde, who always slept lightly, had dozed off [fully clothed]. Blanche said she was still awake, but could hear Buck snoring softly. She did not know about W. D."

Sheriff Coffey began by rapping on the door of Blanche and Buck Barrow's cottage and ordering them to come out. The waiting officers and spectators heard Blanche's soft voice nervously answer, "Just a minute. Let me get dressed." There was a pause, and then she called out, "They're not here—they're in the other cabin." By now Buck Barrow was wide awake. He leaped to his feet and put his hand over his wife's mouth for a moment. Blanche, now thoroughly frightened, began frantically to collect her belongings and throw them into a bag.

Clyde Barrow was alert and on his feet in the other cabin. He flung open the internal connecting door to the garage, threw an armful of weapons into the car, and told W. D. Jones to start the engine. Outside, police were waiting in the darkness for the front door of the searchlit cabin to be opened. They were still unsure whether the occupants were, in fact, the Barrow Gang and did not want to force an entry, especially as Blanche's gentle voice must have given them pause.

Any doubts they had were dispelled when Clyde Barrow swung back the garage door and stood there firing a powerful Browning Automatic Rifle. The police replied, shattering the glass in the windows. Despite his shield, Sheriff Coffey was hit in the neck as more bullets pierced the armored car. Kermit Crawford witnessed the scene from his vantage point in Slim's Castle: "The sheriff sort of spun around, and then the shooting really started. Bullets were whizzing past our heads. I got the women to a safe place, and then headed for my room on the second floor of Slim's for a better view." Crawford saw Buck Barrow run from the cabins spraying the whole area with bullets from an automatic weapon. When he was hit, he slumped backward, his gun still firing.

The police were also in trouble. The deputy in the armored car was wounded in the leg. A bullet damaged the blaring horn mechanism and the car headlights made eerie shadows. The deputy moved the car back out of the line of fire but in so doing unblocked the garage doors. Women were screaming as the Barrow car roared from the garage, Clyde at the wheel with W. D. Jones clinging to the running board and firing a machine-gun. Buck Barrow had been dragged into the back-seat, where he lay in Blanche's arms next to Bonnie Parker. The car, a 1932 Ford V-8, Crawford recalls, scattered the surrounding posse and careered on to the road. A final burst of machine-gun fire from the police punctured the rear tires and shattered the car windows, cutting Blanche's face and blinding her with blood. But there was no one to organize the pursuit of the bandit car, which escaped into the darkness and the safety of a country lane that Clyde Barrow had previously reconnoi-tered as a reliable escape route.

When he knew that they were safe from pursuit, Clyde Barrow pulled the car from the road and turned into a field. There, under the car headlights, he surveyed his gang: Buck was unconscious and bleeding from a bullet wound in the temple; Blanche was moaning with fright and pain, her dress covered with blood from the wounds around her eyes; his burned lover was badly shaken and frightened. Only W. D. Jones was unscathed.

Clyde laid his brother down on newspapers on the grass and poured hydrogen peroxide into his wound and bandaged his head. Buck could not see and was in great pain. Blanche's eyes were bathed with water from a nearby stream, and she was given a pair of sunglasses to conceal her wounds.

At the Red Crown Tavern too the wounded were being tended. The sheriff's son, who had been hurt by a flying bullet, was carried into the dining room of the hotel and then driven to a hospital in Kansas City. His father, ignoring his own neck wound, was busily organizing a pursuit of the Barrow Gang. The injured man from the armored car was taken to hospital while, four miles away, Buck Barrow lay in a field on a bed of newspapers, illuminated by car headlights, bleeding profusely from hideous wounds.

The field belonged to a farmer who found himself awakened after midnight by a group of strangers asking to borrow a car jack to change one of their tires. The following morning the farmer walked down to the field where he had seen the car lights in the early hours and found not just a discarded, punctured tire but blood-soaked sheets of newspaper, soiled bandages, and a bloodstained dress. The farmer told the police that he had seen two women and two not three men. The Platte City deputies now knew for certain that the Barrow Gang had been blooded and that at least one of them was seriously wounded.

17

"DADDY, DON'T DIE"

CLYDE BARROW HEADED north during the early hours of July 20 and crossed into Iowa. At Mount Ayr, a hundred miles from Platte City, he turned the car off the road and stopped near to a running stream. It was now daylight. The scene was later dramatized by Nell Cowan: "Buck was running a high fever, and Blanche was in constant pain. The car held a horrible cargo of agony and death, and Clyde was half frantic about his brother. . . . Bonnie's leg was causing her great suffering and needed dressing badly."

Clyde did what he could to make his three patients comfortable. He was distraught at his brother's suffering and must have regretted bitterly the loss of the hypodermic syringes and vials of atropine and morphine sulfate that the Platte City *Landmark* reported were afterward found in one of the motel cabins at the Red Crown Tavern. He washed the wounds in water from the stream and evidently renewed the bandages, for some half burned bloody ones were later found at their stopping place.

The bullet-riddled Ford V-8 then continued its nightmare journey into Iowa. They were without food and drinking water. Nell Cowan later learned of their sufferings: "Buck asked constantly for water. . . . His delirious ravings and pleadings

153

were driving Blanche to insanity. She said she knew Buck was going to die unless he went to a doctor, and she wanted him taken to one." Clyde argued with her that if Buck were taken to a doctor it would inevitably result in his death—by execution— but if they kept going there was still a chance that he might survive. Buck Barrow regained consciousness in the middle of the dispute and whispered to his frightened wife, "We won't give up, hc..iey. We keep on driving."

As the afternoon wore on, the suffering of the three injured members of the gang became unbearable and Clyde, who had been driving since midnight, needed rest. As they neared the village of Dexter, twenty-five miles west of Des Moines, they came across a pleasant sweep of grass, dotted with trees and surrounded by protective woodlands—a public recreation area, twenty acres in extent. Local people took picnics there on summer weekends, but on this particular Thursday Dexfield Park was deserted.

Clyde drove across the bumpy grass to a secluded spot protected by trees and undergrowth, with a small river near at hand. The two uninjured men made a rough bed on the ground for Buck and another for Bonnie Parker. Despite her damaged eyes, Blanche insisted on sitting up next to her husband, telling the others not to speak about her wounds so as not to worry him.

Yet even the summer peace of Dexfield Park was insecure. It was dangerous to remain throughout the daylight hours in a public place, and a constant watch was necessary. They also needed to reconnoiter the surrounding countryside for potential victims and to plan escape routes along country roads and highways. The weekend was a particularly dangerous time, with the likelihood of courting couples and picnicking visitors coming to enjoy the grassy shade. It must have been for this reason that the fugitives spent Sunday July 23 driving along dusty side roads in intense summer heat.

One of the visitors to Dexfield Park that Sunday afternoon was a local farmer who had heard on his radio that there might be dangerous criminals in the vicinity. As he strolled by the river, he came upon a heap of blood-soaked, partly burned bandages and a car floor mat and considered it worth contacting the county sheriff to tell him of his discovery. The sheriff prudently decided that he would not take risks with such vicious people. He not only mobilized his deputies but also called in the local vigilantes, under the leadership of a special deputy. The two men deployed their forces carefully. During the afternoon they surrounded the temporary campsite and concealed their men carefully in the surrounding woods, while the observant farmer and a deputy hid close by behind some bushes to watch for the fugitives' return.

Two cars, driven by Clyde Barrow and W. D. Jones, drove back into the park in the late afternoon. They seem to have abandoned their earlier caution, for after dusk they lit a campfire to fortify the injured members of the group with warm food and drink. Clyde cleaned and restacked their arsenal of guns. Later, after the others had gone to sleep, he and W. D. Jones tinkered with the car engines by the light of a single pocket torch. Then they too lay down to sleep, neglecting their usual precaution of setting a guard.

During the night, police from Des Moines, National Guardsmen, and even some local farmers with shotguns arrived at Dexfield Park and were deployed in the surrounding woods and at strategic roadblocks. Meanwhile the fugitives slept, unaware that they were the center of a quiet circle of armed men. No attempt was made to approach them. Dawn came, and still the watchers kept silence.

As the sun rose, the sleepers stirred, sensed the morning freshness, and struggled to their feet. Only Buck Barrow slept on. Clyde could see that his brother was deathly ill. He turned away and began to collect and pack their belongings, saying that he was taking Buck back to his mother. Bonnie replied that he could not leave without her and that there was no point in taking Buck to West Dallas because he would soon be dead. But Clyde persisted. He had promised Cumie Barrow that he would take his brother to her if ever Buck were seriously ill or injured, and that was what he intended to do. Blanche said that she would go with them: She would never leave Buck.

The campfire was lit, and they began to prepare breakfast. W. D. Jones was cooking sausages, Bonnie making coffee, and

Blanche frying some eggs; Clyde Barrow stood by smoking a cigarette (unusual for him) after lighting one for his brother, who was now awake.

At this moment the waiting men were at last ordered to move. It was Bonnie Parker who saw the first telltale movement among the trees. She screamed a warning, dropping the coffee on the fire as she did so. Clyde and W.D. moved with lightning speed, grabbed automatic rifles, and began firing at the advancing men, who were now clearly visible. Volleys were fired in reply, but the advance faltered as the posse sought cover. Bonnie was also firing. Even timorous Blanche and her dying husband were seen to pick up guns and start firing.

Then Clyde jumped into one of the cars and started the engine, shouting to the others to join him. W. D. Jones followed. The others staggered after them, with Blanche, still half-blind, trying to put shoes on her husband's feet. Clyde accelerated in a desperate attempt to escape, but a bullet struck him in the arm. The car swerved and smashed into a tree stump, wrecking one of the front wheels. Amid a hail of bullets, Clyde raced for the other car, followed by W. D. Jones. Bonnie and Blanche staggered forward and were helping Buck when a bullet struck him in the back. He fell. They picked him up and he fell again. Bonnie was spattered with buckshot, and blood began to pour from a wound in W.D.'s head. As they reached the second car, the concentrated fire of the posse smashed its windows, pierced the gas tank, and punctured the tires. Buck Barrow fell again, begging Blanche to leave him and run from the ambush, but she refused and crouched down beside him, using a tree stump as protection against the hail of police bullets.

Clyde Barrow was now running toward the woods, with W. D. Jones and Bonnie Parker after him. Buck was still attempting to fire and by so doing attracting considerable fire from the advancing posse. Several bullets thudded into his back, and he slumped down with his head on Blanche's lap. She screamed, begging the surrounding gunmen to stop firing.

"Stop, for God's sake, stop. Don't shoot any more—you've already killed him."

As the posse reached the mortally wounded man and his

7. (left) Clyde's accomplice, Raymond Hamilton, 8. (center) Bonnie's sister, Billie (right) 9. Buck Barrow.

10. (below) Police reenactment of a Barrow robbery

11. (left) Bonnie 12. (center) Clyde and his mother 13.(right) Bonnie and Clyde

14. (below) A .32 Colt revolver, reputedly the one smuggled by Bonnie to Clyde Barrow in the Waco Jail.

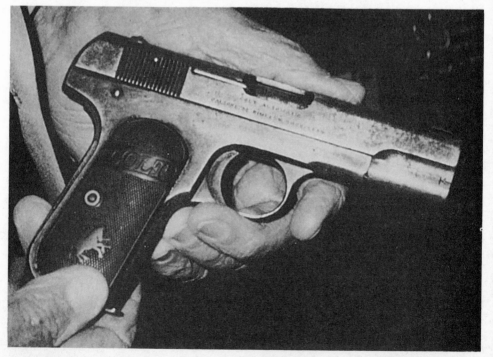

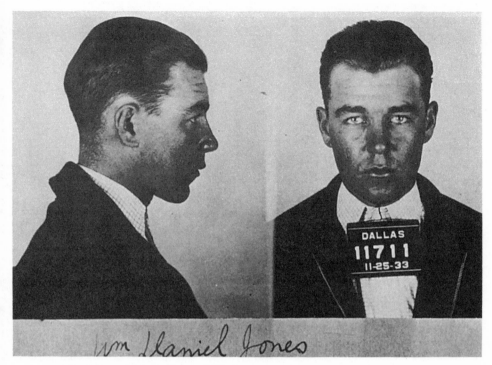

15. (above) Mug shots of W. D. Jones

16. (below) The capture of Blanche and Buck Barrow at Dexfield Park, Iowa, July 23, 1933

17. (above) Four of the hunters of Bonnie and Clyde. *(Left to right)* Smoot Schmid, Ed Caster, Ted Hinton, and Bob Alcorn, with items from Clyde Barrow's car. The photograph was taken after the unsuccessful police ambush at Sowers, November 23, 1933.

18. (below) Mug shots of Henry Methvin

31. (above) Annie and Bart (Peggy Cummins and John Dall) as the gun-toting fugitives in *Gun Crazy* (1950).

32. (below) Bonnie Parker (Dorothy Provine) and "Guy Darrow" (Jack Hogan) in the 1958 film *The Bonnie Parker Story*.

33. An early scene from the 1983 comedy film *Bonnie e Clyde all'italiana*, in which Anorella Muti (Bonnie) and Paolo Villaggio (Clyde) are accidentally trapped into a life of violent crime.

frightened, shrieking wife, a National Guardsman kicked the revolver from Buck Barrow's hand. Two other men grabbed at the slight red-haired woman, each holding her by an arm, and pulled her away from Buck, who sat crouching forward on the ground clad in a blood-soaked vest. Blanche was wearing the corduroy riding breeches, shirt, and boots in which Nell Cowan had thought she looked so pretty when she had paid her last brief visit to Dallas. Her damaged eyes were hidden by dark glasses, stark against her pale face. Her arms were held wider by the firm grip of her captors, with her body slightly twisted, as though crucified. She cried piteously to her husband, "Daddy, don't die—don't die—don't die."

THEY TOOK BLANCHE Barrow twenty miles to the county jail in the small town of Adel. Later she was moved to the prison in Des Moines, where she was interrogated about the recent activities of the Barrow Gang, especially the gun battles at Joplin and Platte City. Both Sheriff Coffey and the prosecutor David Clevenger, who had been Clyde's fellow customer at the drugstore, traveled up from Platte City to interview her about the shooting at the Red Crown Tavern. They got very little from the shaken and frightened woman who, surprisingly, parried their questioning with considerable skill and success. Later, however, she seems to have responded to David Clevenger and told him about the robberies and the killings in which she had been involved. When she was taken back to Platte City, a large crowd collected to see this notorious criminal. The city prosecutor took quite a liking to her and even arranged an accidental meeting between his wife and Blanche Barrow in his office at Platte City. Mrs. Clevenger was quite charmed with her husband's prisoner and still recalls her surprise at finding a woman "so terribly tiny that it was hard to visualize her having the strength to lift a very large weapon." She also remembers that Blanche later wrote to her husband thanking him "for the courtesy he had shown her while she was in jail awaiting trial."

While Blanche Barrow was being questioned and prepared for trial, her husband was close to death in a hospital at Perry, the town from which Clyde Barrow and W. D. Jones had stolen the second car. His room was locked and guarded by armed police officers, while others patroled the corridors and hospital grounds in case there should be any attempt to rescue him.

During periods of consciousness, Buck Barrow was questioned by law officers who remained at his bedside. One of these was the deputy from Alma. The dying man admitted that he and not Clyde Barrow had murdered Henry Humphrey, the town marshal, after he and W. D. Jones had crashed the car at the road block near Alma.

On Wednesday, July 26, 1933, Buck Barrow's mother, his sister Nell, and a younger brother arrived at Perry together with Emma Parker and her younger daughter, Billie. Although desperately weak, Buck was at least conscious when his family entered the heavily guarded room. He recognized his mother and talked lucidly to Emma Parker and her daughter. On the following day, however, he was delirious and confused. Nell Cowan said "he'd be quiet only when his mother or Billie held his hand." She remembered that as they left his bedside at lunchtime Buck begged them, "Take Blanche with you, don't leave her." When they told him that his wife was not with them he repeated, "Please take her—she's hungry. Poor little Blanche—take her with you, mother."

The next day, Friday, he was much worse. His sister said that he called for Clyde and Blanche throughout the day. He deteriorated rapidly on the following day, and at two o'clock in the afternoon of July 29 he died. He was thirty years old.

18

"IT'S HELL OUT THERE"

ON SEPTEMBER 7, 1933, Clyde Barrow and Bonnie Parker returned to the Dallas area. It was four months ₋ince they had last seen their families. Emma Parker was shoc₋ ₋when she saw her daughter: "Bonnie was still unable to w₋ ₋ithout help. She was miserably thin and much older. H₋ ₋ was drawn up under her. Her body was covered in scars.

Clyde still had to lift Bonnie from the car. At this mee₋ g, he put a quilt on the ground and laid her on it so that she co₋ ₋ sit close to her mother. Emma Parker held her daughter's wa₋ted hands as they talked together that evening. Bonnie told ₋ ₋r mother that she and Clyde had not slept in a bed for two month₋ and were living entirely in the car. They needed pillows and additional blankets, for the September nights were becoming chilly. Mrs. Parker agreed to bring some on the following night and also suggested that she should fetch for Bonnie the crutches that Clyde had used after his self-mutilation in Huntsville penitentiary.

Nell Cowan was filled with pride for her daring, handsome brother when she heard how he had guided the wounded fugitives to safety despite four bullet wounds and with one arm hanging useless. He had helped Bonnie and W.D. down to the river and swum with them across to the other bank. Halfway across they had been spotted by the posse, and bullets began to splash into the water around them, but somehow they had reached the other side, where Clyde left them in a cornfield while he ran to a nearby farmhouse, threatened three men with a useless, watersoaked revolver, forced them to give him their car keys and then to lift Bonnie into the back of their car. W. D. Jones had then driven the car at breakneck speed, Clyde moaning with pain in the front seat beside him.

Later they stopped the car and tried to clean themselves up. Bonnie washed the men's bloodstained shirts and her dress in a stream, lying on her uninjured side. At Polk City they stole another car and drove for three days southwest toward Denver, Colorado. Where exactly they went Bonnie could not recall. "We lived in little ravines, secluded woods, down side roads for days that stretched into weeks. We were all so sick that time went by without our knowing it. We lost track of the days."

Later the fugitives were nearly a thousand miles south, in Clarkesdale, Mississippi. Clyde had recovered sufficiently to drive again, but their car was showing signs of wear, and Jones was sent off, with $2.12 in his pocket for gas, to steal another. But he never returned—he had evidently had enough of life with Bonnie and Clyde.

BLANCHE BARROW WAS tried in the Platte city circuit court in early September. She was prosecuted by David Clevenger, without an attorney to represent her, and pleaded guilty to the charges. She was sentenced to ten years in the Women's Prison Pen in Jefferson City, Missouri. The Barrow and Parker families no doubt took a sardonic pride in the fact that the Platte City courthouse was very heavily guarded by armed police in case Clyde Barrow should attempt to rescue his sister-in-law.

The secret family meetings continued during the autumn months. According to Emma Parker, "the kids came in to see us every single night except five. They'd either drive by the house or the filling station. Often they'd stop. If we didn't talk with them they'd tell us where to meet them and we'd drive out and be with them several hours."

Bonnie met her favorite nephew, Buddy (her sister Billie's four-year-old son), at some of the clandestine family meetings. Buddy was very fond of his Auntie Bonnie. When his little sister, Jackie, was unhappy he once comforted her by saying, "Don't cry Jackie. Never mind. Bonnie's coming after a while and she'll sing the Crawdad Song." He seems to have had instilled into him the criminal code of his family, for Emma Parker proudly recounted that he told her, "I shall tell my mother I have been with Bonnie, but nobody else."

It was a bitter blow to Bonnie Parker when she learned in early October that her niece had been taken seriously ill with a "stomach disorder" and had died in hospital. Soon after this came the news that her nephew too had been taken ill with the mysterious disease and died of it. Bonnie must have longed to help her grieving mother and sister in their home instead of adding to their anxieties. Her nomadic life with Clyde Barrow was also becoming more uncomfortable with the chill of advancing autumn and the prospect of winter nights spent in the open or cooped up in an unheated car. They were also running out of funds. Soon she and Clyde would have to risk danger and perhaps kill or be killed.

By early November, they had chosen another victim to sustain their parasitic life—Jim MacMurray, an enterprising oilman who still succeeded in making a profit, despite tumbling oil prices, from his refinery near the small township of Overton. It was on the cool morning of November 8 that Bonnie Parker stepped out of a Ford V-8 and walked over to MacMurray's office, looked in, then turned around and walked back to the car, without attracting any undue attention from the few tanker drivers who were standing around. She soon reappeared with Clyde Barrow and a confederate, brandishing guns. They herded the tanker drivers into the refinery office to join the surprised owner and his manager. Barrow then demanded the keys of the safe: a large metal pipe with a hinged and padlocked lid that had been concreted into the floor. When MacMurray said that he did not have the keys, Barrow pointed his gun at the padlock and blew it apart at point-blank range. He then knelt down, put his hand in the safe, lifted out between two and three thousand dollars, backed out of the office, and ran with the other man to the waiting car, which meanwhile Bonnie Parker had driven up to the office. The three thieves drove away and were not caught at any of the roadblocks that the police set up in the area.

The identity of Clyde Barrow's confederate is a mystery. He was not identified by the local police, and the Parkers and Barrows never mentioned any uncaptured criminal acquaintances in their subsequent written accounts. Certainly Deputy Hinton, who was quickly dispatched from Dallas to the scene of the crime, was unable to name the man who helped Bonnie and Clyde in the daylight robbery of MacMurray's refinery.

ONE WEEK AFTER the robbery in the east Texas oilfields, Clyde Barrow's former confederate was arrested. The sheriff's office in Dallas had received a tip that W. D. Jones could be found at an address in the southern Texas city of Houston. The seventeen-year-old criminal was arrested on November 15, 1933, and immediately began to "sing like a canary." He maintained that he was very relieved to have been taken into custody, for he was fearful of the vengeance of Clyde Barrow. He told his interrogators that he had been forced, against his will, to join Clyde Barrow and Bonnie Parker. He had been innocently enjoying himself at a downtown dance on the previous Christmas Eve when they had appeared and used pistols to "convince" him to go to east Texas with them. They locked him in the trunk of their car, he claimed, and did not let him out until the following morning, when he found himself, to his surprise, at Temple. He also said that Barrow frequently taunted him and had called him, among other things, a "yellow punk," for example when they attempted to steal Doyle Johnson's car on Christmas Day 1932. He could not say much about the murders as he had usually been asleep at the bottom of the car or, for one reason or another, unconscious when they occurred. On one occasion he had been chained to a motel bed, he told his interrogators, and often forced to spend hours at a time unwillingly practicing weapon training in secluded hideouts. "It's hell out there, Mr. Hinton, just hell. Never sleep in a bed, never eat a good meal, always running scared, never knowing when a bullet is going to catch you. God, I'm glad to be in this jail. Don't ever make me leave it while Clyde's alive."

While Jones was holding forth in the Dallas county jail, Sheriff Schmid and his deputies were also receiving information about the activities of the Barrow and the Parker families. A dairy farmer named Stovall who lived near the village of Sowers in Wise County (northwest of Dallas) had noticed a couple of cars that occasionally parked on a stretch of unpaved road near his farm. Stovall told Ted Hinton that he was certain the cars belonged to the Barrows.

Sheriff Schmid was very interested in Charlie Stovall's story and immediately made plans to set up a reception committee for the next family gathering near Sowers. On the evening of November 22, the Dallas county sheriff arranged his ambush. He had with him Ted Hinton (carrying a submachine gun), Bob Alcorn (with an automatic rifle), and Ed Caster (armed with a repeating rifle). Schmid deployed his forces behind a fence beside the highway: Their cars were parked, out of sight, half a mile away. The strategy that the sheriff had devised was for his men to stay concealed until they were certain that their quarries were indeed Clyde Barrow and Bonnie Parker, whereupon Schmid would rise up and call, "Halt." At this point, according to the sheriff's optimistic plan, Clyde Barrow and his companion would recognize the hopelessness of their situation and surrender. Ted Hinton had considerable misgivings about the likely success of Smoot Schmid's scheme.

The first car arrived at dusk. It contained Emma Parker and Cumie Barrow. The car turned into a lane and parked about seventy-five feet from the main highway; the two women were familiar with the place, for they had been there the day before to celebrate Cumie Barrow's birthday. In the fading light they could see the country lane curving down in front of them toward a small bridge; behind them was the main highway along which they expected their children to appear.

After what seemed a long time to the cold, watching law officers, a car drove along the highway and started to turn into the lane, then pulled back on to the main highway, drove on, stopped, turned, and then drove back. This time the car steered into the lane, moved past the one already parked, and then began to turn again. The lights of the stationary vehicle were then switched on, brilliantly illuminating the turning car. There was no doubt to any of the cold deputies crouching uncomfortably behind the fence that it was driven by Clyde Barrow with Bonnie Parker sitting at his side.

Emma Parker, sitting in the stationary car enjoying a gossip with Cumie Barrow, heard a popping sound. She said her first thought was that someone was letting off fireworks. Clyde and Bonnie knew better: They had been ambushed. Barrow immediately stopped turning the car and accelerated it in the opposite direction, down the lane toward the bridge. In a swift reflex, his tiny companion smashed the glass in the back window with her gun and prepared to fire back. But she checked herself, for she realized that she might gun down her own mother. Clyde was firing at the side of the road as he drove. One of the bullets grazed Ted Hinton's neck. Police bullets whizzed around the accelerating car, puncturing the left rear wheel and passing through the vehicle, wounding Clyde and his companion in the legs. In the heat of the moment they felt no pain, and Barrow kept the car bumping forward on three tires across the bridge into the darkening lane. They drove on for a few miles, safe from immediate pursuit, for Sheriff Schmid and his deputies had deliberately hidden their cars well away from the site of the ambush.

When Clyde and Bonnie reached a highway, they parked their bumping vehicle and hijacked a passing Ford coupe. They eventually found their way up into Oklahoma, where they managed to obtain medical attention and spent extremely cold nights in the windowless car until they stole another and returned to Dallas. Clyde Barrow had a score to settle there.

SMOOT SCHMID'S AMBUSH had been a conspicuous failure. Not only had the two criminals escaped yet again, but Mrs. Stovall, the farmer's wife, had been injured in the neck by a piece of glass from a window that had been smashed by a stray bullet that had reached the nearby farmhouse. What is more,

Emma Parker was indignantly claiming that the ambush had not been preceded by the customary call for the fugitives to halt.

All that the Dallas county sheriff and his deputies could do was examine the Ford V-8 that had been abandoned on the highway to the west of Dallas and harvest their clues. There were bloodstains on the seats and ten spent cartridge cases on the floor, together with an assortment of personal belongings, including pillows, cans of food, knives and forks, a stack of car license plates, lipstick, a mirror, and several detective magazines. The damaged car and its curious collection of objects was, however, a poor substitute for the expected capture of Bonnie and Clyde. It did not impress insistent newspapermen or even the Barrow and Parker families, who, according to Emma Parker, "went down to the court house later to look the car over after the officers had brought it in."

Smoot Schmid, who was already worrying about his prospects for the next election, had only one exhibit left: W. D. Jones. The arrest of the teenage criminal had been kept secret: now the hard-pressed sheriff decided to announce the capture of a member of the Barrow Gang in an attempt to retrieve at least partially his public image as the scourge of the Dallas County criminals and in particular the man who was going to destroy Bonnie and Clyde.

SCHMID'S PRINCIPAL QUARRY, consumed with the desire for vengeance against the sheriff and his deputies, returned to Dallas on November 28.

It appears that Barrow, a man who had gunned down unarmed members of the public without compunction, objected to the Dallas sheriff's use of weapons when there were "innocent people about." The fact that his mother and Emma Parker were aiding and abetting the multiple murderer seems not to have weighed at all with Clyde. He told Emma Parker that he was "out to get" Smoot Schmid and the deputies who had taken part in the attempted ambush in Wise County.

As soon as he returned to Dallas, Barrow sought Smoot Schmid's address and tried to telephone the sheriff. He evidently received no answer, for according to Emma Parker, he waited outside Schmid'~ house until three o'clock in the morning to no avail. He also watched Bob Alcorn's house on another evening, again without success.

Emma Parker said that "Clyde was really blind with rage." She recognized that "this deliberate stalking of Schmid and Alcorn was the first time we'd ever known him to try to get a cop." It was Nell Cowan who finally persuaded her brother to abandon his intention of murdering the Dallas county sheriff or one of his deputies. She argued that such an action would only rebound on the family. She also scotched Clyde Barrow's idea of trying to rescue W. D. Jones from the county jail.

Ted Hinton, however, had got wind of Barrow's threat to murder one or other of the Dallas county law officers and was particularly incensed by the rumor that Clyde Barrow had said that the tough young deputy was afraid to meet him face-to-face. Hinton was steamed up by not only the professional affront but also the personal insult, for he had known the Barrow family since he was a lad, when Clyde's younger brother had been his friend.

The deputy decided that he would demonstrate once and for all that he was not afraid of Clyde Barrow. He took an unsuspecting colleague, John ("Preacher") Hays, along to the Barrow Filling Station in West Dallas. When Hays realized their destination, he demurred: "Wait just a damned minute. I don't want any part of this." But Hinton was determined, and when they found Clyde's father standing outside the filling station, the irate deputy told the elderly man in no uncertain terms, "Henry, next time you see that son of yours, tell him from me that I'll meet him alone, any time."

According to Ted Hinton, Henry Barrow was apologetic: "I know, Ted. I know. I'm sorry, Ted. I can't help what the boy says."

The kindly deputy was touched by Henry Barrow's response, and his anger died. Hinton recalls that he then tried to comfort Henry Barrow and gave him the advice that the elderly taciturn father must have received over and over again: "Persuade your son to give himself up to the police, he might then escape the electric chair or death by police bullets." Henry Barrow only shook his head, for he knew that there was no possibility that this would happen.

Henry Barrow, who by this time had been joined by his tearful wife, told Deputy Hinton that he had been subjected to considerable harassment since his son had become an outlaw. The latest trouble had been the firing of a shotgun at night through his window. Henry Barrow said that he knew who had fired the gun. The old man was barely making a living from his filling station and could not afford to pay for the repairs caused by such vandalism.

Ted Hinton recalls that he regretted his outburst about Clyde Barrow, for he sensed that Henry Barrow regarded him as one of his last remaining friends. He picked up the shotgun that lay on the backseat of his car, thrust it into the old man's hands, and told him that if anyone troubled him again, Barrow should "blast his damned head off."

19

Eastham
Farm
Breakout

THE DECAPITATION OF troublesome neighbors is at first sight an unexpected suggestion for a law enforcement officer. Yet it conformed to the simple and often violent values of a society in which there was little to distinguish the cops from the robbers, except for the side of the law from which they operated. Ted Hinton had grown up in the Bog and had known the Barrows since he was a boy. In a strange way he liked Clyde and years later admitted that he still admired him for his guts.

Hinton's admiration was certainly not shared by Lee Simmons, Governor of the Huntsville penitentiary, soon to become Clyde Barrow's implacable adversary. Yet, as a youth, even that pillar of Texas law enforcement had been charged, and acquitted, of murdering someone for no other reason than that "derogatory statements" had been made about the Simmons family.

Lee Simmons had not known convict number 63527 in the Huntsville penitentiary, but the embittered Clyde Barrow had dreamed his dream of revenge, and that would bring him into deadly conflict with Simmons. It is very unlikely that Clyde had really believed that he would one day attack the hated prison as he had told a fellow convict he would in the depths of despair two years before. Yet, when the opportunity came, it was not his idea but originated with Raymond Hamilton, who, together with help from some members of his family, had devised a plan to break out of the Eastham prison farm.

Clyde must have been turning over the scheme in his mind as he sat in the open with Bonnie on a cold Sunday afternoon in January 1934. Earlier that day Bonnie had suffered a nasty attack of rheumatism, an embarrassing affliction for potential outlaw heroines. It was, however, so painful that Clyde was forced to drive her, screaming at every bump, for 250 miles to the outskirts of Dallas, there to seek her mother's and his sister's help. Fortunately for the success of the projected prison raid, Bonnie was speedily cured, by the liberal application of a linament recommended by Nell Cowan ("The best damn medicine I ever saw," according to Clyde).

Two days later, in the early morning of a raw foggy day, Clyde was hiding in a patch of weeds with another of Raymond Hamilton's friends, a man called James Mullen. Behind them, in the fog, fully recovered from her rheumatics, Bonnie was waiting in the car.

Dawn was just breaking when they heard the marching feet of an approaching squad. They knew that the prisoners would be cutting timber close at hand. They also knew that two of them, Raymond Hamilton and an accomplice, Joe Palmer, were armed with .45 automatics that had been smuggled in to them.

The squad duly halted at the edge of the wood. While the prisoners waited, their prison escort called to the mounted, long-arm guard, who rode toward the group of prisoners. It was at this moment that Palmer and Hamilton produced their guns and fired. The long-arm man was hit in the stomach and head and fell from his horse. Then, from close at hand, a machine-gun opened up through the swirling fog. Clyde Barrow was covering their escape. From behind came the dismal blare of the car horn, Bonnie Parker's signal for the position of the escape car.

Palmer and Hamilton sprinted toward the car, taking with them Henry Methvin, a twenty-one-year-old friend of Hamilton's. Two other escapees, a hard-faced, stooping man by the name of Hilton Bybee and another violent criminal, J. B. French, also ran with them through the obscuring fog to the sound of the blaring horn.

At the car there was considerable confusion and much dispute caused by the unexpected appearance of three additional convicts. Everyone was shouting at once. Raymond Hamilton tried to take charge and bawled at the top of his voice, "Everybody go back except Bybee and me" (he had evidently decided to abandon Joe Palmer). James Mullen loomed out of the fog, adding further to the disorder by reverting to the original plan.

"Nobody but Raymond and Palmer going," he yelled.

Then Clyde Barrow entered the proceedings. "Shut your damn mouth, Mullen; this is my car—I'm handling this."

Eventually all of them jammed into the car. Raymond Hamilton sat on James Mullen's lap, between Bonnie and Clyde, while the others were wedged into the rumble seat in some discomfort. Crouched on top of each other, no doubt still engaged in vigorous dispute, they bounced down muddy country roads, avoiding the roadblocks the police had set up on the major highways. By evening they reached Hillsboro, where they had to stop for gas. The gas pump attendant was so excited by the news of the prison breakout that he failed to notice that there were two men in prison clothes squeezed into the front seat or to hear muffled bumpings coming from the back of the car. He announced that Bonnie and Clyde had snatched five convicts, killing and wounding several guards. The garrulous garage hand assured Clyde that all the roads were blocked and that the criminals would soon be captured.

He was wrong, for Clyde Barrow drove 250 miles through the night to Houston, dropping Bybee and French en route, before turning north toward Fort Worth.

BACK AT THE Eastham prison farm, Lee Simmons was finding out for himself what had happened to the timber-cutting detail in the drifting fog that morning. He visited the wounded guard, Major Crowson, who had been taken to the Huntsville hospital. Crowson was feeling very guilty. He had disobeyed the rule that the long-arm man should never approach the prisoners and the other guards, and he was desperately anxious to be forgiven. Simmons tried to comfort the injured man.

"Don't bother about it. I'm for you. Those fellows had their day; we'll have ours. I promise you I won't let them get away with it."

Major Crowson died the following day. His nurse said he was worried to the last about his lapse of discipline and frequently expressed the hope that Mr. Simmons would not "think hard" of him. At the funeral, Crowson's father told Lee Simmons that his son had firmly believed that Simmons would bring his attackers to justice.

Crowson's confidence in his superior was not misplaced; Lee Simmons had every intention of settling accounts with those responsible for the killing of one of his guards. His motives were not purely altruistic, for like Sheriff Smoot Schmid of Dallas County, he was under considerable political pressure to do something to counteract the wave of criminal violence in Texas—especially the activities of Clyde Barrow and his associates. He sought the assistance of the state governor, Miriam Ferguson, and her husband (a former governor who had been impeached). He knew exactly who was needed to hunt down and destroy Clyde and Bonnie: the former Texas Ranger Frank Hamer.

Hamer, a burly fifty-year-old man, had spent most of his adult life in law enforcement, as the city marshal of Narasota and later as Captain Hamer of the Texas Rangers. He was a cryptic, taciturn man and had acquired a formidable reputation as a result of several spectacular captures and the shooting of a number of Texas criminals. In November 1932 he had resigned from the Texas Rangers, before the Fergusons returned to the state governorship, and in 1934 was working for a Houston oil company.

On February 1, after obtaining the approval of the state governor, Lee Simmons went straight out to Frank Hamer's house in Austin, determined to use all his powers of persuasion. They were enough for Hamer. "Well," he replied, "if that's the way you feel about it I'll take the job." It was in many ways a surprising decision for the middle-aged former Texas Ranger

—not least because it involved a substantial reduction in salary, from $500 a month with the oil company to about $180 as a temporary employee of the Texas Prison System. The instincts of the hunter ran strong in Frank Hamer; as a boy, he had spent weeks at a time by himself in the woods of San Saba County learning to stalk, throw a knife, shoot, and follow the trails of men and animals. He was adventurous, capable of spontaneous decisions that, in the words of a friend, were "not calculated to promote his interests," and had developed a genuine loathing and contempt for criminals. Frank Hamer was probably also not unmindful of the fame and the rewards that the destroyer of Bonnie and Clyde would win, for their exploits were now regularly emblazoned in banner headlines, trumpeted in radio programs, exaggerated in crime magazines throughout America, and even recorded on the back pages of some staid European newspapers.

DESPITE THE DISCOMFORT, danger, and fatigue, the long drive after the raid on the Eastham prison farm was an occasion of personal triumph for Clyde Barrow. He was elated by scoring so conclusively over the prison system he hated. He had three grateful comrades with him who owed to him their liberty. He had used his driving skill and knowledge of the network of minor roads to elude the police roadblocks. He was in business again with his friend Hamilton, and with the addition of Henry Methvin and Joe Palmer, he was once more a gang leader.

This was the very stuff of legend: the outlaw hero with his companions, free once more in the greenwood. The reality was distinctly less romantic. For one thing, Clyde was probably beginning to recall just how irritatingly garrulous his old companion could be as Raymond Hamilton dominated the conversation, exuberantly outlining grandiose schemes for criminal profit. Joe Palmer, a thin silent man with a widow's peak and prominent ears, was feeling car-sick and was more than usually uncommunicative. Henry Methvin, thickset and pimply faced, also sat in uncomfortable silence—outtalked by Hamilton and overawed at finding himself with the legendary killer Clyde Barrow. James Mullen, a thin beetle-browed man with protruding teeth, was still on board—probably to protect his investment (he had been promised $1,000 for his part in the prison breakout) or possibly because the others were frightened that he might betray them for further profit if they let him go.

Raymond Hamilton had one thought uppermost in his mind as Clyde's motley gang were driven first toward Fort Worth (to order some new clothes), then, on the following day, northwest to Vernon, in the Red River Valley (to pick them up), and then down to Louisiana (most probably to contact Henry Methvin's father, who farmed near Gibsland). Hamilton was badly in need of female companionship, and he knew exactly whom he wanted to provide it: Mary O'Dare, an attractive and elaborately painted woman whose husband, Gene (the man arrested with Hamilton, on roller skates, in Bay City, Michigan), was safely out of the way serving a fifty-year sentence for armed robbery. At this time she was dallying with another man whose name she temporarily adopted, calling herself Mary Pitts. Fortunately for Hamilton, Mary O'Dare lived in Wichita Falls, not far from the hideout that the Barrow Gang had established near Vernon on returning from Louisiana.

Hamilton went off with James Mullen to contact the woman who had been the object of his inflamed thoughts during the seemingly endless driving of the previous days. He seems to have had little difficulty in persuading her to abandon the unfortunate Mr. Pitts. He picked her up at her mother's house in Wichita Falls, took breakfast in a tourist camp, and returned triumphantly with her to the gang's hideout in a car stolen especially for the occasion.

Despite her many desirable attributes, Mary O'Dare did not receive an enthusiastic welcome when she stepped from Raymond Hamilton's stolen car on his return to the Red River hideout. Clyde Barrow in particular took an instant dislike to his friend's sexy new girl. However, he accepted her on the very comradely basis that any friend of Ray's was a friend of his and soon began to discuss ways of raising money to cover their living expenses and to pay James Mullen his promised $1,000.

Another urgent necessity was to arm the new additions to the Barrow Gang. On February 19 they robbed the National

Guard Armory in the small town of Ranger (quiet again after the abortive oil boom of a decade earlier) and returned in high feather to their hideout with a number of automatic rifles and pistols and a great deal of ammunition. James Mullen departed after this, presumably satisfied that his clients had sufficient weaponry to obtain his fee for him.

A week later, the fugitives emerged again from their hideout and made off in the direction of Lancaster, a community on the southern outskirts of Dallas, there to rob the local bank. They left one car with Bonnie Parker, Mary O'Dare, and Joe Palmer (who was still feeling sick) at a lonely spot near Bluebird Farm in the south of Dallas County, while Clyde Barrow drove one according to one account or two others according to another into Lancaster and successfully held up the glass-fronted bank of R. P. Henry & Sons. Clyde threatened the banker and two customers with a shotgun as Hamilton loaded the cash into a sack fastened to his belt. They escaped with cash estimated in different accounts at $2,400, $3,800, $4,128.50, $4,433, $4,800, and $6,700.

At Bluebird Farm they abandoned the car they had used in the robbery and all piled into the other. Bonnie had the engine running, and Clyde jumped into the driver's seat, squeezing Bonnie between him and Henry Methvin. Raymond Hamilton and Joe Palmer were in the backseat, with Raymond's auburn-haired girlfriend between them.

Clyde drove off in his usual reckless manner. Raymond Hamilton began counting the money, carefully watched by the driver, who was evidently able to divide his attention even during a getaway. The two men began to argue about the division of the spoils, which Hamilton first proposed should be split equally between himself and Clyde, who refused, insisting that the money be divided equally among the six of them.

Raymond Hamilton was furious at his partner's decision. He argued and raged from the backseat of the speeding car but eventually subsided into sulky acquiescence. Clyde, who was still watching in the driving mirror, then saw his accomplice slip some of the banknotes that he was counting into his own pocket. From that moment all confidence between the two criminals disappeared.

20

DISTRUST
AND
DISAGREEMENTS

BY LATE FEBRUARY the Barrow Gang was the antithesis of a happy outlaw band. Raymond Hamilton still wrangled with Clyde Barrow about the division of the money stolen from the Lancaster bank and nagged him for his limited criminal ambitions, especially his preference for robbing wayside garages. He maddened Clyde with his boastings and his ambitions as a big-time bank robber. Barrow retorted by sneering at Hamilton, called him a yellow punk, and reminded him of occasions when his conduct had been less than heroic.

Poor Joe Palmer was unwillingly drawn into their rows at this time. "I was asleep in the blankets in the bottom of the car, and Raymond was going to kill me because I had called him a punk blabbermouth braggart, and he had to take it. So Clyde slapped him and cursed him, and went into the ditch and broke the left wheel."

Hamilton's sexy girlfriend also added to the ill feelings within the group. Joe Palmer recalled that "Clyde, Bonnie, and Henry hated Mary O'Dair [*sic*] and called her the 'Washerwoman.'" According to Palmer, "Mary would get all over Henry—and he wouldn't fool with her at all. The three talked about getting Mary and bumping her off after Raymond got caught, as they thought the law would get Raymond."

Despite these appalling disagreements the six fugitives left for what seems to have been their spring holidays. In late February 1934 they drove north into Oklahoma and then northeast across Missouri and Illinois into Indiana. By early March they were near the town of Terre Haute, on the Wabash River just over the border from Illinois, intent on fun and high living. According to Emma Parker, the "boys ordered suits and overcoats, all tailored and matching. They also bought hats, shoes, and gloves to suit. The two girls purchased some dresses and coats." They visited theaters and ate in good restaurants, but still they got on one another's nerves. Even Clyde Barrow and Bonnie Parker quarreled. During one of these rows, Clyde stormed off and left Bonnie sobbing and declaring that she would go home to Mother. Mary O'Dare took her aside and said that if she were Bonnie she would "fix him" before she left. Bonnie agreed that she would. However, she got a great surprise when she learned that Mary O'Dare meant literally to poison, or at least to dope, her lover. "Then while he's out, you take his roll and beat it." Bonnie Parker was shocked by this suggestion and duly recounted it at the next family meeting.

Raymond Hamilton added still further to the tension within the gang by attempting to flirt with Bonnie as well as with Mary O'Dare. Hamilton is said to have suggested to Bonnie that they could "knock off" Clyde and the three of them depart together. It was probably just a joke, but it did not amuse Bonnie and no doubt further inflamed Clyde when he was told about it later.

By March 6, despite the pleasures of Terre Haute, the antipathies within the group had reached such a pitch that Hamilton and Mary O'Dare left and headed back to Texas. Hamilton, the consummate car thief, stole a vehicle for their journey.

The remaining fugitives at once abandoned their hideout near the Wabash River. They realized that there was a very real possibility that Raymond and Mary might betray them with a telephone call to the local police. Four days later Clyde Barrow and Bonnie Parker, with Henry Methvin and car-sick Joe Palmer, were also back in Texas. On a chilly March day they were just south of Dallas, where they selected a cemetery for a family reunion. Nell Cowan, who had been alerted by the usual warning telephone call to the Dallas hairdressing shop in which she worked, drove the two mothers there on March 10 to hear all about the difficulties that Bonnie had in getting her hair permanently waved and of their holiday in Indiana, which had been so ruined by the nasty Raymond Hamilton and his moll.

WHILE BONNIE AND Clyde were unburdening themselves of their troubles in the cemetery, three men were planning fresh problems for them only a few miles away on that very evening. Sheriff Smoot Schmid had become quite desperate in his hunt for Bonnie and Clyde and, together with his deputies Bob Alcorn and Ted Hinton, had devised a plan of startling boldness to trap or even literally to flatten their quarry. The scheme involved a very large and clumsy four-wheel-drive gravel mover that Sheriff Schmid had hired from a Dallas excavating company. The machine was parked just off the Industrial Boulevard, the two-lane road that ran across the flat boggy land that then divided the poor white area of West Dallas from the center of the city. At the controls sat Ted Hinton. Half a mile along the Boulevard, Smoot Schmid was on the lookout in a car with Bob Alcorn. They had heard that Clyde and Bonnie were in the vicinity and had set their trap. The idea was that if Clyde Barrow was seen driving along the Boulevard, Ted Hinton would set the gravel mover in motion to block the road or even to run down Barrow's vehicle. Smoot Schmid was to judge the feasibility of the project from his vantage point in the parked car. The sheriff was worried, very reasonably, that if the traffic was too heavy there could be danger to other motorists as a large gravel mover lurched on to the highway or, if Bonnie and Clyde were not squashed, from any subsequent shooting. The sheriff was to signal the appearance of Clyde Barrow with a single flash of his car headlights. If heavy traffic made the plan too risky, then Smoot Schmid would give two flashes.

Just after midnight Ted Hinton, perched uncomfortably on top of the gravel mover, saw a single flash from his superior's headlights. He started the engine, and the machine began to lumber forward. As he did so, Schmid flashed his headlights twice more—the attempt was off. Hinton saw a car, driven by Clyde with Bonnie at his side, shoot by, followed by Smoot Schmid and Bob Alcorn several vehicles behind. There was not the remotest chance of catching up.

RAYMOND HAMILTON'S HATRED for Clyde Barrow continued to fester after they parted. The memory of Clyde's blistering scorn still rankled and he could not resist goading his former friend. At the end of March Hamilton, flushed with success at the robbery of $1,500 from a bank in Grand Prairie, wrote a long derogatory letter to the assistant district attorney of Dallas, dissociating himself from Barrow and accusing him of senseless murder and of being merely a petty robber of filling stations—so very different from his own spectacular career as a bank robber.

Hamilton's letter was published in the Dallas newspapers, and as might be expected, Clyde Barrow was furious. Emma Parker, too, was very cross, like an indignant mother dealing with a naughty schoolboy. "Raymond seemed to have overlooked that the desperado, Clyde Barrow, had delivered him from the Eastham farm, and he was plenty good enough for that."

Clyde was determined to exact revenge. Three times he dispatched his quiet, ailing friend Joe Palmer to search for Hamilton. At the third attempt Clyde admitted to Palmer that he intended to kill Hamilton. After this Joe Palmer took himself off, too weak with stomach problems to keep up with Clyde. The Barrow Gang now consisted of Bonnie, Clyde, and Henry Methvin.

On March 31 Clyde heard on the car radio that Hamilton and Mary O'Dare had robbed another bank, this time south of Dallas, and had kidnapped a mother and her four-year-old son to assist their getaway. Barrow guessed that Hamilton and his moll would make for their favorite hideout (a lonely spot on low hills, just north of Fort Worth and Dallas), a place that was also used for the secret meetings of the Barrow and Parker families. An ambush was set for the following morning, Easter Sunday. With the three avengers was the pet rabbit that they hoped to give Bonnie's mother for an Easter present later in the day. As Clyde, Bonnie, and Henry waited and time dragged on they realized that Raymond Hamilton was now unlikely to put in an appearance. He had, in fact, gone with Mary O'Dare to Houston. The three fugitives relaxed: Clyde was asleep in the backseat, Bonnie was fondling the rabbit, and Henry Methvin was pacing up and down by the roadside. It was Bonnie who first detected the distant sound of approaching motorcycles. She woke Clyde, and Henry moved quickly toward the car. Both men had their guns close at hand.

Two state highway patrolmen drove up and began to park their motorcycles. They were making a routine search following Raymond Hamilton's recent bank robbery. Clyde Barrow was in danger of being caught in the trap he had set for his former friend.

Clyde later said that he intended only to kidnap the two officers. This, he claimed, is what he meant by his cryptic order "Let's take 'em." But Henry Methvin, a hunted convict, was scared and perhaps befuddled, for he and Bonnie had been drinking. To him, Barrow's order meant only one thing: to fire. He did so, and as Emma Parker related, both officers fell to the ground: "Bonnie was petrified with fear and Clyde was white with rage." According to this version of events, Clyde Barrow did not fire and cursed the pimply young man at his side for the unnecessary killings.

But three weapons were fired at the two unsuspecting patrolmen, for spent cartridges from a shotgun, an automatic rifle, and a pistol were afterward found on the ground. Furthermore, a farmer called William Schieffer who watched these events from a distance had a very different story to tell. He maintained that there were two bursts of gunfire from the car and that he saw a small woman run over to the bodies of the fallen officers. She put her foot on one of them, turned him on to his back, and, as the body still twitched, fired several shots at it. However, Schieffer saw some other, very curious, things. He later identified the woman as Bonnie's sister, Billie Mace, and

Fig. 5 Comment by the *Dallas Morning News* on the Grapevine murders

one of the men as Raymond Hamilton's brother, Floyd. These errors cast considerable doubt on the farmer's evidence. Furthermore another witness, a Mrs. Giggal, who was out for a Sunday afternoon drive with her husband, said that she saw a *man* standing over the prostrate bodies of the patrolmen. But the farmer steadfastly maintained that he saw a woman fire at one of the wounded patrolmen.

THE THREE FUGITIVES fled north into Oklahoma after the murders in Grapevine on Easter Sunday 1934. Two days later Ted Hinton and Bob Alcorn followed them, now joined in the chase by Frank Hamer and his freshly recruited assistant Manny Gault. They were led northward by the reports from the various garages at which the fugitives stopped.

On April 4, the four pursuers drove through Sherman and Denison and crossed the Red River into Oklahoma. That afternoon they were in the town of Duvant, twenty miles from the Texas border. It was a pleasant spring day, and the streets of the little town were crowded with cars and people. Ted Hinton was driving, with Bob Alcorn at his side. In the following car were Frank Hamer and Manny Gault.

"Here they come!" Bob Alcorn suddenly exclaimed.

There, driving past them in the opposite traffic lane, were Clyde Barrow and Bonnie Parker, with Henry Methvin in the rear seat of the car. But there was little Hinton and Alcorn could do. They were under strict orders from Sheriff Schmid not to start a gunfight anywhere that members of the public could be injured.

The next morning the frustrated lawman received a reliable report that Barrow and Methvin, with Bonnie Parker, had been spotted in a drugstore in Texarkana, about 150 miles east, just across the Texas border into Arkansas. Bonnie Parker had walked into the drugstore with one of the two men and had left a partly eaten sandwich. Later in the day they were reported a few miles north of Texarkana, buying drinks at a wayside stall. The proprietor noticed that there were guns in the car. Later still, after midnight, they were spotted when their car was stuck in the mud after drenching rain.

On the following day, April 6, 1934, the fugitives were still in trouble. They were now 230 miles north in the flat countryside of northeastern Oklahoma. Heavy rain had been falling there too, and again their Ford V-8 became bogged down on a side road in a strange landscape dominated by mountainous piles of white mining spoil between the small towns of Miami and Commerce. Barrow and Methvin flagged down a passing truck and ordered the driver to tow them out of the mud, telling him that they would shoot him if he didn't get a move on. These threats were overheard by a passing man, who also noticed that the windshield of the car was pierced by a bullet hole and reported what he had seen and heard to the police.

Two officers drove out to investigate: Percy Boyd, the police chief from the nearby town of Commerce, and a constable, Cal Campbell. Boyd was tough, balding, and in his midthirties; his subordinate was a sixty-three-year-old man. When they arrived at the muddy rutted road they found that the Ford V-8 had been hauled from the mire and was still occupied by the three tired fugitives.

Again it was Bonnie Parker who gave warning of the police officers' approach. As Boyd and Campbell walked toward the car with weapons drawn, there was a burst of fire from two machine-guns. The two officers replied with three or four shots. Then Cal Campbell fell, spilling blood on to the muddy road, killed by a single shot through the heart. Percy Boyd staggered as he was hit in the head. With blood streaming down his face, Boyd flung down his pistol and raised his hands. Clyde Barrow ordered the wounded man into the car, where he slumped on the backseat next to Henry Methvin. Barrow then turned the vehicle westward along the glistening, treacherous road.

Three miles further on the car stuck again. The fugitives forced another passing motorist to pull them out and sped on, crossing the tree-lined Neosho River, continuing west, and then turning north into the flat Kansas countryside. After half an hour Percy Boyd had recovered sufficiently to attempt some conversation with his captors.

He turned to Henry Methvin and timidly asked, "I don't like to get personal, but isn't that Clyde Barrow?"

AS THE CAR wove its way through the neat geometrical pattern of side roads across the sodden Kansas landscape, Bonnie Parker began to talk to Percy Boyd. She told him that they were sorry to have shot the other policeman, but according to Percy Boyd, "they kept joking about it all of the time they held me."

Boyd and Bonnie seem to have got on very well together, exchanging gossip about their families. He was introduced to Sonny Boy, now scheduled as a Mother's Day gift for Emma Parker. Bonnie even extracted a promise that if anything should happen to her while he was in the car, he would see to it that her mother received the rabbit. She also got him to agree to "tell the world" that she did not smoke cigars (as she had been widely portrayed in the newspaper photograph). "She said she didn't want her public to think of her as a girl who smoked cigars," Boyd later reported, "because nice girls don't smoke cigars. She was pretty mad about it."

The three criminals and their hostage reached the small town of Fort Scott, close to the Missouri border, by the late afternoon. There they bought a newspaper and read, in a stop-press account, that Cal Campbell had been killed and the chief of police of Commerce, Oklahoma, kidnapped by the murderers.

At Fort Scott they also bought food, which they ate, picnic-fashion, in the seclusion of some nearby woods, under a canopy of fresh spring leaves still soaked from the heavy rains. The fugitives were in a relaxed mood and seem to have been on their best behavior, clearly enjoying the unexpected social encounter with their wounded victim. They joked together as they ate and read the newspaper, and Boyd noticed that they had no fear of being captured.

As the strange picnic party gossiped in the pleasant afternoon sunshine, the hostage took the opportunity to observe Barrow's latest apprentice in crime, the pimply Henry Methvin, who, although cocky like Clyde Barrow, was clearly not the kingpin of the gang. Boyd said that Clyde "acted as though he owned the earth. He thinks quite a lot of himself. Bonnie is a lot like him, but she thinks quite a bit of Barrow, you can tell that."

Later that night the party drove back into Fort Scott to look for a replacement for their hard-driven, bullet-holed V-8 but were unable to find a car that satisfied them. Toward dawn they dropped Percy Boyd near a farmhouse, despite the considerable risk that Boyd would at the first opportunity signal their presence in the vicinity of Fort Scott. But the three criminals had taken a great liking to their captive; Bonnie in particular had enjoyed the opportunity to talk to someone new, while Clyde Barrow clearly admired Boyd for his courage. Joe Palmer later recalled that Clyde and Bonnie said Boyd had more real guts than any man they ever saw, but their admiration for the captured policeman was certainly not reciprocated, and after his release, Percy Boyd did not hesitate to telephone his position to his headquarters.

During most of the night, hundreds of lawmen had been searching for Boyd and his captors through the countryside where the state borders of Oklahoma, Arkansas, and Kansas converge. With them were Frank Hamer, Manny Gault, and the two Dallas deputies Ted Hinton and Bob Alcorn. At dawn they were in the sheriff's office in Coffeyville, seventy-five miles south of Fort Scott. There they received a telephone call telling them of Boyd's release and giving the most recent position of Bonnie and Clyde. The four Texas lawmen lost no time in getting to Boyd to learn as much as possible about the latest doings of the Barrow Gang. Ted Hinton described the strain on the hunters as they drew closer to their quarry and drew comfort from the thought that things could only be worse on the fugitives' side.

We had scoured the swamps in the Louisiana back country and the smoky hills of Arkansas. We came to know each place in northeastern Oklahoma, where Bonnie had spent some time when she was growing up and where she had friends and relatives. We had met with local law enforcement people, generally no more than one or two good men in each area, and shared our experiences with them. . . . Gradually, we felt, the area in which the fugitives would go without attracting attention was shrinking. We told ourselves that if their physical

Fig. 6 Cartoon from the *Dallas Journal* of 9th April 1934

resources were being drained as ours were, living in our car for the most part and taking sandwiches along for snacks as we searched, then we could be reasonably sure that they would make a fatal mistake somewhere.

THE LAWMEN WERE also drawing close to Raymond Hamilton. The small excitable gangster had caused a considerable furore by his recent bank robberies and was still being sought for the murder of the guard at Eastham prison farm. In addition, he was uncomfortably aware that Clyde Barrow intended to murder him at the first opportunity.

It was probably for these reasons that Hamilton and his painted girlfriend left Texas for New Orleans in early April 1934. Their presence there was revealed when Hamilton sent another fingerprinted letter (with a New Orleans postmark and written in a scrawling hand on Hotel Lafayette paper) to a Dallas lawyer disclaiming any part in the recent killings by Clyde Barrow and his companions. A few days later, Mary O'Dare was spotted nearly seven hundred miles away in the bustling oil city of Amarillo, in northwest Texas, where she had rented an apartment. There was no sign of Raymond Hamilton, and after three days of watching, the police arrested her. Intensive interrogation drew from Hamilton's girlfriend an admission that she did not love him and that she only went with him for the money that he provided to buy "nice things."

Hamilton's affairs had now reached a very low ebb. He had spent all his money and was reduced to riding on freight trains, presumably to avoid police roadblocks. On April 25, Hamilton was trapped on the main highway to Oklahoma just south of Sherman. He gave himself up without any resistance. "I'm Raymond Hamilton and I don't intend to give you any trouble. I'm just fresh out of ammunition, money, whisky, and women. Let's go to jail."

CLYDE BARROW WAS far to the east in Memphis, Tennessee, when he read in the newspapers of Raymond Hamilton's capture. Characteristically, Barrow could not resist sending a vindictive letter to his enemy, dictated to Bonnie. Clyde gloated

Fig. 7 Cartoon from the *Dallas Journal* of 26th April 1934

over his former friend's predicament, referring to Hamilton's "long boastful tongue," and then harked back to the original cause of their dispute. "When you started the rumor about Bonnie wanting a cut of the loot you sure messed yourself up. I have always taken care of Bonnie and never asked any thief to help me."

After posting this letter, Clyde and his confederates drove across Arkansas to Joplin, Missouri, where they met Joe Palmer.

Strangely enough, Clyde Barrow seems not to have borne Palmer any ill will, despite the fact that the man had not returned from his last errand to lure back Hamilton. Even worse, Palmer had thrown in his lot with Barrow's enemy for a while, though clearly he liked Clyde: "Maybe [he] was a murderer and killed folks; but he sure was good to me and the boys, and he toted fair." Palmer also had a great respect for Henry Methvin. "He carried me four miles on his back in Iowa when I was shot. He had one shell in his gun and I had two in mine. He said: 'If they get us, I will use this one on them and you hold your two—and shoot me with one, and do what you please with the other one.'"

A WEEK AFTER their meeting with Joe Palmer in Joplin, the fugitives were in West Dallas. Despite intense police activity, Clyde Barrow drove openly past his father's filling station and told his family where they should meet. He had chosen a quiet country road, some few miles east of the city, where Emma Parker joined them and sat on the ground in the pleasantly mild, moonlit evening, talking to Bonnie for nearly two hours. Bonnie showed her mother some recently taken photographs of Clyde and herself. As she did so, Bonnie ran her carefully manicured fingers across one of the photographs and got her mother to promise that "when they kill us, don't ever say anything—ugly—about Clyde."

It was at this meeting, according to Emma Parker, that her daughter gave her a copy of another poem she had written, which would epitomize the legend that bore her name: "The Story of Bonnie and Clyde" (see p. 192).

Clyde himself was engaged in more modest literary efforts in the early days of May 1934. He had evidently obtained the use of a typewriter (perhaps during a break-in at some business premises or perhaps with the assistance of a relative), for the Dallas assistant district attorney received the following epistle, which bore his authenticated fingerprint and which had not, apparently, received the usual literary assistance of Bonnie Parker:

```
Mr,KIng

        So Raymond Hamilton nev er killed anybody.  If
he can make a jury believe that I8m willing to come
in and be tryed my self.  Why dont you ask Ray about
those two pol icemen that got killed near Grapevine?
And while you are [at] it bwetter talk it ov er
with his girl friend.  Bonnie and me were in
missouriwhen that happened but where was Ray?coming
back from the West bankjob wasnt he?  Redhot too
wasn8t he?  I got it straight.  And ask hi m about
that escape at East-ham farm wherethat gard was
killed.  Giess he claims he doesnt know fire any
shots there don8t ge?  Well if he wasnt too dum to
know how tp put a clip in a automatic hed hace
fired a lot m ore shots and some of the vrest of
the gards would got killed too.  He wrote his lawyer
he was too good for me and didnt go my pace,well it
makes a me sick to see a yellow punk like that
playing baby ad making a jury cry over him.  If he
was half as smart as me o the officers couldnt catch
him either/  He stuck his fingerprints on a lett er
so heres mine too just to let you k now thjis is on
the leve;
                X Clyde
P s AsK Ray why he was so dam jumpy to get rid of
those yellow wh eels on his car and akshis girl friend
how they spent easter
```

The Story of Bonnie and Clyde

You've read the story of Jesse James—
Of how he lived and died;
    If you're still in need
    Of something to read,
Here's the story of Bonnie and Clyde.

Now Bonnie and Clyde are the Barrow gang,
I'm sure you all have read
    How they rob and steal
    And those who squeal
Are usually found dying or dead.

There's lots of untruths to these write-ups;
They're not so ruthless as that;
    Their nature is raw;
    They hate all the law—
The stool pigeons, spotters, and rats.

They call them cold-blooded killers;
They say they are heartless and mean;
    But I say this with pride,
    That I once knew Clyde
When he was honest and upright and clean.

But the laws fooled around,
Kept taking him down
And locking him up in a cell,
    Till he said to me,
    "I'll never be free,
So I'll meet a few of them in hell."

The road was so dimly lighted;
There were no highway signs to guide;
    But they made up their minds
    If all roads were blind,
They wouldn't give up till they died.

The road gets dimmer and dimmer;
Sometimes you can hardly see;
    But it's fight, man to man,
    And do all you can,
For they know they can never be free.

From heart-break some people have suffered;
From weariness some people have died;
    But take it all in all,
    Our troubles are small
Till we get like Bonnie and Clyde.

If a policeman is killed in Dallas,
And they have no clew or guide;
    If they can't find a fiend,
    They just wipe their slate clean
And hang it on Bonnie and Clyde.

There's two crimes committed in America
Not accredited to the Barrow mob;
    They had no hand
    In the kidnap demand,
Nor the Kansas City depot job.

A newsboy once said to his buddy:
"I wish old Clyde would get jumped;
    In these awful hard times
    We'd make a few dimes
If five or six cops would get bumped."

The police haven't got the report yet,
But Clyde called me up today;
    He said, "Don't start any fights—
    We aren't working nights—
We're joining the NRA."

From Irving to West Dallas viaduct
Is known as the Great Divide,
    Where the women are kin,
    And the men are men,
And they won't "stool" on Bonnie and Clyde.

If they try to act like citizens
And rent them a nice little flat,
    About the third night
    They're invited to fight
By a sub-gun's rat-tat-tat.

They don't think they're too tough or desperate,
They know that the law always wins;
    They've been shot at before,
    But they do not ignore
That death is the wages of sin.

Some day they'll go down together;
And they'll bury them side by side;
    To few it'll be grief—
    To the law a relief—
But it's death for Bonnie and Clyde.

—Bonnie Parker

21

FINAL
BULLETS

THE HUNTERS OF Bonnie and Clyde had discovered early on their quarries' most vulnerable trait: the strong psychological dependence on their families. Even so, all efforts had failed to trap the fugitives at their regular meetings with their kinsfolk, either in the shabby streets of West Dallas or at a secret rural rendezvous. When it was realized that Clyde Barrow had acquired another assistant, Smoot Schmid sent his deputies to investigate Methvin's origins and family ties.

Like Clyde Barrow, Henry Methvin was a country boy. He had been born twenty-one years earlier, in northern Louisiana, thirty miles south of the Arkansas and fifty miles east of the Texas borders. Henry's father, Irvin Methvin, had a small farm on the pinewooded slopes that rose from swampland. It was a landscape of neat farmhouses and traditional red barns, peopled by friendly country folk in close-knit communities. But times were hard during the Depression, and Irvin Methvin could barely make a living for his family from the cotton that he grew in forest clearings.

Hinton and Alcorn made several visits to Bienville County during the early months of 1934. They drove around the country south of the small community of Gibsland, where Methvin, senior, farmed, taking great care not to attract attention. They had also contacted the local sheriff, Henderson Jordan, to enlist his help in the search. The two Dallas deputies were by this time certain that Clyde Barrow, Bonnie Parker, and Henry Methvin had been hiding in the neighborhood. It must have been as a result of their efforts that Frank Hamer could boast that he had located the criminals' hideout on February 17, only days after his first briefing by Hinton and Alcorn in Dallas. "There was always plenty of signs in the camp: stubs of Bonnie's Camels—Clyde smoked Bull Durham—lettuce leaves for their white rabbit, pieces of sandwiches and a button off Clyde's coat. I found where they had made their bed."

Clyde Barrow had, in fact, driven Henry Methvin through this part of Louisiana on at least two occasions and in early March 1934 had visited the Methvin farm with Bonnie Parker. He seems to have been quite taken with Henry's family and even discussed the possibility of buying a house on the farm, which he imagined his and Bonnie's families using during the summer, so enabling family visits on a more regular basis. Emma Parker was not impressed with the idea.

IN EARLY MAY, 1934, immediately after the last family meeting near Dallas, the fugitives drove southeast to Nacogdoches County, a region of red soil and pine trees some fifty miles from the Louisiana border. Clyde's uncle, a brother of Cumie Barrow, lived there in the quiet, inaccessible country of the Nacogdoches River bottoms. Dee Brown had been a bootlegger and still plied his trade in illicit homemade whiskey. His property was well guarded with a wire gate at its entrance that was always kept firmly locked. There the fugitives could live in relative security and no doubt enjoyed the company of Clyde's cousin "Jelly." Jelly Brown was the same age as Clyde and a very personable young man—noted, in the words of a contemporary, for "his dandy dress and sweetness of appearance."

Clyde, Bonnie, and Henry Methvin stayed on in their Nacogdoches sanctuary as the late spring days moved toward the promise of early summer. Yet even there they were not safe from squealers. Their betrayal came about by the chance capture of a suspected counterfeiter, by Clint Peoples, the tough young deputy sheriff of Conroe (then a rapidly growing oil town north of Houston). After his arrest the counterfeiter whispered to Peoples, from his cell, "Do you want to catch somebody that's wanted real bad . . . Clyde and Bonnie?" He told the surprised deputy that he "saw them real often" at Dee Brown's place where they "came in to hole up all the time."

Peoples acted quickly. He contacted the sheriff of Nacogdoches County and at midnight was waiting with the sheriff, a motorcycle patrolman, and a Texas Ranger at a disused filling station near Dee Brown's place. The counterfeiter had been sent off to discover if Clyde and Bonnie were still there. The hours dragged by, and the four lawmen were half-asleep when at four o'clock the counterfeiter returned. He aroused them by tapping on the car window and then told them, "I won't be able to deliver, they left two days ago." All he could say was that Clyde and Bonnie had gone into Louisiana.

The elusive fugitives were, in fact, by then moving toward their hunters, for on the evening of May 19, Bob Alcorn and Ted Hinton were driving into the Louisiana town of Shreveport. They were tired and hungry after several days on the road living off sandwiches and snatching what sleep they could by taking it in turns to doze in the passenger seat while the other remained at the wheel.

Just before midnight the two deputies, followed in another car by Frank Hamer and Manny Gault, arrived at the Inn Hotel and booked rooms for the night. They had chosen this motel for a reason that would have commended it to Clyde Barrow: their car could be parked beneath their rooms and could be reached quickly by a single flight of steps. The deputies stacked their arsenals of weapons on the back seats and carefully covered them with blankets.

The four lawmen slept soundly that night and had a large breakfast on the following morning. Ted Hinton recalled that he spent most of that Sunday morning and afternoon relaxing, writing letters, and playing cards. In the early evening he telephoned the chief of the Shreveport police to announce their presence in town and also to arrange an introductory meeting with Frank Hamer and Manny Gault. The police chief hinted

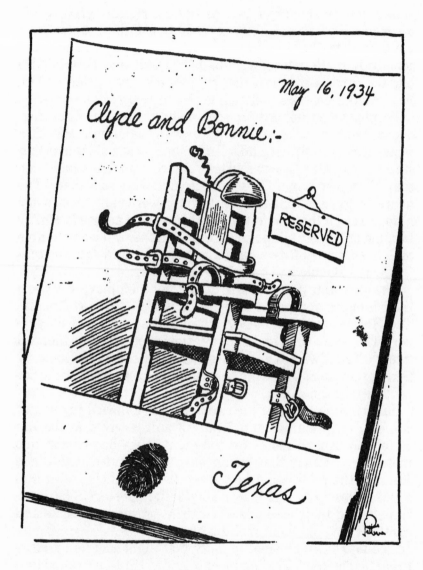

Fig. 8 Cartoon from the *Dallas Journal* of 16th May 1934

at some interesting information he might pass on to the four Texans if they were to pay a visit to his office.

At the Shreveport police headquarters they learned that Clyde Barrow and Bonnie Parker had been seen in the town on the previous night. The pair were sitting in a parked vehicle outside the Majestic Café when a patrolling police car drove slowly past. Barrow evidently thought they had been detected, for without hesitation he started the engine and recklessly accelerated away. As the car shot past them, the two patrolmen recognized the driver and his passenger and gave chase but were soon left far behind, to return disconsolately to the Majestic Café to question the staff. There at least they made a discovery: There had been a third person in the car, a young man who had waited in the café to collect a stack of sandwiches and some soft drinks to carry out to the others. When his companions drove off, the young man left abruptly without paying or taking any refreshments with him.

The third man was identified as Henry Methvin. Whether he had become separated from his companions by accident or design, it was deemed likely that Clyde and Bonnie would eventually go in search of him at his father's farm. Accordingly, the Texan lawmen decided to set up an ambush, left Shreveport, and headed east along the main highway toward Arcadia, fifty miles to the east, to pick up the county sheriff. Henderson Jordan had an unrivaled knowledge of the surrounding countryside and would be able to suggest the most suitable place for the ambush. As usual, Ted Hinton and Bob Alcorn were driving together, followed by Gault and Hamer in the other car.

Twenty-five miles along the road they passed through the town of Minden, where they encountered some road construction works and were forced to take a detour around a bridge. As they moved slowly along the detour, Hinton saw, to his intense surprise, a tan-colored Ford V-8 drive past them in the opposite direction. Clyde Barrow was driving in dark glasses with Bonnie Parker at his side. Before either Hinton or Alcorn could react, the pair had driven on past Hamer and Gault, who did not recognize them.

The four lawmen decided not to attempt pursuit but to continue on to Arcadia. It was late afternoon when they reached the sleepy little town and contacted the county sheriff. It was agreed that Jordan would bring along his deputy, Prentis Oakley, and would meet the four Texans later at the agreed spot, about eight miles southwest of Gibsland, where they would lie in wait for their quarry.

According to Ted Hinton, "We settled in at about 9 p.m. Monday [May 21] for an all-night vigil." Frank Hamer, on the other hand, later wrote that "By the night of May 22, we had good reason to believe that Clyde would visit this mail box within a short time. About midnight we drove out to Gibsland. . . ." There are a number of other discrepancies between the accounts left by the two men, for reasons that will be discussed later.

THE PLACE SELECTED for the ambush was on a long, straight stretch of road that ran roughly east to west through dense woodland. Their cars safely hidden, the lawmen had stationed themselves on a roadside bank obscured by undergrowth and backed with tall trees. The road sloped away on each side, giving them an unrestricted view for half a mile in each direction along the only graveled road that led to the Methvin farm. There, crouched on the damp ground among the trees and dense bushes, they tried, unsuccessfully, to make themselves comfortable. They talked only in low voices and gradually became conscious of the forest sounds: the wind rustling the leaves, the calling of birds, and once the slithering of a snake at their feet. Later they heard stealthy movements in the undergrowth as Henderson Jordan and his deputy arrived, their cars ensconced among the trees further down the road.

Ted Hinton recalled, years later, the discomforts of their vigil. He was especially troubled by voracious Louisiana mosquitoes, which bit him viciously not only on his neck and ears but even in his mouth and nostrils. Only once during that night of torment did the waiting officers see the lights of an approaching vehicle. They were instantly alert, with their weapons ready, but it was only a van and not, as Jordan confirmed, Irvin Methvin's old Ford truck.

As dawn light slowly filtered through the moss-covered trees, the six men stretched their tired, cold limbs and breakfasted from a pile of sandwiches that they had bought the night before in Arcadia. They continued their watch as the sun rose higher and morning passed into afternoon. There was no sign of the tan-colored Ford V-8—only occasional trucks carrying logs and a few passing cars.

The six ambushers tried to sleep by turns, two at a time, in the parked cars, their dozing periodically interrupted by the sounds of approaching vehicles. As the afternoon dragged on to evening, they prepared for another night of cramped waiting. They were dirty and unshaven, their eyes red with fatigue and their skins blotched with blood from the attacks of persistent insects. Their only food was the dwindling pile of stale sandwiches.

For Ted Hinton, the second night's ordeal was even more abominable and tedious than the first. The tall deputy was on the right of the firing line, armed with a powerful automatic rifle. On his left was his friend Alcorn, the Arcadia deputy Prentis Oakley next to Henderson Jordan, and at the end of the line beside Manny Gault, Frank Hamer.

Slowly the hours passed without sound or sight of the tan-colored Ford V-8. And then, with the approach of dawn, the waiting line of men heard an engine in the distance. It was unmistakably that of a Model-A Ford truck. As it approached, the officers could see, as they had suspected they would, that the old truck was driven by Irvin Methvin, and the decision was taken to intercept it. Methvin, senior, must have been extremely surprised at his dawn encounter with six armed men. According to Ted Hinton, the elderly farmer protested loudly and would not say where he was going. He claimed to know nothing of his son's whereabouts.

Then the county sheriff stepped forward and told Methvin they were going to take him "right over here easy like." The unhappy farmer was handcuffed so that his arms were extended around the trunk of a tree at some distance from the lawmen's concealed position. While this was going on, Bob Alcorn had turned the farmer's truck around and parked it on the far side of the road from the ambush position, facing to the right. The truck was then jacked up and right front wheel removed. Thus immobilized, the vehicle would, they hoped, act as a decoy for Clyde Barrow. At least it might cause him to slow down to discover whether Henry's father needed help.

The light grew stronger as the sun rose on the morning of May 23. Ted Hinton said that he could hear Irvin Methvin cursing his captors, claiming violation of his citizen's rights and threatening that he would inform the FBI of this outrage.

By nine o'clock the ambushers were utterly depressed. They had spent two wretched nights and a day with no better result than that of nourishing the local insects. Furthermore, according to Ted Hinton's account, they had carried out an illegal arrest and violated the rights of an angry citizen. It was decided that the party would wait for another half hour. The tired and hungry men must already have been dreaming of cups of hot coffee and soft, clean beds. Then, at about quarter past nine, they heard the sound of an approaching car, though it could not be seen, for it had not yet reached the crest of the hill on the right of the line of lawmen. Hinton, the nearest officer, was first to spot the tan-colored Ford V-8.

"This is him," he whispered to Bob Alcorn, who passed on the news to those on his left.

THE CAR WAS traveling at considerable speed. Inside, Bonnie Parker was eating a sandwich taken from a brown paper bag on the backseat. They had just been shopping, and she had bought a magazine to read. She was wearing a red dress and red shoes. Her hair was freshly tended and neat. On her knee was a road map of Louisiana. As usual Clyde Barrow was driving in his stockinged feet. His dark glasses, which he usually wore in the daytime, were on the dashboard, for the morning sunlight was at his back. Behind him were the carefully cleaned weapons covered by a folded blanket.

As the gradient of the road increased, the V-8 slowed. Clyde turned the steering wheel to pull over into the left-hand lane and then braked to stop the car opposite Old Man Methvin's truck, which seemed to have a puncture. He slipped the gears into neutral as he looked around for Henry's father. A muffled shout was heard, and Bonnie screamed as she saw a movement among the bushes of the high bank on the left. Barrow grasped his automatic rifle, found it was jammed, and reached for his pistol. And then there was an explosion of sound. The car rocked under a massive input of bullets. The windows shattered, the back of Clyde's head exploded, dozens of bullets plowed into his and Bonnie's bodies. He fell back, drenched in blood, his mouth open; she slumped forward, her face pale and spattered with blood.

As the driver's foot slipped from the clutch pedal, the wrecked vehicle began slowly to roll downhill, while shots from the six ambushers continued to pour into it. Ted Hinton had emptied his automatic rifle, blasted five shots from his shotgun, and was now loosing off his pistol. In a cloud of dust, the car rolled on to the left, the ambushers in pursuit, and ran into a ditch. Ted Hinton, with Bob Alcorn at his side, grasped the handle on the driver's door. They could see Clyde Barrow slumped backward, the back of his head a bloody pulp. Wedged against the bank, the door would not open, and Hinton had to scramble over the car bonnet to wrench at the other door.

Bonnie's tiny body slipped sideways. Hinton smelled her perfume and gazed at her blood-spattered face. He lifted her up, knew that she was dead, and laid her back in the seat. Leaning across her body, he pulled the pistol from her lover's hand. It was cold, for it had not been fired. As he moved back, Hinton noticed a half eaten sandwich and saw that the hand of the little waitress who had once served him in the café in Houston Street had been shot away. On the floor lay the blood-stained road map of Louisiana.

22

TEARS
AND
BURIALS

TED HINTON RECALLED in old age that he felt no elation after the killing of Bonnie and Clyde. His head was still ringing from the thunder of the guns. He was tired, and they still had to tidy up. Someone returned the wheel to the Ford truck. One of the officers released the handcuffed farmer.

Irvin Methvin was furious. He was convinced that his son had been killed but was reassured when he looked down at the bodies of Clyde and Bonnie and lifted the blanket that covered their backseat arsenal. Nevertheless, Methvin was determined to exact vengeance, swearing that he would inform the FBI of his illegal shackling to a tree. Frank Hamer took the irate farmer to one side. The former Texas ranger had considerable powers of persuasion, which he now used on Irvin Methvin. Eventually the two men reached agreement: Methvin, senior, would not make his complaint, and in return, Hamer would use his influence to obtain lenient treatment for Methvin, junior. Furthermore, Irvin Methvin reluctantly agreed to go along with the story that his family had betrayed Bonnie and Clyde— at least to the extent of not denying it. The unfortunate farmer was, after all, not in a strong bargaining position with a son threatened with the electric chair.

Frank Hamer seems also to have negotiated an agreement

with the lawmen who killed Clyde Barrow and Bonnie Parker: that none would reveal how Irvin Methvin had been treated as long as more than one of them lived. Toward the end of his life, Ted Hinton, the last survivor of the six, told his son of the secret agreement and in his autobiography published in 1979 gave his version of the events that occurred between May 19 and 23, 1934.

This agreement accounts for Hamer's reticence at the time in talking of the killing of the two fugitives and of the curious inconsistencies in his version of events, as later recounted to his friend Walter Prescott Webb. The agreement also laid the foundation for an important element in the legend: the betrayal of Bonnie and Clyde.

AFTER IRVIN METHVIN was released, the deputies took the pile of weapons from the bullet-riddled vehicle and stacked them in Henderson Jordan's car. As they were doing this, Deputy Oakley noticed smoke rising from among the trees about six hundred yards down the road. Ted Hinton and Prentis Oakley drove down to investigate. At the bottom of an incline they found an overturned truck. Its engine was still running, and its load of logs spilled on the ground. Three blacks cautiously emerged from the trees. They had abandoned the truck, frightened by the fusillade of shots, and left it to roll down the sloping road and crash into a ditch. This incident was also to be incorporated into inaccurate versions of the destruction of Bonnie and Clyde.

THE LAW OFFICERS' next task was to fetch the county coroner to the scene and to arrange for the criminals' car to be towed away. Bob Alcorn, Manny Gault, and Prentis Oakley remained to guard the car while the others drove into Arcadia. There Ted Hinton telephoned the news to Smoot Schmid, and Frank Hamer contacted Lee Simmons. The director of the Texas state penitentiary said that "in ten minutes I was on the road to Arcadia, Louisiana, with Luther Berwick, my convict-driver." Berwick "was stepping down hard on the gas." Simmons, with an eye to his political future, was not going to miss this opportunity for some sensational publicity.

Fig. 9 Cartoon from the *Dallas Journal* of 24th May 1934

In West Dallas Emma Parker also received a telephone call, before ten o'clock. She was sewing. All her family were at home, except Billie Mace (who was being detained as a suspect in the Grapevine murders). The caller said that he was a newspaper man and asked to speak to Emma's sister or to Buster. When Emma Parker stubbornly insisted that he speak to her, the reporter blurted out that Bonnie and Clyde were dead. Emma Parker said that she had received dozens of such messages in the past but that this time she knew it was true and wept for her daughter.

At ten o'clock on that May morning, Joe Palmer, Clyde's car-sick confederate, was at the Lee Huckins Hotel in Oklahoma City. He was not a registered guest but was merely sitting in the lobby. On the radio he heard the following announcement: "Pardon me, ladies and gentlemen. I have authentic information that Clyde Barrow and Bonnie Parker have just been killed in Arcadia, Louisiana, by Captain Hamer of the prison system and others." The taciturn gangster said he "hated" that news and later confessed that he had "been in misery most of the time, especially since Clyde and Bonnie got killed." Joe Palmer left Oklahoma City at 1:30 P.M. that day for Tulsa and then, despite the danger of capture, found his way back to Dallas so that he could attend the funeral of the two criminals who had been kind to him.

FROM ALL OVER America, newspapermen and an incredible variety of sightseers were making for Arcadia, Louisiana. When Hamer, Hinton, and Jordan returned to the scene of the ambush at Gibsland they were astonished to find about two hundred cars parked along the road and a large crowd of people gathered around the wrecked Ford V-8 and its gruesome cargo. The three lawmen were appalled, for their colleagues had been unable to keep the crowds away from the car. Hair had been hacked from Bonnie's head, material cut from her blood-soaked dress and from Barrow's gory shirt. One man had attempted to amputate Clyde's trigger finger; another had tried to cut off his ear, to pickle it in alcohol. Splinters of glass from the car windows were picked up; the hubcaps were stolen.

Despite the rain, men and women were crawling on all fours searching for empty cartridge cases or attempting to dig embedded bullets from the surrounding trees.

After the coroner had completed his work, the Ford and its corpses was towed along narrow country roads toward Arcadia. The rain had cleared, and the morning was bright and warm. At the front of the convoy was the county sheriff and his deputy, followed by Frank Hamer and Manny Gault and then the towed car with the two bodies. From their position behind, Ted Hinton and Bob Alcorn could see the bloody top of Clyde Barrow's head gently rocking with the motion of the car. Behind, there was a procession of cars containing the excited sightseers. Ted Hinton remembered that his head was still aching. He was sweating in the heat of the morning sun, itching from hundreds of insect bites and dreadfully tired.

As the macabre convoy was driving into Arcadia, it came to a sudden halt when the towing truck broke down right outside the school. Ted Hinton was horrified to see the schoolchildren pouring out into the road to look in at the broken bodies in the wreck. Before he and Alcorn could prevent it, the children had thrust their hands into the car to smear their fingers in blood, tear hairs from Bonnie's head, and rip more strands from her tattered red dress.

When the driver of the towing truck got it to start again, the convoy moved on into the small country town and stopped outside the local furniture store, which also served as the funeral parlor. The law officers were forced to push a path through a rapidly growing crowd so as to be able to carry the two bodies into the store and lay them on tables in a back room. As they left, the killers of Bonnie and Clyde were cheered and even kissed. Behind them the crowd was pushing into the furniture store to see. Ted Hinton was feeling sick and Bob Alcorn was shaking.

Outside, people were again picking souvenirs from the car: men in shirt-sleeves and straw hats, women in summer dresses were stealing fragments of glass and torn bits of upholstery. A way was cleared through the mob and the car towed to safety behind a tall wire fence near the county jail.

Newspaper reporters were arriving, alerted by radio news-flashes. Frank Hamer was in charge, posing for photographs with the other officers in front of the car they had smashed with their bullets. Later Lee Simmons drove in. He walked up to Frank Hamer and shook him by the hand and then turned to congratulate the other five. Hamer used Simmons's arrival to deflect the bombardment of questions from insistent reporters.

"Now here's the boss. I've been acting on his instructions. If any statement is to be given out, he is the one to make it."

Simmons described his role in the affair and that of the other men. When pressed with questions about the Methvins, the lean Texan replied, "There are some things which the public is not entitled to know."

Smoot Schmid also arrived that afternoon. More photographs were taken and fresh statements made. He told his two tired deputies that no less than $26,000 in rewards had been promised for the capture or killing of Clyde Barrow and his moll. But he warned Hinton and Alcorn that the enthusiasm of reward promises tended to diminish when the deed was accomplished.*

By dusk it was estimated that Arcadia's normal population of 3,000 had increased to 12,000 by the influx of sightseers, newspapermen, and officials. The roads into the little town were choked with vehicles. A constant stream of people still poured through the back room of the furniture store to gape at the bodies of the two lovers, still covered with congealed blood. The plate-glass windows of the store had been broken and furniture damaged. The undertaker was unable to embalm the corpses, so great was the press of the crowd, and eventually he resorted to squirting embalming fluid to drive the crowd back.

That evening Henry Barrow arrived. He had driven in the hearse of a Dallas undertaker to collect the body of his son. The elderly, taciturn man was seen sitting in a rocking chair in the front part of the furniture store, his head buried in his hands, weeping.

---

*Sheriff Schmid was right: Ted Hinton and Bob Alcorn received only $200.23 each.

Buster Parker drove in at ten o'clock that night. He too had hired a hearse with an undertaker, to collect the tiny body of his sister. They had left Dallas at noon but had lost their way. Buster was terribly upset and raged against the men who had murdered his sister in such a cowardly manner.

THE BODIES OF Clyde Barrow and Bonnie Parker were taken to Dallas on the following morning. Despite Bonnie's wish that she and Clyde should in death lie "side by side," their bodies were separated. Clyde Barrow's corpse was taken to the Sparkman-Holz-Brand Chapel and Bonnie Parker's to the McKamy-Campbell Chapel in Dallas. Both were put on public view, for as at Arcadia, great crowds gathered outside the two funeral homes and queued to file past the body of the multiple murderer and the corpse of the woman who had died at his side.

Clyde Barrow's funeral took place late in the afternoon of Friday May 25. The service was supposed to have been only for family and friends, but a large crowd gathered and tried to push its way into the chapel. The service was punctuated by the noise and taunts from the mob outside. To Emma Parker it was a nightmare. Cumie Barrow sobbed at the familiar words.

> Man that is born of a woman is of few days, and full of trouble.
> He cometh forth like a flower, and is cut down: he fleeth also as a shadow, and continueth not.
> And dost thou open thine eyes upon such a none, and bringest me into judgment with thee?
> Who can bring a clean thing out of an unclean? . . .

Henry Barrow wept as his son's coffin was carried from the chapel.

Clyde Barrow was buried next to his brother Buck on a bare slope in the West Dallas Cemetery. At the graveside the press of the crowd was so great that the family mourners who could get to it were nearly pushed into the open grave. Nell Cowan could get no closer than forty feet to it. As the crowd dispersed, a low-flying airplane dropped a gigantic floral wreath.

Ted Hinton was present at his victim's funeral. He had known the Barrows since his childhood in the squalid streets of West Dallas. Joe Palmer was also there. He had risked capture and the electric chair to pay homage to the man who "was good" to him and "always toted fair."

THE FUNERAL OF Bonnie Parker took place the following day, Saturday, May 26, 1934, in South Dallas. Her body had not rested at her home, as she had asked that it should, for the size and behavior of the crowds had made this impossible. Neither was she to be buried next to her lover, as she had predicted in her poem. Mrs. Parker was reputed to have said that "Clyde had her for two years and look what it did to her."

Emma Parker used the money from an insurance policy on her daughter's life to give Bonnie a respectable burial. Bonnie's mutilated hair was waved and curled into its former neatness. Her nails were manicured. She was dressed in a blue silk negligee and placed in a silver casket. One hand held a small bunch of lilies chosen from van loads of flowers and wreaths. The largest wreath of all was sent by the newspaper boys of Dallas. They, at least, had benefited from the exploits of Bonnie and Clyde, which had so dramatically increased newspaper sales.

Bonnie's sister was brought under police escort to the funeral service. She was still being held for her supposed involvement in the Easter Sunday murders of the two highway patrolmen. Billie Mace fainted when she saw her elder sister's face in the open casket. Her mother also collapsed and had to be carried from the chapel.

They buried Bonnie Parker in the Fishtrap Cemetery in West Dallas next to the graves of Buddy and Jackie, who had been so fond of their Aunt Bonnie and loved to hear her sing the "Crawdad Song."

23

EXECUTIONS
AND
EXCUSES

ON THE DAY Clyde Barrow was buried in the small roadside cemetery, Raymond Hamilton was taken back to the Huntsville penitentiary chained by the neck in the "one-way wagon." His previous sentence of 263 years' imprisonment had been increased to 362 years. Shortly afterward Joe Palmer was captured in Missouri, tried, and also brought back to the Walls by Uncle Bud, the prison transfer officer. He too had received an increased sentence that even before could not have been served out. Lee Simmons was determined that they should face trial for the murder of his prison guard Major Crowson and, what is more, should die in the electric chair. Both men were tried yet again, and both were sentenced to death. Simmons said that he worked closely with the prosecution in both these cases. The district attorney told him after the trials that without Simmons's help there would have been no death penalties.

The two criminals had no intention of remaining longer than necessary in the death house. On July 22 they escaped. The breakout was engineered by another murderer, Charlie Frazier, with the help of a bank robber, Whitey Walker. They bribed a prison guard to smuggle in .45 automatics. While most of the inmates were watching a basketball match (between the Prison Tigers and the Humble Oilers of Brenham) on that hot Sunday afternoon, Frazier, with Hamilton and Palmer and a fourth man, Blackie Thompson, forced their way out of the death house. They were joined by Walker and two other convicts. The seven criminals used a fire ladder to attempt to climb over the prison wall. Raymond Hamilton and Joe Palmer were first over, shortly followed by Blackie Thompson. They ran to waiting escape cars. But as the others were climbing the ladder, a prison guard opened fire. He stood his ground against the response from the criminals' automatic pistols. Charlie Frazier was twice shot off the ladder before he gave up, and Whitey Walker was killed. He had given his life to free his friend Blackie Thompson from the death cell.

WITH HIS NEWLY gained freedom, Raymond Hamilton resumed his trade of bank robbery. By the end of the year his exploits were regularly reported in the nation's newspapers alongside those of John Dillinger and other famous gangsters.

On February 17, 1935, he stole eight machine guns from the National Guard Armory in the leafy oil town of Beaumont, Texas; a week later he escaped a carefully laid police trap in McKinney, Texas, and captured three hostages en route; March 28 with Ralph Fults (a youthful friend of Clyde's), he robbed a bank in Prentiss, Mississippi, and surprised and disarmed at gunpoint a pursuing posse of fifteen men.

On April 6 Hamilton was captured by Smoot Schmid and five deputies near one of his old haunts in Grapevine between Dallas and Fort Worth. In an effort to throw off his pursuers, Hamilton had disguised himself as a tramp and was spotted by Sheriff Schmid plodding along a railway cutting with a group of hobos. Hamilton gave himself up without a fight. He was much cast down and refused to speak to his captors as they drove him back to Dallas.

"How do you feel, kid?" Smoot Schmid asked the small, dejected gangster as he was marched into the county jail.

"Well, how do you think I feel?" Hamilton snarled.

Joe Palmer had also been captured. He too had taken to hiding on the railway. He was seen on an embankment near the town of Paducah on the Ohio River in Kentucky sound asleep

with a loaded .45 automatic lying at his side. The two policemen who spotted him quietly walked up, kicked his revolver to
one side, and handcuffed him.

"The Lord had his arm around those two cops," Joe Palmer,
normally a man of few words, was later moved to comment. "If
I hadn't been dead tired for sleep, you'd have to bury them."

Raymond Hamilton was returned to Huntsville on the day of
his capture. He met Palmer briefly before the quiet gangster
was taken off to court and sentenced to be executed on May 10,
1935, for the murder of Major Crowson, the Huntsville prison
guard. After he heard his fate, Palmer pleaded for Hamilton's
life, claiming that it was he, and not his friend, who had killed
the guard. The plea was rejected and Hamilton was later also
sentenced to be executed on May 10.

Joe Palmer accepted his fate with resignation, but his excitable friend refused to believe that he would be electrocuted and
grew frightened and very restless, hoping for a reprieve. On
the day of the execution Hamilton realized that there could be
no last-minute reprieve and broke down completely. Lee Simmons said that fear took complete charge of him. Palmer
talked quietly to him and told him of his belief in an afterlife.

Raymond Hamilton was allowed to choose which of the two
would go first into the electric chair, but he either could not or
would not make the choice. Joe Palmer, therefore, offered to go
first. Before he left to walk to his death, he turned to Raymond
Hamilton and said, "Good-bye old pal. We're going to be happy
in a few minutes. We'll meet on the other side."

The steel door to the death chamber was opened, and Lee
Simmons and a warden accompanied the first man to the chair
just after midnight. Before he was strapped in, Joe Palmer
read a statement that he had prepared that afternoon for the
newspapermen who were assembled to watch his end. He
addressed himself to the prison chaplain:

> Father Finnegan, I have many things to thank you for—chiefly
> for introducing me to our God. You have always been very
> patient and kind, and I am well aware I would have exhausted
> one with less patience.

I have enjoyed our acquaintance for a number of years, and each year I have found something more to admire in you.

I hope I may embrace death as willingly as any of the seventy-four or eighty men you have prepared.

If anyone has injured me, I forgive them whole-heartedly, and ask the pardon of those whom I have injured.

I ask God to accept my ignoble death in atonement for my sins.

So far as my death is acceptable to God, I unite it to the sorrows and death of Jesus Christ.

My friends in Christ, I bid you good-bye.

Five minutes later Raymond Hamilton was led into the execution room. Lee Simmons said that he was entirely changed in his manner. He crossed himself, expressed his gratitude to Joe Palmer, and asked Father Finnegan to tell "Mama and Katy [his last girlfriend]" that he was glad to atone for his sins. Then he said, "I don't need any more time; I'm ready to go now."

ANOTHER OF CLYDE Barrow's confederates also faced the consequences of his crimes. In March 1935 Henry Methvin was charged in the district court of Ottawa County, Oklahoma, with the murder of Cal Campbell on April 6, 1934 "while acting conjointly with Clyde Barrow and Bonnie Parker, and with premeditated design to effect the death of Cal Campbell."

The court proceedings resulted in a mistrial, for the jury failed to agree on its verdict. A second trial was therefore set in September 1935. Methvin was found guilty of murder and sentenced to death. However, he appealed against the verdict and his case was referred to the Criminal Court of Appeals of Oklahoma.

Henry Methvin's appeal was considered on September 18, 1936. He maintained that the fatal shot was fired not by him but by Clyde Barrow. Methvin used the argument (which had been employed earlier in similar circumstances by W. D. Jones) that he was asleep in the back of the car at the time and had been awakened by the shots that had killed Cal Campbell.

Furthermore, he claimed, again like W. D. Jones, that he had been held by Barrow against his will and frequently threatened with death if he did not obey Barrow's orders.

The court was not convinced by either of these aguments. However, it did take account of a mitigating circumstance, namely "that the defendant had agreed with the authorities in Louisiana to aid and assist federal and state officers to apprehend his codefendants, Clyde Barrow and Bonnie Parker, and in pursuance of said agreement did give to the authorities in Louisiana information that led to their justifiable killing by officers of the law." Because of this, Methvin's sentence of death was reduced to one of life imprisonment.

Evidence for Methvin's betrayal of Bonnie and Clyde was given by a neighbor of the Methvins, John Joiner. He testified that the Methvins had asked him on "about the first of March, 1934" to contact the county sheriff. Joiner claimed that he had two meetings with Henderson Jordan, at the second of which there were also present Lester Kandale—a Department of Justice man from New Orleans—Frank Hamer, and Bob Alcorn. Joiner testified that he told these officers that Henry Methvin was willing to put Clyde Barrow and Bonnie Parker "on the spot" in exchange for his freedom. He also claimed that "Mr. and Mrs. Methvin had directed that any arrangement must be made in writing" and furthermore that he had seen a written agreement that was "turned over to Sheriff Jordan for safe keeping." This agreement, Joiner said, was signed by Miriam Ferguson, governor of Texas, and the superintendent of the state penitentiary of Texas, Lee Simmons.

"On May 21, 1934," Joiner said, he "received word from the Methvins that Clyde Barrow and Bonnie Parker would be there the next morning." He therefore "notified Sheriff Jordan, who, in turn, notified the officers at Dallas, Tex."

Henry Methvin's mother, Ave, told a somewhat different story. She testified that her son came to their farm on "about first March, 1934, with Clyde Barrow and Bonnie Parker." She said that Henry Methvin talked to her and her husband "about making arrangements with the authorities for the apprehension of Clyde Barrow and Bonnie Parker." According to her account it was she and her husband who talked to Frank Hamer, Henderson Jordan, and Bob Alcorn. She claimed her son came home again in early April, when she told him that an agreement had been made with the law officers. She next saw Henry Methvin with his two companions on the "night before Clyde Barrow and Bonnie Parker were killed," when they called at the farm. Ave Methvin said that she and her husband "went that night and told the sheriff that Barrow and Parker would be back there next day."

Henry Methvin testified that he had visited his parents on May 21, 1934, and learned that an agreement to betray Clyde Barrow and Bonnie had been concluded with the law officers. He told his mother that he intended to escape from the other two in Shreveport and that this would bring them back to the farm to look for him. Henry Methvin then told the court that after the killings he stayed at his parents' home until arrested on the charge of murdering Cal Campbell.

THESE THREE TESTIMONIES given before the Oklahoma Criminal Court of Appeals differ totally from Ted Hinton's posthumously published account of the events surrounding the killing of Bonnie and Clyde. Hinton's story insists that Bonnie and Clyde were not betrayed by the Methvins and that Irvin Methvin was illegally detained by the ambushing lawmen and forced to agree to a false story of betrayal to save his son from the electric chair.

Now there are obvious inconsistencies between the testimonies of Ave and Henry Methvin and their neighbor Joiner. First, Henry Methvin said that he visited his parents with Bonnie and Clyde on May 21. Ave Methvin, on the other hand, told the court that they appeared on "the day before Clyde Barrow and Bonnie Parker were killed," that is May 22. Secondly, Joiner claimed that on May 21 the Methvins asked him to take the message to the sheriff that Clyde and Bonnie would be around the next morning. Ave Methvin told the court that it was *she and Irvin Methvin* who went to see Henderson Jordan that day. Thirdly, John Joiner said that he saw a document signed by the Texas Governor and Lee Simmons that stated that "if Henry Methvin delivered Clyde Barrow and

Bonnie Parker over to the authorities, he was to have his freedom from the state of Texas." Yet the document produced as evidence in court was written weeks after the killing of Clyde Barrow and Bonnie Parker. It was dated August 14, 1934. However, this inconsistency can be explained, for in his account of events Lee Simmons refers to a letter (written on April 24, 1934 to Captain Hamer) that was seen by the governor and that, in Simmons's words, "was delivered to the friends of Henry Methvin."

If Ted Hinton's version of events is true, then Ave and Henry Methvin and John Joiner committed perjury in their evidence. This could account for the inconsistencies in their testimonies. However, the discrepancy could just as well have arisen from genuine confusion on their part as to the timing of events.

Hinton's account clearly implies that Frank Hamer deliberately encouraged belief in a false story of betrayal by the Methvins. Such interpretation would also involve Lee Simmons as his accomplice and would imply that Simmons deliberately lied to Miriam Ferguson when he referred to a letter (written on April 24, 1934) that he said was seen by the friends of the Methvins. This seems unlikely. It is equally improbable that Ted Hinton, a truthful man, would have deliberately fabricated his story toward the end of his life to tarnish the posthumous reputations of Frank Hamer and Lee Simmons.

One possible explanation of this curious affair is that Ted Hinton was unaware of Frank Hamer's negotiation with the Methvin family. Both in their accounts maintained that of the ambushers, only Frank Hamer, Henderson Jordan, and Bob Alcorn were present at the negotiations. It also seems likely that both Hamer and the Methvins would have wanted to retain maximum secrecy, for any leak about the plan would have been disastrous for all parties. It may well have been that all present were sworn to secrecy.* If that was the case, why was it necessary to detain Irvin Methvin illegally and shackle

---

*Federal Marshal Clint Peoples, who was a close friend of Frank Hamer, is convinced by this theory. He says that Frank Hamer "wouldn't tell anybody anything." Clint Peoples also emphasizes the fact that "the early-day law-enforcement officer had a reputation that he could be trusted and would not divulge where he got his information—even to his colleagues."

him to a tree immediately before the ambush of Bonnie and Clyde?

The most obvious explanation is that it would provide an alibi for the elderly farmer. After all, if the ambush had failed, then he would have been in a very awkward position, for Clyde Barrow would certainly have attempted to murder his betrayers. Shackled to a tree and protesting vigorously, he had a good alibi for the presence of his truck, which was an important element in the strategy of the ambush.

When the ambush was successful, Hamer might well have wished to dispense with any reference to this embarrassing incident. Furthermore, he could not have been sure that Irvin Methvin (who seems to have been a wily old man) might not have attempted to turn the tables on him and claim kidnapping to use in future bargaining for his son's life.

Such a hypothesis implies that Bonnie and Clyde were betrayed by Henry Methvin, as was generally supposed from the outset.

Joe Palmer was outraged by the idea. He told Lee Simmons as he waited in the death house, "If a fellow were to sell my father out, like Old Man Methvin did Clyde and Bonnie, I would hunt him up, kill him and carry him over and dump him on their doorstep." He believed that something like this would happen to Henry Methvin. "Don't you know Old Lady Barrow and Mrs. Parker won't stand for that? They will have Henry either killed or put in the electric chair."

But Henry Methvin survived: For ten years in an Oklahoma prison, then for a time as a restaurant owner in Minden, Louisiana, before he was killed in a train accident. Perhaps Old Lady Barrow and Mrs. Parker were not as bloodthirsty as Joe Palmer supposed. Perhaps, like him, they could not really believe that Henry Methvin had betrayed Bonnie and Clyde. Joe Palmer (who was the closest approximation to a gentleman in the Barrow-Parker ménage) said, "I believe in Henry, for he could have turned on me, as he knew exactly where I was. And I think he thought more of Clyde than he did me."

OLD LADY BARROW and Emma Parker had their own troubles with the law to add to their suffering after the killing of Clyde and Bonnie. Together with eighteen other relatives and friends, the two mothers stood trial in Dallas in February 1935. They were brought to court in police vans. The men were chained together by their necks under the watchful eyes of armed federal officers. The two mothers wore black hats, Emma Parker looking defiantly at the excited crowds and Cumie Barrow concealing her face with a handkerchief. They were charged with harboring two dangerous criminals: Clyde Barrow and Bonnie Parker. Cumie Barrow was described by the prosecuting council as "the ringleader of this conspiracy." Like Emma Parker, Mrs. Barrow pleaded "mother love" as a reason for their clandestine meetings with their daughter and son. The able young defense lawyer waxed eloquent in his defense of Cumie Barrow:

> Let me remind you, dear friends—in reverence, of course— that the Mother of Christ was such a woman as she; a woman from the ranks of the poor whose bed of labor was a pile of straw in a manger. My client has not the fashionable frocks of many of the elite of Dallas, nor are her finger-nails glowing with pink tint, nor is her face made smooth by the practiced hand of a tonsorial artist. Her dress is made of calico, her nails are worn from constant scrubbing of diapers and bare floors, her face is lined with marks of sorrow. I wonder if the face of the Immaculate Virgin was not lined as this poor woman's after the Divine Mother beheld her bleeding son dangling against the sky on a cross! This poor woman before you looked at cruel wounds made by machine guns and automatic rifles in the body of a boy she bore. . . .

The jury was not convinced by the plea and found both of the mothers guilty. Strangely, the judge, William Atwell, allowed the women to choose their own sentences: thirty days in jail. Raymond Hamilton's mother received the same sentence; Billie Mace, Mary O'Dare, and Blanche Barrow were each sentenced to a year and a day in prison. Clyde Barrow's sister Marie was sentenced to "one hour in the custody of the United States marshal." W. D. Jones and Henry Methvin had also been brought from prison for the occasion. They were sentenced to two years and a year and a day, respectively, to be added to their existing sentences. Nell Cowan, surprisingly, was never tried. The others were all imprisoned for varying periods: Floyd Hamilton and his wife, Clyde's younger brother ("L.C.") and his wife, Mary O'Dare's father (Joe Chambless), James Mullen, Steve Davis (Raymond Hamilton's stepfather), and Hilton Bybee.

24

FROM
HOOVER
TO FILM
NOIR

PUBLIC REACTION TO the deaths of Bonnie and Clyde had been immediate and in many cases horrifying. Even the men who had killed them—hard-bitten men who acted with consciousness of right on their side—were sickened by the crowds of struggling people who fought each other for bloody relics from the bullet-shattered Ford V-8 in the warm Louisiana sunshine. No one could have predicted the excited crowds that gathered in Dallas to gaze at the bodies and follow the coffins to their graves. The violent deaths of two young psychopaths had stirred the minds of some twentieth-century Texans at a primitive level. Two months later, the killing of John Dillinger outside the Biograph cinema in Chicago provided the same intense and macabre public interest: Men dipped their handkerchiefs and women the hems of their skirts in his blood. Thousands of people queued to stare at the gangster's body as it lay in the mortuary, propped up so that it could be seen better. Someone even tried to buy Clyde's body from the police.

With the wave of hysterical interest in Bonnie and Clyde that swept through America, the relics were now prized objects. Lee Simmons had given permission for the killers of Clyde Barrow and Bonnie Parker to take what they wanted from the blood-stained car in Arcadia. He told Frank Hamer, "You take what you want and then divide the souvenirs with the boys that did the job." They had quite a selection from which to choose. There were three automatic rifles, two sawn-off shotguns, one Colt revolver, nine automatic pistols, and thousands of rounds of ammunition. Subsequently an enterprising showman capitalized on public fascination with the relics by acquiring the wrecked Ford V-8 and constructing around this spectacular item a slide show that depicted the gory details of the killing.*

The Barrow and Parker families were not slow to realize the potential value of the relics. Both the mothers tried to get possession of their children's murder weapons, which were already worth a good deal of money. Cumie Barrow wrote to Frank Hamer on July 28, 1934.

> Mr. Hamer, we have been told here by Sheriff Smoot Schmid in Dallas that you have in your possession some guns that were in the car at the time you and the officers killed my boy Clyde. Now Mr. Hamer, I do hope you will be kindly enough to give me those guns as you know you have no right to try and keep those guns. I feel you should think you have caused me enough grief and hardships without trying to cause me more trouble now. I have been told you got out of the car three pistols and one saw off shotgun. Now I do know that my boy did buy most of the guns he had so I don't see why you should not return the ones you have to me. You don't never want to forget my boy was never tried in no court for murder and no one is guilty until proven guilty by some court so I hope you will answer this letter and also return the guns I am asking for. (signed) Mrs. C.H. Barrow.

The desire for any objects, however remotely connected with the psychopath murderer and his girl, continued unabated for years. Even the bricks of the Red Crown Tavern in Platte City,

---

*The car was still being exhibited forty years later at $2.50 a time. *Time* magazine reported that the car had been auctioned in Princeton, MA, in 1973 for $175,000—$20,000 more than was paid for Hitler's Mercedes.

Missouri, where Buck Barrow was shot and Blanche Barrow nearly blinded were treasured. Thirty years later, when the Red Crown Tavern was demolished, the bricks were sold for a dollar each, and as the local newspaper reported, "Everyone wanted one, and they would have paid five dollars for them or more." Before the motel cabins were demolished, tours were arranged for the local schoolchildren. Even Platte County's "official poet laureate," O. V. Cecil, was moved to write a commemorative poem commencing with the stirring lines:

> History was made in thirty-three
> In our county known as Platte
> When the Barrow gang stopped by
> With dope, fast cars and gat.

Mob hysteria was not uncommon in the 1930s in the southern states, where lynchings still sometimes involved mutilation and the taking of grisly souvenirs. It seems unlikely, however, that the people who struggled around the bloodstained car were primarily motivated by latent sadistic impulses, for they took anything that could be wrested from the vehicle.

The compulsive urge to possess material relics from certain special, dead creatures is a widespread human phenomenon. Such objects can be greatly valued or regarded with considerable veneration. They can range from pieces of rhinoceros horn to the blood of dead saints or that most sacred of medieval relics, the foreskin of Jesus. Objects that have been, or were supposed to have been, in physical contact with certain dead persons can be similarly prized or revered. They can vary from pieces wrenched from the car of the dead James Dean to the Shroud of Turin or bits of the True Cross.

Anthropologists maintain that such relics serve as manifestations of the "power" or the "life force" of the dead person from which they were taken. Such people are regarded as exceptional beings: abnormal or even supernatural. The fact that the corpses and possessions of Clyde Barrow and Bonnie Parker were treated in such a way is an eloquent testimony of the intense excitement that their crimes had evoked.

WITH THE KILLING of Clyde Barrow and Bonnie Parker the American public breathed a sigh of relief. Everywhere in the United States at that time there was concern at the wave of gangster crimes, and the news that two of the more notorious had been destroyed on May 23, 1934 was greeted with grateful enthusiasm in the press. The two young criminals were portrayed in unflattering and often inaccurate terms—for example in *The New York Times*:

> Clyde Barrow was a snake-eyed murderer who killed without giving his victims a chance to draw. He was slight, altogether unheroic in physical appearance.
>
> Bonnie Parker was a fit companion for him. She was a hard-faced, sharp-mouthed woman who gave up a waitress job in a Kansas City restaurant to become the mistress of Raymond Hamilton, Texas bank robber. Barrow took her away from him.

Even the adverse opinions of their former criminal friends were sought and gleefully quoted in the general press euphoria that followed the killing of Bonnie and Clyde. Under the headlines Death of Outlaws Relief to Former Allies in Forays, the *Dallas Morning News* reported that W. D. Jones was "a very willing prisoner since he was put in the Dallas County jail ... fearing that he would be killed by Barrow or some of his friends." Mary O'Dare recorded how "Raymond suspected that Barrow and Parker might be trying to put us on the spot."

The top man in the profession, John Dillinger, also had a very low opinion of Clyde Barrow, regarding him as an amateur who was "giving decent bank robbers a bad name." Another professional told the writer John Toland that he and his fellow criminals despised Clyde Barrow and Bonnie Parker for their purposeless, harebrained career.

The lawmen who had previously been criticized in the press for their lack of success in putting an end to the Barrow Gang's reign of terror were now riding on a wave of popularity. The tactics of the hunt and the method of killing received general approval. The *Austin American* of May 24, 1934, for example, reported,

> Justice travels with leaden heel, but it strikes mighty hard. Clyde Barrow and Bonnie Parker made their last stand in Louisiana. They were trailed by a highway patrolman, two Deputy Sheriffs and Frank Hamer, who had been given orders to "get their man."
>
> Well, they were trailed to their hideout. They reached for their guns. They were shot into the world of oblivion. They will sleep in dishonored graves.
>
> Congratulations to the fearless officers of the law who trailed these enemies of the social order.

Frank Hamer, in particular, received rapturous praise from all sides for his part in the affair. He and the other lawmen were even lauded from the floor of Congress, and a special resolution was passed thanking them for their part in restoring law and order to the nation.

In Austin, their hometown, Frank Hamer and Manny Gault received a heroic welcome. The local newspaper, the *Statesman*, ran gigantic banner headlines announcing:

HAMER-GAULT HERO DAY IS SET

The day would be May 28, 1934. There was to be a testimonial dinner with speeches from Hamer's old political enemies the Fergusons and other state and city dignitaries. Hamer himself would have none of it. He detested such affairs and excused himself in his usual brusque manner—thus further enhancing his reputation by his modesty.

The burly Texan was pestered on all sides for press and radio interviews but stubbornly refused to give them. Lee Simmons recalled that Frank Hamer received an offer from the National Broadcasting Corporation while the two men were together. The offer, for a few minutes' talking, was to be $1,000—then a princely sum.

"Hell, no!—I won't do it—What do you think I am—Hell, no!" Hamer spluttered into the telephone.

AS THE EXCITEMENT subsided, some discordant notes could be heard among the widespread praise of the final dispatch of Bonnie and Clyde. Even before their end there had been criticism of police methods, and after the event the *Dallas Times Herald* detected the "development of widespread resentment against officers who stamped out the terrors of this section." This resentment was apparently not confined to the poor whites in West Dallas, for the newspaper also confided to its readers that "at one of the country clubs where the elite gathered, the feeling was voiced on all sides that Hamer and Hinton, Alcorn and the others were 'cowardly murderers.'"

Another newspaper article reported that "at a bridge game in which women, mothers of children, were playing, the opinion was not controverted that 'the officers didn't have much guts to shoot down a man and a woman that way.'"

The accusations of cowardly murder was also the stock-in-trade of the showman who was displaying the death car in the major Texas towns. When the show reached Austin, Frank Hamer and Manny Gault went along to see it. Hamer was outraged at what he heard and objected to the lies that were being told about him. The ex-Texas ranger confronted the car's owner and "slapped him across the room." As the shaken man rose to his feet, Hamer issued a dire threat.

"If you ever use my name again, even if you are in South America, I will come to you if I have to crawl on my hands and feet."

Quite apart from ill feeling about the killing, there was evidently much admiration for what the *Dallas News* described as "the glamour that small minds saw in the sneaking and bloody exploits . . . of Clyde Barrow, 24, and Bonnie Parker, 21 [he was, in fact, twenty-five and she was twenty-three]."

As the crime reporter of the Dallas newspaper well knew, there were many small minds in America at that time. The director of the recently inaugurated Federal Bureau of Investigation was also aware of the dangerous glamour of the gangsters. J. Edgar Hoover once fulminated to a member of the Department of Justice about it:

> I'm going to tell the truth about these rats. I'm going to tell the truth about their dirty, filthy, diseased women. I'm going to tell the truth about the miserable politicians who protect them and the slimy, silly or sob-sister convict lovers who let them out on sentimental or ill-advised paroles.

The late Bonnie Parker received the full benefit of this approach in a book (with a foreword by Hoover) written by Herbert Corey:

> Bonnie Parker was quite as devilish as Shoe Box Annie [a well-known thief, swindler and murderess, who showed great enterprise in the disposal of her victims' bodies] but with every will in the world to give her place on the big-time it must be admitted that she was a cheap and noisy killer. "A scourge of the filling-stations," someone called her. Not a kind word may truthfully be said of Bonnie Parker or her mate, Clyde Barrow. They were physically unclean. The woman boasted that she never took a bath. They slept in the cars they stole, hiding in woods and fields. Their activities were possible through the kindness of the Governor of Texas, who not only granted them whatever a "general parole" may be, but also released Clyde's brother Buck to keep them company.

WHILE THE ESTABLISHMENT was trying to degrade the public image of Bonnie and Clyde, their families were engaged in exactly the opposite process.

The intrepid Cumie Barrow caused a considerable stir at the Capitol Theater in Elm Street, Dallas, when she tore down photographs of Clyde's and Bonnie's bodies. On May 31, Billie Mace was released from jail, freed of the charge of involvement in the killing of the two highway patrolmen at Grapevine. Within a week the *Daily Times Herald* announced that she would make her stage debut at the State Theater in Wichita

Falls and was optimistically awaiting the "tenders of movie contacts in Hollywood" to tell her part in the story of her elder sister and Clyde Barrow. On July 8 the Dallas newspapers announced that Henry and Cumie Barrow and Emma Parker were being sought by two publishers to write books about their dead children.

In September, only four months after the deaths of Clyde Barrow and Bonnie Parker, a slim volume appeared in book-shops the length and breadth of America. The book's black-and-red dustcover is adorned with the head-and-shoulders drawing of a smartly dressed man, his well-groomed hair glistening. With his head held slightly to one side, he looks like a rather intellectual Hollywood film star. Also on the cover (linked to the picture of the young man by the radiating head-lights of a car emerging from beneath his portrait) is the picture of a friendly looking young woman, with a neat hat, a broad smile, and dimples. *Fugitives. The Story of Clyde Barrow and Bonnie Parker* purports to be written by "Bonnie's Mother (Mrs. Emma Parker) and Clyde's Sister (Nell Barrow Cowan)." Originally published in Dallas, it was "compiled, arranged and edited" by a professional journalist, Jan Fortune. The hand of Fortune is occasionally very evident in the writing, her style more reminiscent of Barbara Cartland than of the two tough women from the criminal fraternity of West Dallas. "There she sat, so lovely—only twenty three—with the May moonlight sifting through her yellow hair and making shad-ows on her cheeks. . . . Bonnie looked at me—as if she were a million years older than I was, as if she knew things I'd never learn if I lived for centuries. . . ."

Apart from these patches of moonshine, the book is a reason-ably accurate account of the lives of the daughter and brother of the two authors. They clearly tried to tell the story of Bonnie and Clyde as they experienced it and with the loyalty of their kind; only occasionally did they use fictitious names (to avoid trouble for others) or knowingly distort the facts. The overrid-ing impression given by Emma Parker and Nell Cowan is of two respectable, if somewhat seedy, families and their friends struggling to lead honest lives in difficult circumstances. From their writing it is hard to realize the extent of their criminal connections. No one would guess, for example, that Bonnie's husband (Roy Thornton) was an experienced crook, that Bonnie's sister, Billie Mace (alias Billie White) was married to a convict, or that Clyde's younger brother (L.C.) was serving a five-year sentence at the time the book was written. Nell Cowan took a pathetic pride in writing of the young Clyde Barrow that "the most respectable and educated people were his friends."

The two women were also anxious to emphasize the charm and beauty of their two subjects. Nell Cowan was outraged at "the many stories which describe Clyde Barrow as small and undersized, with a weak chin and shifty eye." She repeatedly spoke of her brother's "delightful personality," "his boyish, lovable grin" and of how this "very handsome boy" was so "thoroughly lovable and full of fun." Here clearly was an example of the psychopath's ability "to win and bind forever the devotion of women."

Bonnie Parker's exceptional good looks and her appealing charm were a constant theme of both the women, a theme that was expertly embroidered by Miss Fortune. Her affectionate nature and genuine love for Clyde Barrow were central to the book.

Nell Cowan and Emma Parker were surprisingly detached in their attitude to Clyde Barrow's murders. They refused to accept that he was involved in the killing of two elderly shopkeepers (John Bucher and Howard Hall) despite convincing evidence to the contrary. Nell Cowan also refused to believe that Clyde murdered Doyle Johnson. She accepted her brother's story that it was W. D. Jones who had shot him. Emma Parker changed the date of the killing from December 25 to December 5. Presumably she could not accept the obscenity of a murder on Christmas Day.

Emma Parker and Nell Cowan's book leaves the impression that Bonnie and Clyde were both physically attractive and charming young people driven to a life of crime by unfair police harassment. Essentially the same theme was used in Arthur Penn's film re-creation of the lives of the two fugitives, *Bonnie and Clyde*, thirty-four years after their deaths.

THE APPEAL OF Arthur Penn's film *Bonnie and Clyde* is uncomplicated. As played by Warren Beatty and Faye Dunaway, the fugitives are just beautiful, folksy amateurs. Even their murders are handled with delicacy. In fact, apart from a few toppling cops, only one is shown—the fictional shooting of a bank employee who tries to prevent their escape after a robbery. As one critic commented, "There are few reminders that these beautiful, dapper, corny people are killers as well." The film was even embellished with incidents borrowed from the exploits of another 1930s gangster, John Dillinger. Dillinger's biographer, John Toland, was quick to spot this: "What the movie-makers did was to borrow adroitly many scenes from the career of that much more interesting and relatively likeable criminal John Dillinger—and to give Clyde a number of Dillinger's more appealing characteristics." These included the refusal of Warren Beatty's Clyde to take money from a customer during a bank holdup: He robbed only banks. Buck Barrow's straw-hatted, and quite uncharacteristic, leap over the barrier in the bank was lifted from Dillinger, who had himself been influenced by the Hollywood athleticism of Douglas Fairbanks: a complex case of artistic inbreeding.

In Arthur Penn's interpretation of Newman and Benton's script, Bonnie and Clyde die happy in a slow-motion, balletic representation of the Gigsland shooting by the evil Hamer, for Clyde has finally achieved that most sacred of modern goals—orgasm. Bonnie was most appreciative: "Hey. You did just perfect." The film writer Carlos Clarens summed it up a decade later:

> The message that came through, raising the most eyebrows and selling the most tickets, was that it was better to live fast, die young, and leave good-looking images in the collective mind than to conform to the indignities of growing old and being co-opted by the straight, practical world. Beyond a cer-

tain moment, Bonnie and Clyde had to die, not because history decreed their death, but because the film's particular fiction was of the sixties, and death had to rescue them from adulthood, domesticity, and the middle class, fates far worse than death in the age of the dropout.

THE RELEASE OF *Bonnie and Clyde* raised a storm of controversy and reopened issues that had been hotly debated three decades earlier during J. Edgar Hoover's attempt to destroy the glamor of the gangster. The furor began immediately after the world premiere in Montreal. The film critic of *The New York Times*, Bosley Crowther, was particularly vociferous in his dislike and started a controversy that another critic described as making "the 100-Years-War look like a border incident."

In his article of August 7, 1967, Crowther expressed his surprised disapproval that the film "was wildly received with gales of laughter and given a terminal burst of applause." But he comforted himself with the observation that "Some more sober visitors from the United States attending this festival ... were wagging their heads in dismay and exasperation that so callous and callow a film should represent their country in these critical times." He went on to complain that "It seems but another indulgence of a restless and reckless taste, and an embarrassing addition to an excess of violence on the screen."

Crowther's views were shared by another American critic, Joseph Morgenstern. Writing in *Newsweek*, immediately after seeing the film, he classified it as "a squalid shoot-'em-up for the moron trade." A week later, after seeing which way the wind was blowing, he had changed his mind: "I am sorry to say I consider that review grossly unfair and regrettably inaccurate. I am sorrier to say I wrote it." The contrite critic of *Newsweek* admitted that "I had become so surfeited and preoccupied by violence in daily life that my reaction was as excessive as the stimulus. ... And yet precisely because *Bonnie and Clyde* combines gratuitous crudities with scene after scene of dazzling artistry ... it is an ideal laboratory for the study of violence, a subject in which we are all matriculating these days. . . ."

Morgenstern's late enthusiasm was widely shared, and the popularity of the film increased, not only in America but in Europe, particularly in Great Britain and France. Indeed *Bonnie and Clyde* became a spectacular box-office success. Yet controversy still raged, especially in the correspondence columns of some American newspapers, where Hoover's battle of thirty years before was fought again. John Toland, with all the authority of the biographer of John Dillinger, entered the lists and compared the real Bonnie and Clyde unfavorably with his subject. Even an aged gangster from the 1930s, Raymond Moseley (then serving a forty-year sentence in Indiana State Prison), informed the readers of *The New York Times* that the Barrow Gang was held in little regard by his fellow inmates and had not been "mentioned in years." Other correspondents fulminated against the portrayal of "the shoddy history of these things" and in turn were attacked by the defenders of Warner Brothers' golden egg. An assistant professor of art history at Columbia University gave it as her opinion that "this film just may be the greatest one produced in America since the first days of glory in the movies."

For many American intellectuals of the late 1960s *Bonnie and Clyde* became a symbol of their own disgust and discontent with capitalism and for their country torn apart and troubled with the Vietnam War. These were the years of student revolt, of urban guerrillas, and later the Symbionese Liberation Army with Patty Hearst as their version of a bank-robbing girl with a machine-gun. For a newspaper correspondent from Cambridge, Massachusetts:

> Bonnie and Clyde, of the movie at least, represent a needed nihilism—not in a philosophical way, of course, but in a very activist way. They waste few words—only enough to make their message clear—and show by their actions that it is proper to attack the repressive institutions of our society and to ignore the ethic we have built up to protect those institutions.

BY THE END of 1967 *Bonnie and Clyde* was an international sensation. There were plenty of people ready to cash in on the craze, as there had been in the aftermath of the killing thirty-three years before. Bonnie's sister, Billie Jean Parker (formerly Mace), produced a record album to tell her version of the lives and deaths of Bonnie and Clyde. Emma Parker and Nell Cowan's little book, ghosted by Jan Fortune, was reissued. Another writer, Miriam Allen DeFord, quickly produced a slim paperback *The Real Bonnie and Clyde*, which reverted to debunking in the Hoover style, ending with the wholesome thought, "Why do we not apotheosize people like Gandhi or Einstein or Dr. Schweitzer? Why do we not transform them into legends, instead of people like Bonnie and Clyde?"

David Newman and Robert Benton's screenplay was also swiftly converted into a novel, *Bonnie and Clyde*, by Burt Hirschfeld, while Sandra Wake and Nicola Hayden edited *The Bonnie and Clyde Book*. Here was an example of art feeding on art. It described the production of the 1967 film, included a lavishly illustrated version of the screenplay together with some assorted, largely adulatory writings by various critics and contributions by Arthur Penn and Warren Beatty, still basking in the glow of their fabulous box-office success.

The pop industry also benefited from the craze. In October 1967, CBS Records in Britain issued a single of "Foggy Mountain Breakdown," the lively hillbilly tune played by Flatt and Scruggs and the Foggy Mountain Boys. By January 1968 "The Ballad of Bonnie and Clyde" had been cut by the pop singer Georgie Fame and was heading toward the top of the British charts. The record incorporated the sound of a machine-gun firing and, for this reason, was banned in Norway and censored on French and American radio. The Country and Western singer Merle Haggard recorded "The Legend of Bonnie and Clyde." Other pop songs followed, including "A Day in the Life of Bonnie and Clyde," "Saga of Bonnie and Clyde," and "Bonnie's Song." A record album appeared of Charles Strouse's music for the film with excerpts from the dialogue. Then came a release "Original Theme from Bonnie and Clyde as Performed in the Motion Picture by Flatt and Scruggs."

The New York Times was taken aback by this manifestation of the Bonnie and Clyde legend: "Bad-man ballads are as old, in world folklore, as bad men. But this rash of recordings to be inspired by a film 34 years after the death of the principals involved may be without precedent in the recording industry or, perhaps even more remarkably, the motion-picture industry."

FOR MILLIONS OF people in the Western world the film image of the slim young woman in the beret, jumper and the knee-length skirt had become almost as familiar as that of the outlaw in Lincoln Green. But the re-creation of Bonnie Parker's costume for Faye Dunaway differed in one major respect from that of the original. The real Bonnie's skirt reached down nearly to her ankles, for short skirts, bobbed hair, and straight lines had vanished by the time that they took to the road. The early 1930s were the hard, no-nonsense years of the Great Depression, and the nonconformist dress of the previous decade gave way to curving lines and long skirts. Despite the much-vaunted visual verisimilitude of Arthur Penn's film, Faye Dunaway was clothed in a knee-length skirt. For Dunaway's Bonnie to have worn an ankle-length skirt would have been an absurdity for the audiences of the late 1960s wallowing in the nihilism of *Bonnie and Clyde*. Such authenticity would have appeared after an interval of thirty years to have been merely amusing and entirely inappropriate to the film's basically romantic representation of Bonnie Parker's outlawry and death. Like the professional balladeers and minstrels of the fourteenth and fifteenth centuries describing the exploits of the Outlaw of Sherwood, the Hollywood image makers were adapting their story to the audience of the time.

25

GROWTH
OF
LEGEND

THIS BOOK HAS traced the lives of two underprivileged products of a raw society. The man was unprepossessing in appearance and a psychological cripple. Ill-educated and incapable of sustained work, he slid into petty crime and, in his criminal incompetence, into purposeless killings. The woman was an exhibitionist. Her affectionate nature responded to the childlike appeal of the psychopath and to romantic images of Western criminal outlaws. As fugitives, the couple gained confidence from the fear that murder generates in others, and for two years they eluded capture by the badly organized forces of the law.

Not at first sight promising material for the growth of legend. But glorious things can grow from very humble origins. The supreme figure of British legend was certainly not what he finally appeared to be in the writings of Malory or Tennyson. In early Welsh scripts, King Arthur was one of the "Three Red Ravagers" and was guilty of "Three Wicked Uncoverings" (including digging up a human head). His adventures were conceived in yokel terms in this rustic incident related in the *Triodd Ynys Prydein (The Welsh Triads)*:

> The third was Trystan son of Tallwch, who guarded the swine of March son of Meirchion while the swineheard had gone on a

message to Essyllt to bid her appoint a meeting with Trystan.
Now Arthur and Marchell and Cai and Bedwyr undertook to
go and make an attempt on him, but they proved unable to get
possession of as much as one porker either as a gift or as a
purchase, whether by fraud, by force or theft.

It would appear, after all, that those fabulous figures (Arthur,
Tristan, Isolde, Mark, Kay, Bedvere) could engage in nothing
more heroic than herding and pig stealing.

The man who in legend became Sir Robin of Locksley, or
even the rightful Earl of Huntingdon, had very different origins more than six hundred years ago. The fifteenth-century
work *Scotichronicon* contains the following entry for the year
1266:

> Then arose the famous murderer, Robert Hood, as well as
> Little John, together with their accomplices from among the
> dispossessed whom the foolish populace are so inordinately
> fond of celebrating both in tragedy and comedy.

According to Professor J. C. Holt "the famous murderer" was
probably a dispossessed yeoman. His low social status was
evidently as important an element in the initial growth of the
legend of Robin Hood as it was of his nineteenth-century Australian counterpart Ned Kelly or Kelly's contemporaries, the
legendary desperadoes of the American southwest. Richard
Meyer has emphasized that "the American outlaw hero is a
"man of the people"; he is closely identified with the common
people." Bonnie and Clyde were certainly in this tradition.

Another essential ingredient, recognized by Eric Hobsbawm, in the immortalization of the heroic bandit is roots in
the countryside; he is "rural, not urban." The outlaw hero,
however, is unlikely to appear in a stable agricultural society
such as existed in western Europe for the past few centuries.
The societies that produce outlaw heroes, according to Hobsbawm, are those that "know rich and poor, powerful and weak,
rulers and ruled, but remain profoundly and tenaciously traditional." This could be the Texas of Bonnie and Clyde: a society

of small, impoverished farmers, of prosperous ranchers and those growing rich from the newfound wealth of the oil fields, of powerful and indeed some corrupt politicians, of semirural poverty on the fringes of Dallas—a violent society recently exposed to images of conspicuous wealth on the radio and cinema screen. Despite accelerating social change, it was a society still primitively capitalistic and politically conservative.

A seemingly universal feature of the bandit legend is that the criminal hero is unfairly forced into outlawry by unreasonable authority. Such emphasis can be found in descriptions of American and Australian criminal heroes, of Carpathian, Sicilian, Calabrian outlaws, and, as Hobsbawm quotes, of Sardinian bandits. "The career of a bandit almost always begins with some incident which is not in itself grave, but drives him into outlawry: a police charge for some offense brought against the man rather than for the crime; false testimony; judicial error or intrigue. . . ."

This ingredient is, however, a fictional addition to the legend of Bonnie and Clyde: first, in the account of his sister (which represents Clyde Barrow as being unfairly harassed by the police) and, secondly, by Bonnie Parker's poem.

> But the laws fooled around,
> Kept taking him down
> And locking him up in a cell,
> Till he said to me,
> "I'll never be free,
> So I'll meet a few of them in hell."

The "Robin Hood" theme—taking from the rich to give to the poor—is as much an embellishment in the Bonnie and Clyde legend as it was apparently in the growth of the myth of the English prototype. It is introduced into the 1967 film when (borrowed from Dillinger's exploits) Clyde Barrow is shown refusing to take money from a customer in the bank and sympathizing with dispossessed farmers.

The legend of Bonnie and Clyde gained strength from the

audacity of their exploits, an audacity born from their realization of the fear that their random killing caused. Like all bandit outlaws, Clyde Barrow was adept with weapons. This clearly fascinated many Americans, as Robin Hood's mythical skill at archery had thrilled simple folk in medieval England and Ned Kelly's marksmanship had no doubt absorbed some nineteenth-century Australian rustics. As Eugene Hollon commented, "Americans have not known a true frontier for more than three generations, yet we refuse to grow out of our cowboy mentality and our love of guns. What started out as necessity for survival has become part of our national culture."

Above all, the deaths of Bonnie and Clyde conformed to archetypal legendary pattern. They could not be caught by "fair" means and were only brought to their ends by trickery. Whatever was the truth of the matter (for Ted Hinton's version of events introduces some uncertainty) there was no doubt in the minds of the newspaper readers of 1934 and of the cinemagoers in 1958 and 1967 that Bonnie and Clyde were betrayed by someone whom they had trusted: so were King Arthur, Robin Hood, Ned Kelly, Jesse James, Sam Bass, Billy the Kid, and Pretty Boy Floyd.

To all these evocative ingredients was added the piquancy of the tiny, very feminine figure that stayed with Clyde Barrow through the dangerous and uncomfortable years of outlawry and gave rise to a sexual titillation so thoroughly exploited by Hollywood and the Hearst press.

THE SPECTACULAR GROWTH of this legend is a surprising phenomenon for the middle years of the twentieth century. There were no equivalent, universal legends in late nineteenth- or early twentieth-century Europe despite some remarkable and brave criminal exploits. According to H. Ashton-Wolfe's account, Jean Cavaillac ("la Terreur de Marseilles") was a handsome giant of a man who took to a life of crime after murdering his unfaithful wife. His exploits far exceeded those of Clyde Barrow, or Jesse James or Ned Kelly for that matter. Cavaillac committed at least fourteen murders, was detained, and escaped from the medieval stronghold of Good King René at Tarascon. He held out with a band of followers in the Château d'If (the prison that figured in *The Man in the Iron Mask*) against police and a gunboat. Cavaillac then hijacked a cargo ship, was captured, and taken to a French prison colony in New Caledonia and escaped to Peru, there to become leader of a band of brigands. He was eventually killed in a gun battle against an overwhelming force of Peruvian soldiers. But elderly French people whom I have questioned have no recollection of la Terreur de Marseilles. For them Cavaillac was probably the name of a French politician. Similarly that romantic figure Nance Romanetti (King of the Corsican outlaws) killed by gendarmes in 1926 is now virtually forgotten.

The hard-headed French at the turn of the century had no need to create heroes from their criminals, however romantic or spectacular their exploits, for they had the confidence bred of many centuries of civilization. French culture teems with colorful characters from Joan of Arc to Napoleon, Roland to Jean-Paul Sartre. It is not at all like the raw young societies that produced Ned Kelly or Bonnie and Clyde and quickly converted them into romantic figures—by essentially the same mechanisms that in earlier times transformed some European criminals into outlaw heroes in the minds of ordinary people.

The full traditional role of the archetypal outlaw is to protect the underprivileged, to right wrongs, and even to change society. Bonnie and Clyde were, of course, not remotely interested in such things. Their legend is merely antiauthoritarian, perhaps equivalent to the early stages of that of Robin Hood, when in 1266, the "famous murderer" was celebrated by the "foolish populace." However, many contemporaries of Bonnie and Clyde derived vicarious pleasure from their exploits, for in the words of Eric Hobsbawm, "one of the chief attractions of the bandit was, and is, that he is the poor boy who has made good, a surrogate for the failure of the mass to lift itself out of its own poverty, helplessness and meekness." For many Americans in the latter years of the 1960s, *Bonnie and Clyde* became symbols of defiance against materialist capitalism and their nation's conflict in Vietnam.

Perhaps the images of Bonnie and Clyde and the earlier

criminal heroes satisfied a deep need in their countrymen; they occupied the vast southwestern landscape so recently cleared of Indians and Mexicans, so empty of history and the legendary and historical figures that were the birthright of their European forefathers. Geoffrey Ashe has shown how a Celtic chieftain who engaged in pig stealing grew with the skill of storytellers to become the great King of the Round Table, the hero of the matter of Britain, and the English rival of Charlemagne and Roland. The tiny waitress from Dallas and the murderer she loved are now part of the matter of America and are probably more familiar to hundreds of millions of people throughout the world than either Charlemagne or Roland.

APPENDIX:
BONNIE
AND CLYDE
IN THE
CINEMA

PERHAPS MORE THAN any other modern legend, the story of Bonnie and Clyde has been manipulated by Hollywood. In many ways the film maker's role has been analogous to that of the professional balladeers and storytellers who developed the legend of the outlaw of Sherwood Forest or of another American psychopathic killer, Jesse James, who became Clyde Barrow's boyhood hero.

The first film to use the theme of Bonnie and Clyde followed swiftly after their deaths. Its director, newly arrived in Hollywood, was the brilliant refugee from Nazi Germany Fritz Lang. His first American film, *Fury*, had been a boxoffice disaster; Lang's pessimism did not provide the escapist appeal to the cinemagoers of the Great Depression, who had enough troubles of their own.

His second film, *You Only Live Once*, was released in January 1937. It portrayed two fugitives: Eddie Taylor (played by Henry Fonda) and his young wife, Jo (Sylvia Sidney). Eddie, a truck driver, is wrongly accused of murder during a bank robbery and sentenced to death. Like Clyde Barrow he mutilates himself, in this case by slitting his wrist, and arranges for Jo to smuggle him a gun into the prison hospital. He escapes just as the news of his pardon is received; he shoots the prison doctor and then the chaplain who tries to bar his way. The escape is given a nightmarish quality: the prison yard is choked with fog pierced by moving searchlight beams and blaring loudspeaker voices.

Eddie picks up Jo (who has been contemplating suicide), and they escape by driving down endless country roads. They obtain gas at gunpoint but do not rob the filling station (the till is subsequently robbed by an attendant). Their flight attracts considerable publicity. They are portrayed in the newspapers as legendary figures: robbing, killing, and living fast. Jo's sister, like Clyde's, complains that "They're being blamed for every crime committed in the country."

In reality the two fugitives are in desperate straits. Jo is forced to have her baby in an abandoned shack. In a touching scene, Eddie picks a bunch of wildflowers and brings it to her. But the hope of birth is followed by the certainty of death. Eddie and Jo are shot down: they are last seen crucified by the crosslines in the sights of a police sniper's rifle as the murdered chaplain's voice is heard calling, "Open the Gates."

Fritz Lang's portrayal of the two fugitives was entirely sympathetic. Jo and Eddie, the "three-time loser," were inevitable victims. Early in the film Eddie showed Jo some frogs in a pond and told her that they mated for life and always died together.

Although not a re-creation of the Bonnie and Clyde story, the screenplay by Gene Towne and Graham Baker incorporated a number of features from their lives and deaths. In several ways the film is closer to Emma Parker and Nell Cowan's improved portrait of Bonnie and Clyde than to the reality of their lives: Eddie Taylor is not a psychopath but an ordinary man who is harshly treated by society; he and Jo rob only for the essentials of life; Eddie murdered only because he was trapped; and above all Eddie genuinely loves Jo from the beginning.

By his brilliant artistry, Fritz Lang filled the screens and minds of 1930s cinema audiences with the powerful images of a man and a woman both young and beautiful, ill treated by society, fleeing from and resisting authority as outlaws on the country roads of America until gunned down in a police ambush.

Persons in Hiding, the next film portrayal, was very different from Fritz Lang's sympathetic interpretation. It was part of J. Edgar Hoover's campaign to strip the gangsters of the great American crime wave of their glamorous appeal. Hoover realized that the rustic desperadoes of the Great Depression were potentially more attractive than the earlier Mafia gangsters of the Chicago era. The Hearst press and the pulp magazines had turned Bonnie and Clyde into colorful characters, but they were also seen by many people as just ordinary folk who had struck back at life and managed to share some of the wealth depicted in Hollywood films and glossy magazines.

Hoover had produced a book (actually written for him by a journalist, Courtley Riley Cooper) that purported to show criminals for what they really were and gave rather too much credit to the FBI for the destruction of the gangsters of the mid-1930s. The title of this book was also used for the film, which set out to destroy the fake glamour of Bonnie and Clyde. *Persons in Hiding* was released in early 1939, the first of a series of four films of the same name. Its story was only loosely related to that of Clyde Barrow and Bonnie Parker.

For all the film's eagerness to discredit the gangsters, the Bonnie Parker role in the story was given to an extremely attractive young actress called Patricia Morison. Dorothy Bronson, as Hoover renamed her, is a thoroughly bad lot. Born on a remote farm and reared in great poverty, Dorothy is shown to be deeply attached to her mother, old Ma Bronson. At the opening of the film Dorothy is working discontentedly as a hairdresser. She pines for a more glamorous life, which includes unlimited supplies of perfume. She meets a small-time criminal, Freddie Martin (played by J. Carrol Naish), and predictably (given Miss Morison's inappropriately stunning looks) he falls in love with her. Soon she reveals her dissatisfaction with life and, once married to him, sets to work to convert him into a "big-time" crook.* After that, in the words of Gra-

---

*In this ambition she does, in fact, resemble Kathryn Thorne rather than Bonnie Parker. Kathryn Thorne married and succeeded in converting the small-time bootlegger George Kelly Barnes into that well-known but rather incompetent gangster George "Machine Gun Kelly." Dorothy Bronson changes her husband to Freddie "Gunner" Martin.

ham Greene, who reviewed the film, "it's all speeding cars and montage."

Mr. and Mrs. Martin blaze a trail of robberies and holdups across the countryside and eventually attract the attention of the FBI. They are pursued by a G-man, Pete Griswold. In contrast to the sordid life of the fugitives, the wholesomeness of the Griswold family is carefully emphasized, as Graham Greene observed. "With every intonation and weary cock of the head we get the whole contented bourgeois home, the comradely wife and the furniture from a plain van, the melancholy crack over the breakfast table, the law-abiding background to the dangerous life."

Eventually Freddie Martin is captured while attempting a risky car holdup, driven to it by the desperate need for money to satisfy his wife's uncontrollable desire for perfume. Poor Freddie breaks down when he learns from the G-men that Dorothy has been negotiating with them to betray him. The betrayal was to take the form of a trade-in. Freddie was to have been exchanged for Ma Bronson, who, like Emma Parker, had been arrested for complicity in hiding her daughter and son-in-law.

Finally the wicked Dorothy is taken in (a victim of her primary obsession) as a result of a tip-off when she is seen buying another bottle of the fatal perfume.

The film was only a moderate box-office success. Contemporary critics applauded its propaganda: "As a result of clever direction and excellent acting by J. Carrol Naish and Patricia Morison—a newcomer to pictures—the whole horrible atmosphere has been perfectly caught. These people are real, anxious, suffering human beings learning by bitter experience that 'crime does not pay.'"

Forty years later, Carlos Clarens wrote:

> After the disproportionate build-up in the Hearst papers came the forseeable Hoover debunking: Bonnie and Clyde were just a couple of petty criminals, one a silly girl who hankered for expensive dresses and perfumes, and the other a gritty ex-con who inveigled her into a series of holdups. Nevertheless, this little B-film, with its B-film ambitions and a meager shooting

schedule of eighteen days, could not quite suppress the romantic aspect of an outlaw couple meeting by the roadside or hiding out in shabby rented rooms. As it stands, the picture came out so soon after the actual event that it cannot help but fascinate us today: this was surely the way Americans thought about Bonnie and Clyde in the thirties—as picturesque but unglamorous second-raters.

STILL THE LEGEND grew and J. Edgar Hoover could not stop it. While he was attempting to erase the romantic image of the two young fugitives, another equally compelling version of their lives emerged.

In *Gun Crazy*, released in 1950, the two leading characters, Annie and Bart, share an obsession with guns. Bart Tare (played by John Dall) has grown up to be a superb marksman. He meets Annie Laurie Starr (Peggy Cummins) in a marksmanship contest at a fairground, where she is a sharpshooter in a sideshow, and is recruited to join the act. They later abandon the fairground and take to a life of crime to satisfy Annie Laurie's desires for excitement and "things . . . lots of things, big things." They progress from garage holdups to bank robberies, with Peggy Cummins's Annie Laurie wearing a Bonnie beret and taking explicitly sensual pleasure in using her gun. Bart is repelled by the thought of killing, but to Annie Laurie it is an exciting prospect, and she eventually shoots two people while making her escape from a bank robbery.

The fugitives are by now nationally known criminals and are hunted by the police. They finally seek refuge in the mountains near Bart's hometown but are discovered. The posse sent out against them is led by two of Bart's childhood friends, Clyde Boston and Dave Allister. Rather than allow Annie Laurie to shoot Clyde and Dave, Bart kills her and is then himself shot down.

Gun Crazy, which later became a cult among the admirers of *film noir*, links sexuality with violence. Annie Laurie sexually blackmails Bart into violent crime and then initiates him into the sensual thrill that it gives her. She corrupts and dominates their relationship until they are trapped in a maze of violence and death.

This film, more than any other, emphasizes the powerful attraction of weaponry in the growing legend of Bonnie and Clyde. Critics of *film noir*, such as Ed Lowry, attributed great significance to the implied phallic symbolism: "Guns are clearly related to sex, both are repressed by a benevolently castrating authority, and the individuals' exercise of the power they represent takes the form of clearly antisocial acts."

The theme of the dominating female with her obsession with guns and violence is an obvious distortion of the relationship between Bonnie Parker and Clyde Barrow. In reality *he* dominated *her*. Yet the photograph of Bonnie with a cigar in her mouth and a machine-gun in her hands was an exciting image, which the contemporary newspapers and pulp magazines had exploited to the full. The alternative image of the two young fugitives fleeing from ugly authority that the Hoover propaganda had been so anxious to counter was now all but extinguished.

THE PORTRAYAL OF Bonnie Parker as a lusty and dominating gun moll continued in Hollywood's next variation on the legend of Bonnie and Clyde. In 1958 appeared the first film to represent explicitly the careers of Bonnie and Clyde: *The Bonnie Parker Story*.

In this film version, produced by Stanley Shpetner, Bonnie is working as a waitress in a cheap café in 1932. The heroine (played by Dorothy Provine) is first glimpsed behind the credit titles removing her stockings and unzipping her dress. The next scene switches to the countryside where "Guy Darrow" (played by Jack Hogan) is engaged in what the *noir* critics would no doubt interpret as overt phallic symbolism as he fondles a machine-gun and shoots off the limb of a tree. Guy tells his friend Bobby that he has "Gotta little girl picked out." Bobby warns him that she (Bonnie) "is a real wild cat."

Guy Darrow is not put off by his friend's warning but visits the café, where Bonnie has just repelled the unwelcome advances of its unsavory owner. Guy eventually prevails on her to join him by showing her his machine-gun and promising, "You and me, fifty-fifty. Cause, honey, I am goin' places."

Their first criminal venture so excites Bonnie that she inter-feres with the getaway by moving close to him in the car, saying seductively, "Kiss me. I said kiss me, Guy."

Their activities soon attract considerable police and news-paper attention. They also manage to damage accidentally the car bumper of the film's version of Frank Hamer (Tom Steel) who is already in hot pursuit of the fugitives.

Unlike the real Bonnie Parker, Dorothy Provine's version is discontented with their poor profits and also by their uncom-fortable accommodation in a disused farmhouse: "We're livin' like a coupla animals." She also, very understandably, repels Guy's attempt to make love to her as she is taking what must have been a very chilly bath in a rainwater tub.

Guy attempts to resolve their difficulties by calling in his brother Chuck Darrow, who, unlike his easygoing prototype, is an ambitious and resourceful criminal. Chuck is eventually shot in the film's re-creation of the ambush at Dexfield Park, Iowa. Bonnie and Guy flee, leaving Chuck in the arms of his still-nameless girlfriend. Guy panics badly: "We'll never get out of this one." But Bonnie is now in command. She accom-plishes their escape by the stratagem of floating Guy's jacket down the stream, thus throwing off the pursuing hounds and the posse, who riddle the garment with bullets.

Bonnie (who by this time has become very bossy indeed) next organizes an operation to free her ex-husband, Duke Jefferson, from Clemens Prison. She sends Guy off to hide the guns in the undergrowth near the prison and while he is away encounters two men (Marv and Al) with whom she quickly links arms and walks off into seclusion. Duke Jefferson is duly "sprung" and quickly comes into conflict with poor Guy Darrow for Bonnie's favors. She does not respond to either man (perhaps because of her recent encounter with Marv and Al) and protects herself by scattering tin tacks on the floor around her bed.

Later, Bonnie meets a handsome young architect, Paul, who enters her motel room to use the telephone. Bonnie, who is alone, is much taken with Paul and his educated talk. She sighs, "I never knew anyone like you before."

But Bonnie has to return to work and has soon organized the

ambush of an armored truck carrying a large quantity of money. The execution of her plan is delayed, however, by the appearance of a party of boy scouts.

Just as the delayed ambush is about to reach a successful conclusion, a posse of lawmen arrives (presumably alerted by the boy scouts). In the ensuing gun battle Duke Jefferson is shot, but Guy Darrow and Bonnie escape.

At this stage, Bonnie seeks fresh recruits to replace her late husband and departs with Guy for Athens, Louisiana, to pick up two likely lads. However, the elderly father of the two potential recruits is worried about his sons' descent into further crime and informs Tom Steel.

Steel comes to an arrangement with the old man and sets up an ambush for Bonnie and Guy. The two fugitives are shot down in the now-traditional rain of bullets. As she dies, Bonnie's voice is heard calling, "Paul."

The crude portrayal of Bonnie in *The Bonnie Parker Story* continued the distortion of her character by making her the dominant partner. She becomes a caricature: a 1950s version of Belle Starr set in a bad re-creation of the southwest in the early 1930s. By no stretch of the imagination could Dorothy Provine's Bonnie have produced two stylish ballads. But there is a trace still of the Bonnie who, given a fair chance, could have made a happy life of the sort revealed to her during her brief encounter with the handsome young architect, whose name she utters with her dying breath.

Clyde, on the other hand, appears first as virile and tough and possessed of much sexual bravado but declines into an impotent and subservient figure. There is no suggestion of genuine love between them. In one sense this could contain some semblance of plausibility in representing the psychopath as a man who can attract but not sustain a full sexual relationship.

It is interesting to note that in the 1950s context the hunters of Bonnie and Guy are not ugly or cowardly. There is no strong suggestion of antiauthoritarianism. The Hamer figure (Tom Steel) and his deputies are just straightforward guys doing a necessary job.

THINGS WERE DIFFERENT in the 1960s when the legend achieved its most thorough transformation.

Arthur Penn's film version of the outlawry of Clyde Barrow and Bonnie was originally conceived three decades after their killing in the years of nostalgia for the period of Fred Astaire and Ginger Rogers. The idea belonged to two sophisticates from the staff of *Esquire* magazine, David Newman and Robert Benton. They were film enthusiasts, inspired by the works of New Wave directors like Truffaut, Godard, Antonioni, Fellini. They had also read John Toland's book *Dillinger Days* (published in 1964), which devoted only a few scattered but evocative pages to the exploits of Bonnie and Clyde; they were enough to fire the imaginations of Newman and Benton. Working night after night to the recorded sound of Flatt and Scruggs and the Foggy Mountain Boys (to gain appropriate musical atmosphere), they eventually produced a script. Newman and Benton clearly intended to convey the powerful charm of their two main characters. In the introduction to their script they wrote,

> Bonnie Parker and Clyde Barrow headed one of the notorious gangs, and their names and deeds were well-known across the country. To many they were heroes of a kind, for they showed bravery in the face of incredible odds, daring in their free enterprise, and style in their manner. They took a delight, it seemed, in foiling the law—the small town cops, the sheriffs, the justices of the peace.

In Newman and Benton's hands Clyde Barrow and Bonnie Parker were to become folk heroes—of a kind. If not downright glamorous, they were to have style. They would provide cinematographic fun and games until suffering the traditional fate of the Hollywood bad guys. But there was to be more to it than that: there was to be contemporary relevance.

> If Bonnie and Clyde were here today, they would be hip. Their values have become assimilated in much of our culture—not robbing banks and killing people, of course, but their style,

their sexuality, their bravado, their delicacy, their cultivated arrogance, their narcissistic insecurity, their curious ambitions have relevance to the way we live now.

Newman and Benton's script was rejected by a number of film companies, but Warner Brothers eventually took it. The film was to be produced by Warren Beatty, who would also take the part of Clyde Barrow. Faye Dunaway was to be Bonnie Parker. The film was shot on location during 1966 in some of the clapboard Texas towns that were then virtually unchanged since the times of Bonnie and Clyde. It was completed and ready for release by the next summer. The world premiere of *Bonnie and Clyde* took place with considerable ballyhoo at the Eighth International Folk Festival of Montreal on August 4, 1967.

In *Bonnie and Clyde* the hero and heroine are brought together even faster than in *The Bonnie Parker Story* by basically the same cinematic device. Bonnie first appears partially clothed (virtually nude), standing in her bedroom window from which she sees Clyde Barrow attempting to steal her mother's car. He also sees her, full frontal, from where he is standing. She flings on a dress and runs down to interview the thief. They engage in some particularly banal repartee until he walks her down the street and then shows her his gun. No doubt about the symbolism here because the script decrees that Bonnie should touch it "in a manner almost sexual, full of repressed excitement." Clyde almost immediately uses his gun in the robbery of a grocery store, largely to impress the watching Bonnie Parker. She is not only duly impressed but sexually excited and like Dorothy Provine's Bonnie tries to make love to Clyde as he attempts to drive away from the scene of the crime.

Miss Dunaway discovers Clyde's sexual inadequacy rather sooner than Miss Provine—indeed as soon as the car stops after the getaway from the grocery robbery. She comments after he fails to come up to her expectations, "Your advertising is just dandy. Folk'd just never guess you don't have a thing to sell." However Warren Beatty's Clyde persuades her to stay (despite his limitations) because, as he says, "... you're different, that's why. You know, you're like me. You want different things. You got something better than bein' a waitress."

Despite his sexual inadequacy Clyde Barrow is not dominated by Faye Dunaway's Bonnie Parker as Guy Darrow was by Dorothy Provine's Bonnie. During the ambush it is he and not Bonnie who organizes their escape. He is tough and resourceful, if not particularly intelligent.

PROBABLY THE MOST memorable aspect of Arthur Penn's *Bonnie and Clyde* is the impression of verisimilitude that it conveys. The film was shot with brilliant camerawork under the huge Texas skies on the dusty plains that Bonnie and Clyde knew. Furthermore, it attempted to portray, more accurately than its predecessors, some real events from the lives of Clyde Barrow and Bonnie Parker. Even so, the film was still historically inaccurate for two reasons. First, because it was obviously impossible to portray in 111 minutes all the participants and incidents that occurred during the months of outlawry. It was, therefore, necessary to simplify the story and to eliminate characters. Thus Raymond Hamilton, W. D. Jones, and Henry Methvin were combined into a single fictional person, C. W. Moss, who is casually picked up at a country gas station. The Dallas county sheriff does not appear, and Sheriff Coffey of Platte City, Missouri, becomes Sheriff Smoot of Platte City, Iowa.

Historical inaccuracy resulted, secondly, from the needs of artistry; as Voltaire said, "The secret of the arts is to correct nature." The artistic "corrections" in Arthur Penn's film are fascinating because the growth of the legend primarily results from the need to distort or "re-tell the story," in terms that will be exciting and readily understandable to later audiences. He must, in the jargon of the 1960s, introduce "contemporary relevance." Purely fictional events are used to suggest their concern for the underprivileged victims of the Great Depression. Thus, early on in the film, Bonnie and Clyde meet a dispossessed farmer. He is about to leave his farm, where they stop for Clyde to give his newly acquired girlfriend some necessary, and no doubt sexually symbolic, target practice, in which Bonnie discharges a pistol at a suspended car tire. At Clyde's instigation the dispirited farmer takes a loaded gun from him and shatters the windows of his former home: a last gesture of defiance. An old Negro sharecropper who is standing by also joins in. They part with warm handshakes and much good will.

In another scene (after the film's version of the ambush in Dexfield Park) the wounded fugitives find themselves, at dawn, outside an Oakie campsite. Several poor families are seated around a campfire, cooking. The exhausted C. W. Moss (now enacting his role as W. D. Jones) walks up to them and asks for drinking water. As the leader of the group hands C. W. a drinking cup, he recognizes Moss's companions and says ("in really hushed and reverent tones" according to the script), "That's Clyde Barrow and Bonnie Parker." The poor Oakies crowd around the car. A woman gives C. W. a bowl of hot soup. As he gets into the car, the people press closer for a final look. Clyde "nods his head in a barely perceptible gesture by way of saying 'thank you' to the people." As they drive away, a girl says, "Is that really Bonnie Parker?"

Here then is the image of Clyde and Bonnie as friends of the poor, accepted by the dispossessed—robbing the bankers who ruin poor farmers and destroying the uniformed protectors of the wealthy.

The role of Frank Hamer was also fictionally embellished by the makers of *Bonnie and Clyde*. He is portrayed most unsympathetically; in the cast list he is described as being "Tall, strong, contemptuous of almost everyone and particularly women and criminals; some hidden evil in him sometimes shows in his face." In another scene the script decrees that Hamer shall have a "quality of sinister frenzy beneath his calm."*

A ludicrous incident is fabricated in which Clyde Barrow surprises and outshoots Frank Hamer in what the script des-

---

*The Hamer family later filed a law suit against Warner Brothers claiming $1,750,000 damages for the film's misrepresentations of Frank Hamer.

cribes as "a real razzle-dazzle display of grandstand marksmanship." The gang then tease their captive. This involves Bonnie "coyly" stroking Hamer's mustache (another fictional addition) with a revolver, the nasty Hamer spitting in her face, an outraged Clyde Barrow knocking the handcuffed lawman about and setting him adrift in a skiff.

The hunter of Bonnie and Clyde in 1967 is thus a very different article from wholesome Pete Griswold of thirty years before in *Persons in Hiding* or the straightforward Tom Steel (from *The Bonnie Parker Story*) of a decade before. But the Hollywood scriptwriters of the 1960s had produced nothing more sophisticated than a twentieth-century version of the unattractive sheriff of Nottingham whose wicked antics so entertained simple folk in the audiences of fifteenth-century England.

THE LONG SEQUENCE of Bonnie and Clyde films degenerates into farce with the Italian contribution *Bonnie e Clyde all'Italiana*, made in 1983. Here the two fugitives are incompetent clowns, accidentally trapped into violent crime—a Latin parody of the tough-guy image of the Hollywood outlaw hero. Yet even this is reminiscent of the incompetent young criminal and his girl who fell off the donkeys at Kaufman in their inglorious flight from the police.

Bibliography

CONTEMPORARY NEWSPAPERS WERE useful sources of information. I consulted the following: the *Austin American*; the *Daily Times Herald* (Dallas); the *Dallas Dispatch*; the *Dallas Journal*; the *Dallas Morning News*; the *Des Moines Register*; the *Des Moines Tribune*; the *Fort Worth Star Telegram*; the *Hillsboro Evening Mirror*; the *Indian Citizen Democrat* (Atoka, Oklahoma); the *Joplin Globe*; the *Kansas City Star*; the *Kansas City Times*; the *Landmark* (Platte City, Missouri); *The New York Times*; the *Southwest American* (Fort Smith, Arkansas); the *Statesman* (Austin, Texas); the *Sunday Springfield News and Leader*; the *Temple Daily Telegram*; *The Times* (London); the *Wellington Leader*.

I also consulted articles in the following magazines and journals: the *Pacific Reporter*, *Vogue*, the *New Yorker*, *Today*.

The following books, written by, or about, participants in the events described in this book, provided invaluable insight.

Fortune, Jan I., ed. *Fugitives. The Story of Clyde Barrow and Bonnie Parker. As Told by Bonnie's Mother (Mrs. Emma Parker) and Clyde's Sister (Nell Barrow Cowan)*. 1934, The Ranger Press, Dallas.

Frost, H. G., and Jenkins, J. H. *I'm Frank Hamer: The Life of a Texas Peace Officer*. 1968, Pemberton Press, Auston.

Hinton, Ted (as told to Larry Grove). *Ambush: The Real Story of Bonnie and Clyde.* 1979, Shoal Creek Publishers, Austin.
Simmons, Lee. *Assignment Huntsville: Memoirs of a Texas Prison Officer.* 1957, University of Texas Press, Austin.

I also used the following unpublished sources:

Dallas County Sheriff's Department. Statement made by W. D. Jones. File 6048.
Dallas Police Department. Mug Shot Book. Dallas Public Library.
Russell, Bud. "The Clyde Barrow-Bonnie Parker Harboring Case." Manuscript. Archives of the Dallas Historical Society.
Schmid, R. A., Sheriff. Scrapbook. Dallas Public Library.

The following books and articles provided background information:

Ashe, Geoffrey. *King Arthur's Avalon.* 1957, Collins, London.
――――, ed. *The Quest for Arthur's Britain.* 1971, Paladin, London.
Ashton-Wolfe, H. *Outlaws of Modern Days.* 1927, Cassell, London.
Baker, Marilyn (with Sally Brompton). *Exclusive! The Inside Story of Patricia Hearst and the SLA.* 1974, Macmillan Publishing, New York.
Boulton, David. *The Making of Tania Hearst.* 1975, New English Library, London.
Bromwich, Rachel. *Trioedd Ynys Prydein. The Welsh Triads.* 1961, University of Wales Press, Cardiff.
Brown, Richard Maxwell. "Historical Patterns of American Violence." In *Violence in America. Historical and Comparative Perspectives.* Edited by H. D. Graham and T. R. Gurr. 1979, Sage Publications, Beverly Hills.
――――. *Strain of Violence: Historical Studies of American Violence and Vigilantism.* 1975, Oxford University Press, New York.

Cleckley, Hervey. *The Mask of Sanity*. 1976, The C. V. Mobey Company, Saint Louis.

Collins, Frederick L. *The FBI in Peace and War*. 1943, Putnam, New York.

Corey, Herbert. *Farewell, Mr. Gangster! America's War on Crime*. 1936, D. Appleton-Century Company, New York and London.

Day, James M. *Captain Clint Peoples, Texas Ranger: Fifty years a Lawman*. 1980, Texian Press, Waco, Texas.

DeFord, Miriam. *The Real Bonnie and Clyde*. 1968, Ace Books, New York.

Demoss, Dorothy. "Resourcefulness in the Financial Capital: Dallas, 1929–1933." In *Texas Cities and the Great Depression*. Texas Memorial Museum, Austin.

Drago, Harry Sinclair. *Outlaws on Horseback*. 1964, Bramhall House, New York.

Hobsbawm, E. J. *Primitive Rebels: Studies in Archaic Forms of Social Movement in the Nineteenth and Twentieth Centuries*. 1971, Manchester University Press.

Hollon, Eugene. *Frontier Violence: Another Look*. 1974, Oxford University Press, New York.

Holt, J. C. *Robin Hood*. 1982, Thames & Hudson, London.

Hoover, J. Edgar. *Persons in Hiding*. 1938, Dent, London.

Johnson, Pamela Hansford. *On Iniquity: Some Personal Reflections Arising Out of the Moors Murder Trial*. 1967, Macmillan, London.

Maddox, Web. *The Black Sheep*. 1975, Nortex Press, Quanah, Texas.

Marchbanks, David. *The Moors Murders*. 1966, Leslie Frewin, London.

McCord, William and McCord, Joan. *The Psychopath: An Essay on the Criminal Mind*. 1964, D. Van Nostrand, Princeton.

Meyer, Richard E. "The Outlaw: A Distinctive American Folktype." *Journal of the Folklore Institute 17*. 1980, pp. 94-124.

O'Connor, Dick. *G-men at Work. The Story of America's Fight Against Crime and Corruption*. 1939, Long, London.

Osborne, Charles. *Ned Kelly.* 1970, Anthony Blond, London.
Phillips, John Neal and Gorzell, André L. "Tell Them I Don't Smoke Cigars. The Story of Bonnie Parker." In *Legendary Ladies of Texas.* Edited by Francis Edward Abernathy. 1981, E-Heart Press, Dallas.
Quimby, Myron J. *The Devil's Emissaries.* 1969, Barnes, New York, and Yoseloff, London.
Richardson, Rupert Noval, Wallace, Ernest, and Anderson, Adrian N. *Texas: The Lone Star State,* 4th ed. 1981, Prentice-Hall, New Jersey.
Sann, Paul. *The Lawless Decade.* 1957, Crown Publishers, New York.
Sargant, William. *Battle for the Mind: A Physiology of Conversion and Brain-Washing.* 1957, Heinemann, London.
Syers, Ed. *Back Roads of Texas.* 1979, Gulf Publishing Company, Houston.
Toland, John. *The Dillinger Days.* 1963, Backer, London.
Watson, Frederick. *A Century of Gunmen.* 1931, Ivor Nicholson and Watson, London.
Webb, Walter Prescott. *The Texas Rangers: A Century of Frontier Defense.* 1935, University of Texas Press, Austin.

FILMOGRAPHY

You Only Live Once. United Artists, 1937.

Director: Fritz Lang
Producer: Walter Wanger
Screen Play: Gene Towne and Graham Baker
Starring: Sylvia Sidney ("Jo" Graham) and Henry Fonda
                 (Eddie Taylor)

Persons in Hiding. Paramount, 1939.

Director: Louis King
Producer: Harry Fischbeck
Screen Play: William R. Lipman and Horace McCoy; based
                 on the book *Persons in Hiding* by J. Edgar
                 Hoover
Starring: Patricia Morison (Dorothy Bronson) and J.
                 Carrol Naish (Freddie "Gunner" Martin)

Gun Crazy (Reissue Title: *Deadly Is the Female*]. United
Artists, 1950.

Director: Joseph H. Lewis
Producers: Frank and Maurice King

Screen Play: Mackinlay Kantor and Millard Kaufman; from the *Saturday Evening Post* story by Mackinlay Kantor
Starring: Peggy Cummins (Annie Laurie Starr) and John Dall (Bart Tare)

The Bonnie Parker Story. Anglo Amalgamated, 1958.

Director: William Witney
Producer: Stanley Shpetner
Screen Play: Stanley Shpetner
Starring: Dorothy Provine (Bonnie Parker) and Jack Hogan (Guy Darrow)

Bonnie and Clyde. Warner Bros. Seven Arts, 1967.

Director: Arthur Penn
Producer: Warren Beatty
Screen Play: David Newman and Robert Benton
Starring: Faye Dunaway (Bonnie Parker) and Warren Beatty (Clyde Barrow)

Bonnie e Clyde all'italiana. Fasco Film, 1983.

Director: Steno
Producer: Achilla Manzotti
Screen Play: Luciano Vincezoni, Sergio Donati, and Gianni Manganelli
Starring: Anorella Muti (Bonnie) and Paolo Villaggio (Clyde)

Synopses and film reviews were consulted in *Kinematograph Weekly, Motion Film Bulletin*, the *New Statesman, Newsweek, The New York Times*, the *Observer*, the *Village Voice*, and *Vogue*.

The following books were used:

Clarens, Carlos. *Crime Movies.* 1980, Secker & Warburg, London.

Greene, Graham. *The Pleasure Drome.* 1972, Secker & Warburg, London.

Halliwell, Leslie. *Halliwell's Film Guide*, 3d ed. 1981, Granada, London.

Hirschfeld, Burt. *Bonnie and Clyde: Based on the Screenplay by David Newman and Robert Benton.* 1967, Hodder & Stoughton, London.

Peary, Danny. *Cult Movies.* 1982, Vermilion, London.

Silver, Alain, and Ward, Elizabeth, eds. *Film Noir.* 1980, Secker & Warburg, London.

Wake, Sandra, and Hayden, Nicola. *The Bonnie and Clyde Book.* 1972, Lorrimer, London.

Williams, Mark. *Road Movies. The Complete Guide to Cinema on Wheels.* 1982, Proteus Books, London.